Social Thought on Ireland in the Nineteenth Century

edited by

SÉAMAS Ó SÍOCHÁIN

D1355570

UNIVERSITY COLLEGE DUBLIN PRESS

PREAS CHOLÁISTE OLLSCOILE
BHAILE ÁTHA CLIATH

First published 2009
by University College Dublin Press
Newman House
86 St Stephen's Green
Dublin 2
Ireland

www.ucdpress.ie
© the editors and contributors, 2009

ISBN 978-1-904558-66-8 pb

Cataloguing in Publication data
available from the British Library

*The right of the editors and contributors to be identified as the
authors of their work has been asserted by them*

Typeset in Plantin and Fournier by
Elaine Burberry and Ryan Shiels
Text design by Lyn Davies
Index by Jane Rogers
Printed on acid-free paper in England by
Athenaeum Press, Gateshead

Contents

Preface

This book derives from a conference organised by the editor under the auspices of the Anthropological Association of Ireland (AAI) and held in Headfort House, Kells, Co. Meath on Friday and Saturday, 18–19 March 2005. The discipline of anthropology in Ireland is small and of relatively recent origin. On the relatively few occasions when anyone has talked of the beginnings of an anthropology *of* Ireland (e.g. Wilson and Donnan 2006: 17) they have generally referred to the work of A. C. Haddon at the turn of the nineteenth and twentieth centuries or to the later researches in County Clare of Conrad Arensberg and Solon Kimball (e.g. Haddon 1893; Arensberg and Kimball 1940). Each of these proposed beginnings was chosen, it seems, because it was marked by the conduct of field research. Anthropologist Adrian Peace has characterised the subsequent tradition of field-based anthropological studies of Ireland as involving the presentation of Ireland as a culturally exotic Other, parallel to the presentation of peoples in colonial Africa and Asia. The creation of Ireland as 'object' for study reflected power relations between core and periphery and revealed as much about the observing society as it did about that being observed (Peace 1989).

Yet, while intensive field research by participant observation came to mark anthropology in the twentieth century, the discipline itself had already begun to take on a recognisable form in the nineteenth century (see, for example, George Stocking's well known book, *Victorian Anthropology*). My idea in initiating the present project was to bring into focus the extent to which Ireland was a significant 'Other' during that same nineteenth century, a period formative in the emergence of the discipline of anthropology and considerably before the work of Haddon, Arensberg or their successors, and to suggest that, if a history of the anthropology of Ireland is to be written, it must explore nineteenth-century thought on Ireland. It was clear from the outset that, during that period, Ireland, like India, was a region of considerable interest to major social observers from outside the island. Hence, the project set out to examine the work of selected observers and a few significant themes in which reflection on Ireland featured as an important element.

The selected thinkers are: Gustave de Beaumont (1802–66), friend of Alexis de Tocqueville (1805–59); John Stuart Mill (1806–73); Harriet

Martineau (1802–76); Sir Henry Maine (1822–88); Karl Marx (1818–83) and Friedrich Engels (1820–95); James Anthony Froude (1818–94). In addition, the two significant themes of Celticism and Race, constructs through which the Irish were frequently viewed, are also included; under these headings attention is given to the thought of, for example, Matthew Arnold and Robert Knox.

Professor Vincent Comerford provides a brief historical introduction to the nineteenth century. One of the aims of the project is to seek to relate the social thought being analysed to the Irish and world contexts. The Irish context includes momentous events, such as the 1798 Rebellion, the Act of Union, Catholic emancipation, population increase and famine, the Fenian movement and land agitation, the Home Rule issue, and cultural and political nationalism. The broader, comparative, context included developments in the British Empire (e.g. the loss of the American colonies, involvement in India and the Scramble for Africa), and the Napoleonic Wars. Crucial, too, is the emergence of scientific racism.

Such a project is very much an interdisciplinary one, of course, as the list of contributors involved clearly indicates. It might better be described as an endeavour in intellectual history. In the Preface to his Gill History volume *The Modernisation of Irish Society 1848–1918*, Joe Lee commented that: 'Scholars regularly and rightly lament the neglect of Irish economic history. Several other fields lie equally fallow, scarcely sprouting even a crop of weeds. Intellectual history, the ultimate key to our understanding of both economy and society, has hardly impinged on scholarly consciousness.' It could be argued that Lee's comment still remains valid. In his bibliography he compliments R. D. Collison Black, whose 'deeply researched *Economic Thought and the Irish Question 1817–1870* (Cambridge 1960) makes an enduring contribution to the sadly neglected field of intellectual history' (172). The title of the AAI Conference was an adaptation of that of the late Professor Black. The title of this volume has been altered, however, to better reflect the collection of essays included.

Contributors to the Kells Conference were asked to take account of the following: (a) the general significance of the observers/themes in the history of social thought; (b) the extent of the observers' knowledge of and writings on Ireland; (c) the significance of the latter within the broader corpus of their work; (d) the manner in which they viewed Ireland within a broad comparative context (empire/India/Anglo-Saxons); (e) the effects, in any, of their thinking on public policy; (f) a critical assessment of their thinking in present-day perspective, including, e.g., changing conceptualisations of identity in the context of increasing globalisation and mobility.

The hope in providing these guidelines was that the provision of an over-all framework would throw up fresh insights beyond those derived from the treatment of specific thinkers in isolation: by bringing the analysis within a single frame of reference; by viewing the thinkers in the context of the historical context in Ireland, Britain and the world; by viewing their work in a contemporary analytic framework; and by involving the best of today's available scholarship. The hope remains that this volume will provide a useful building block in an anthropological history of Ireland and point up the significance of Ireland as a case study for the emerging social sciences in the nineteenth century.

Each essay has been revised and expanded since its original presentation in Kells. That on Harriet Martineau was not part of the conference and the editor is grateful to its authors for consenting to its publication here. Finally, we are saddened at the death of one of our contributors, George Watson, gentleman and scholar.

As with every such enterprise, debts to many people have been incurred since its inception. The greatest of these is to the volume's contributors, whose participation in the initial conference helped make it a memorable experience and whose revised essays ensure the quality of the present work. They have also been forbearing over the delay in publication. I am grateful, too, for the detailed and extremely helpful comments of the two anonymous readers, a type of valuable contribution that current assessments of academic performance unfortunately undervalue. Again, without the professional and warm input from UCD Press and, specifically, from Barbara Mennell and Noelle Moran, this work would not have seen the light of day. My thanks, too, to Jane Rogers for the indispensable index.

Without financial assistance neither the initial conference nor the book would have materialised. Accordingly, we acknowledge important contributions from the National University of Ireland Publications Scheme and, for support for the Kells Conference, from the Department of Anthropology, National University of Ireland Maynooth, and from University College Dublin's College of Human Sciences.

Publication is the final phase of what began in 2005 with the Kells Conference. For making that event such a pleasant one, I wish to thank Dermot Dix and Headfort School for providing the location, facilities and a warm welcome; Kells Chamber of Commerce for their sponsorship of a drinks reception; and the Anthropological Association of Ireland, under whose auspices the conference was held and who provided financial and publicity assistance. Finally, to the many others who contributed along the way my sincere gratitude.

While the book was in a late stage of preparation, news of the death of George Watson came as a shock to all who had come to know him. I would like to express my thanks to Dr Richard Watson and to Professor Patrick Crotty for their kind help in providing biographical information on George.

SÉAMAS Ó SÍOCHÁIN
NUI Maynooth, 2009

Bibliography

Arensberg, Conrad M. and Solon Kimball, 1940. *Family and Community in Ireland.* Cambridge Mass.: Harvard University Press.

Black, R. D. Collison, 1960 [reprinted, Gregg Revivals, 1993]. *Economic Thought and the Irish Question 1817–1870.* Cambridge: Cambridge University Press.

Haddon, Arthur C. and C. R. Brown, 1893. 'On the Ethnography of the Aran Islands, Co. Galway', *Proceedings of the Royal Irish Academy*, Third Series, Vol. 2, 768–830.

Lee, Joe, 1973. *The Modernisation of Irish Society 1848–1918.* Dublin: Gill and Macmillan.

Peace, Adrian, 1989. 'From Arcadia to Anomie: Critical Notes on the Constitution of Irish Society as an Anthropological Subject', *Critique of Anthropology*, 9(1), 89–111.

Stocking, George, 1987. *Victorian Anthropology.* N.Y.: The Free Press.

Wilson, Thomas M. and Hastings Donnan, 2006. *The Anthropology of Ireland.* Oxford: Berg.

Contributors to this Volume

PETER J. BOWLER is Professor of the History of Science at Queen's University, Belfast. His most recent book is *Monkey Trials and Gorilla Sermons* (Harvard University Press, 2007) and he is currently working on popular science in the early twentieth century.

CIARAN BRADY is Associate Professor of History and currently Head of the Department of History at Trinity College Dublin. He is the author of *The Chief Governors: The Rise and Fall of Reform Government in Tudor Ireland, 1536–88* (1994), of a biography of *Shane O'Neill* (1996) and is currently completing a study of the Victorian historian and man of letters, James Anthony Froude.

RICHARD VINCENT COMERFORD is a graduate of Maynooth and Trinity College, Dublin. He has been professor of Modern History at National University of Ireland Maynooth since 1989. His books include *Ireland* (2003) in the series Inventing the Nation.

BRIAN CONWAY is lecturer in the Department of Sociology at the National University of Ireland Maynooth and has been a visiting fellow at the Institute for Social and Economic Research, University of Essex, and CEPS, Luxembourg. His book on Bloody Sunday memory is forthcoming from Palgrave.

DERMOT DIX trained in history at Trinity College Dublin and Pembroke College, Cambridge, and is Headmaster and Head of the History Department at Headfort School in Kells, County Meath, Ireland. His research is focused on British imperial ideology in the eighteenth and nineteenth centuries, with particular reference to India, Ireland and America.

GRAHAM FINLAY is a lecturer in Politics and International Relations at University College Dublin. He has published on the history of political thought and post-colonial thought and on contemporary issues involving civic education, migration and global justice.

TOM GARVIN is Professor Emeritus at the School of Politics and International Relations, University College Dublin. His books include *The Evolution of Irish Nationalist Politics* (Gill & Macmillan, 1981), *Nationalist Revolutionaries in Ireland, 1858–1928* (Clarendon, 1987), *1922: The Birth of Irish Democracy* (Gill & Macmillan, 1996), and *Preventing the Future: Why was Ireland so poor for so long?* (Gill & Macmillan, 2004).

PETER GRAY is Professor of Modern Irish History at Queen's University Belfast. He is the author of *Famine, Land and Politics: British Government and Irish Society 1843–50* (1999) and *The Making of the Irish Poor Law, 1815–43* (2009).

ANDREAS HESS is Senior Lecturer in Sociology at University College Dublin. He is the author of *American Political and Social Thought: A Concise Introduction* (New York University Press, 2000), *Concepts of Social Stratification: European and American Models* (Palgrave-Macmillan, 2001), and his latest book is *Reluctant Modernization: Plebeian Culture and Moral Economy in the Basque Country* (Peter Lang, 2009).

MICHAEL R. HILL is currently a senior tutor in the Department of Athletics at the University of Nebraska-Lincoln and editor of the journal *Sociological Origins* and author of *Archival Strategies and Techniques* (Sage, 1993).

CHANDANA MATHUR lectures in the Department of Anthropology at the National University of Ireland Maynooth. Informed by the perspectives of anthropological political economy, her work is based on research conducted in North America, South Asia and among the South Asian diaspora.

SÉAMAS Ó SÍOCHÁIN was Senior Lecturer in the Department of Anthropology, National University of Ireland Maynooth, until recent retirement. His publications include *The Eyes of Another Race: Roger Casement's Congo Report and 1903 Diary* (eds Séamas Ó Síocháin and Michael O'Sullivan, UCD Press, 2003) and *Roger Casement: Imperialist, Rebel, Revolutionary* (Lilliput Press, 2008) and he is editor of *The Irish Journal of Anthropology*.

GEORGE J. WATSON (1942–2009) was Emeritus Professor in the Research Institute of Irish and Scottish Studies at the University of Aberdeen from his retirement in 2005, having served as its Director and Associate Director. He won international renown for his book *Irish Identity and the Literary Revival* (1979; repr. 1994), a meticulously researched illumination of the political context of the achievement of W. B. Yeats, James Joyce, John Millington Synge and Sean O'Casey. He was a founding member in 1985 of the British

Association of Irish Studies, and later helped create the Research Institute of Irish and Scottish Studies at Aberdeen, one of his signal achievements. His wide network of friends and contacts among the poets, novelists, scholars, historians and politicians of Ireland and Scotland was crucial to the success of the Institute in its early years. He was also a distinguished Director of the Yeats International Summer School in Sligo, 1998–2000. He died on 2 February 2009.

CHAPTER I

Introduction

Ireland's Nineteenth Century

R. V. Comerford

Ireland's 'long nineteenth century', like that of most western European countries, began in the period of French revolutionary turmoil and ended in 1914. Arguably, it had ended for Ireland before the actual outbreak of the Great War: the successful establishment of two mutually antagonistic private armies, the Ulster Volunteer Force in 1912 and the Irish Volunteers in 1913 meant that by early 1914 the British government had in a significant respect lost control of Ireland. 1800 and the passing of the Act of Union provides a neat starting point for those satisfied with either convenient calendar dates or the defining power of constitutional arrangements. 'Ireland under the union, 1800–1921' is a well-entrenched formula. Currently, most historians begin their accounts of nineteenth-century Irish politics in the 1790s, more specifically around and about the polarisation of opinion and policies in Ireland, Britain and elsewhere that accompanied Britain's going to war with revolutionary France in 1793.

Few western countries had the British experience of a nineteenth century progressing through enormous and frequently painful secular changes without a calamitous disjuncture. The United States had its Civil War; France experienced revolutionary change of government in 1830 and 1848 and suffered defeat by Prussia; Germany and Italy had their wars of unification; and Ireland had the Great Famine, attempted risings in 1848 and 1867, and the rupture of civil life associated with the Land War. Famine and land troubles, apart from being major subjects of study, have their own claims as turning points. The title of F. S. L. Lyons's influential survey, *Ireland since the Famine* (1971), suggests advancement of the famine as a watershed, although the effect is somewhat blunted by the amount of cover included on the pre-famine period. Most treatments of the nineteenth century in fact highlight the famine and the Land War. *A New History of Ireland* divides its long nineteenth century on the basis of the arrival of the Land Question to prominence, taking as the turning point, however, not the upheaval of the late 1870s but the introduction of Gladstone's first land legislation in 1870.[1]

The fact that so many perspectives on Ireland in the nineteenth century yield a strikingly different profile from that of the country with which it was linked in a United Kingdom is an enduring challenge for students of the history of both Ireland and Britain. It is perhaps the fate of countries subordinate to larger neighbours either to be ignored or treated as exotic. But peculiarities of the British constitutional system are a large part of the story of Anglo-Irish exchange in the nineteenth century. The absence of a written constitution, the survival of the legislative veto of the House of Lords into the twentieth century (1911 to be precise), the unwillingness to charter the liberties of the citizen, and the failure to put religious equality on a statutory footing, may be seen as elements in a constitutional compromise that masked and facilitated the smooth development of a modern political society in Britain. This constitutional archaism did not work as happily in Ireland, where the development of democracy was indeed validated by Westminster, but seldom in such a fashion as to command appreciation or gratitude.

The influence was not all one way, and the presence of Irish issues on the table at Westminster frequently affected the way in which British politics was played. Irish influence on parliament may have favoured change in some instances – Catholic Emancipation in 1829 being an example – but at several points may have facilitated the maintenance of the relics of a society of orders, which in turn continued to exacerbate Irish problems. Counterfactual history is a largely pointless exercise, but for one purpose: to serve as a reminder that at certain points things might have taken a different direction. The crisis in Ireland was crucial to the repeal of the corn laws in 1846. Would the church have avoided disestablishment in England and Wales in the late 1860s if Gladstone had not had the Irish branch to sacrifice? Would the landed interest in Britain have escaped virtually intact through the final quarter of the century if Parnell and the Irish National Land League had not caused anti-landlord sentiment to be equated with disorder and subversion? Much writing on Irish history is done with one eye on England. This is not of itself to be regretted. The problem is that all too often the aspect of England in focus is a static image of interest and influence that misses both the complexity of English politics and the dynamics of the relationship between the two countries. England in the early generations of the industrial revolution was not the haven of social tranquillity imagined by admiring Liberals on the continent, even if its political stability was the envy of bourgeois Frenchmen. The Gordon Riots, Peterloo, the Luddites and the Chartists were all manifestations of a society in turmoil.

Ireland had its own partly overlapping version of this turmoil. The threat of separation rather than any intimations of convergence had provided the background to the Union. Ireland retained its distinctive legal code and even the formalities of a lord lieutenancy, a highly anomalous institution within what was in legal theory a united polity. Nevertheless, the Union raised in many minds the prospect of assimilation, of an Ireland rescued for religion and civilisation by religious and cultural conversion, something not widely dreamt of since the seventeenth century. The thrust for this came not from official but from private sources, particularly Evangelicals envisaging the conversion of the Roman Catholics of Ireland to reformed religion. In the early decades of the century they enjoyed considerable influence with officials of church and state.

Any prospect of accommodation of the generality of Catholics to the new regime was rendered hopeless by the evangelising agenda that went hand in hand with the maintenance of legal disabilities against Catholics. The removal of most of the remaining disabilities by the Roman Catholic Relief Act of 1829 ('Catholic Emancipation') was a concession to popular political pressure that had been directed through influence on parliamentary elections. There was no concession of the general principle of religious equality in 1829 or for many decades to come. However, governmental rejection of a policy of assimilation on exclusivist Protestant terms was signalled in 1831 with the institution of a state-supported national school system that was determinedly neutral as between the confessions. For the next half century the dominant mode of policy was that of integration on broadly liberal terms, but with a preparedness, however reluctant, to suspend some of the legislative guarantees of liberty when that was required to counteract unrest. When Gladstone advocated Home Rule for Ireland in 1886 he was conceding that liberal measures within a United Kingdom framework were no longer adequate to meet the needs of the Irish situation.

Gladstone's Irish question was a simplification. Like many commentators, then and later, he had come to see in the confession-based division of the island's allegiances a conflict between ascendancy and a previously repressed majority. In fact, that horizontal division had been giving way since the 1830s to a more modern, vertical one. This involved the emergence of separate, confessional social systems extending into many areas of social life. The fate of the national school system inaugurated in 1831 illustrates the development admirably. The government's grand design for schools serving children of all denominations in a parish had been altered under pressure from the churches into a system wherein the one parish would have totally separate 'national' schools catering for the different denominations. In due course hospitals and other institutions of public life followed suit, and the pattern extended to wide areas of social and recreational life. This 'pillarisation' was a consequence of liberalism with which liberals were generally uncomfortable. The confessional university was the ultimate expression of

3

the movement. Hence the inordinate delay in finding a 'solution' to the university question, until the Irish Universities Act of 1908 provided an elaborate formula guaranteeing something closely approaching de facto confessionalism in a framework that satisfied the deep-rooted objection of many liberals to any semblance of state endowment of religion.

Especially after disestablishment in 1871, Protestant strength, while making full use of inherited advantages, was based on modern associational structures, of which the Orange Order was a remarkable example. The open conflict over land from the late 1870s onwards further deepened the division and had the effect of making the Protestant/unionist pillar appear more 'aristocratic' than it actually was. In any event, Protestants in late nineteenth-century Ireland were not a shrinking remnant. As a proportion of the population they rose at every census from 1861 to 1911, by which year they constituted approximately twenty-six per cent.

The nineteenth century was a time of bursting nets for the churches in Ireland. The identification of religious with political affiliation – never complete, but substantially effective – acted as a counter to indifference. Religion also came to be identified – in a way that the reformers and counter-reformers of the sixteenth century would have approved – with social propriety and the general advance of good manners. By the end of the century the message that cleanliness is next to godliness was getting through to all but the most marginal sectors of Irish society. There would always be those who could break free from the conventions, but the respectable society of late nineteenth-century Ireland had roles for most of its members defined by reference to class and gender.

The impact of Britain on the economy of Ireland is a very long story. As far as the nineteenth century is concerned, good proximate starting points are the take off of industrialisation in Britain, and the inception in 1793 of the war with France that would not end until the final defeat of Napoleon over two decades later. During that contest English demand for Irish corn increased enormously. The consequence was a booming agricultural economy that encouraged the continued expansion of an already burgeoning population of cottiers largely reliant on the potato to feed themselves and their families. With the collapse of prices and markets after the war's end, the economy on which they depended suffered a dramatic setback. The so-called 'golden age' of Irish agriculture was at an end.

Geographical proximity to England was at least as important as the constitutional link, and the consequent freedom of trade, in bringing the impact of the industrial revolution to bear on Ireland. The frequently repeated conceit that Ireland 'escaped' the industrial revolution – as if to keep the ground clear for the success of the 'Celtic tiger' two centuries later – is valid in one respect only: the country was not endowed with large quantities of the

4

new industrial infrastructure, and what there was of it came to be con-
centrated in the north east. However, the products of the 'dark satanic mills'
of Lancashire and Lanarkshire had a profound impact on life in Ireland.
This included the boon of an abundant supply of cheap cloth, and other
basic goods, and the concomitant growth of retailing. The corollary was the
devastation of the existing structures of domestic production and the impov-
erishment of those engaged therein, both in urban and rural economies.
Perhaps one third of the population came to depend totally on the annual
potato production of their small plots of potato ground. Given time, they
might have been absorbed into the commercial economy. But time ran out
in 1846, when the near-total failure of the potato owing to an airborne blight
not only left millions without their only sustenance but destroyed the faith of
all in the future of the subsistence potato economy. Since rural Ireland had
nothing else to offer them, and urban Ireland scarcely anything more, the
only prospects for those directly affected lay in swift flight to where they
might find opportunity, which primarily meant North America or Britain.

Given the scale of the problem, no government could have prevented
widespread suffering and death in Ireland in 1846–7. The government of the
day was less generous in its good intentions and less efficient in their delivery
than might have been, although it did have good intentions that it tried to
implement. The reasons for the deficiencies were complex and included the
fashionable and convenient shibboleth that government interference could
only make any economic problem worse. Currently acceptable approxima-
tions are for one million deaths (by hunger and the diseases that thrive on
famine) and one million famine emigrants.

The famine years intensified an existing pattern of emigration and
hastened the development of a rural economic system that gave primacy to
the family farm as an impartible inheritance. For the remainder of the
century the population was in constant decline with emigration exceeding
natural growth and immigration. The result was a dramatic divergence from
British demographic and political patterns. The demographic divergence
reflected the sparsity of industrial development in Ireland, which in turn
produced a very different balance of socio-political forces. Coming midway
between the reform acts of 1832 and 1867 that are such landmark events in
the evolution of democracy in Britain, the Irish Franchise Act of 1850
recognised the distinctive character of the Irish socio-political scene by
introducing a franchise based on occupation of property as distinct from
proprietorial interest, the principal intention and effect of which was to give
the vote to the tenants of even quite moderately sized farms.

In 1841 Ireland, with just over eight million people, was more densely
populated than Britain with about eighteen and a half million. However,
several millions of the Irish were caught in an outmoded subsistence economy,

while millions in Britain had made the frequently traumatic transfer to an industrial order capable of sustaining dramatic demographic growth. By 1901 the British population had surged to forty millions, while Ireland's had dropped to four and a half million. The nationalist inclination to process these statistics with a moral calculus is little help towards understanding them. In any case, the declining Irish population enjoyed a rising – if very unevenly spread – standard of living, as represented, for example, by the extensive streets of handsome shops at the heart of so many towns spread throughout the length and breadth of the country.

As a consequence of emigration, the nineteenth century saw the emergence in the English-speaking world of significant concentrations of Irish population. Particularly in the USA, Irish Catholics came to constitute a vibrant social and political influence. The interest of these Irish Americans in the politics of the homeland, albeit intermittent, was to have significant consequences, particularly in the radicalisation of nationalist politics. The Fenian movement owed its immediate origins, its ideological stance, and most of the strategic credibility that it intermittently achieved, to Irish America. The agrarian crisis of the late 1870s led to the identification of the land question with nationalist politics – and the radicalisation of both under the leadership of Charles Stewart Parnell – because of the intervention of Irish America in the person of John Devoy. The consequent Land War crystallised the basic attitudes and interests that would dominate the politics of the island over the following generations.

In almost everything that involved the printed word Ireland and Britain in the nineteenth century constituted a common market largely centred on London. Fifty per cent of the inhabitants of Ireland may have been speakers of Gaelic at the beginning of the century, but that language failed to take off as a medium of popular print culture. The writing, publication and reading of a wide range of literature in English flourished in Ireland over the century. The nationalising thrust of the age supported several assertions of the distinctiveness of some of this work as 'Irish literature in English' or 'Anglo-Irish' literature, before leading on in the 1890s to a movement for the revival and cultivation of literature in Gaelic. This went hand in hand with a movement to restore the old language as part of a wider cultural revival that was a belated manifestation of nineteenth-century cultural nationalism, and that also chimed with contemporary English reaction against the undermining of older ways by the progress of the age.

Nineteenth-century essentialism reached its apogee in the elaboration of racial paradigms linked to language. By the 1840s older origin myths had yielded to the notion that the indigenous Irish were Celts, and thus cousins of the Scots and Welsh. All of them stood in the shadow of the Anglo-Saxons, the supposed methodical builders of states, instinctively gifted for rule. This nonsensical farrago still provides many with their primary conceptual tools for analysing Irish history, politics and culture.

As frequently happens in writing about Britain, this essay has moved over and back between England and the entire island as the term of comparative reference to Ireland. But there is also much scope for getting perspective on Ireland through comparisons with Scotland or Wales. Ireland is also a European country, and there is scarcely anything about its experience that cannot be better appreciated on the basis of continental comparisons: Norwegians, Finns, Poles, Czechs, Slovaks, Hungarians, Serbs, and even Belgians, spent some or all of the nineteenth century in thrall to larger powers; the Netherlands and much of Germany developed confessionalised social systems; Finland suffered a serious famine in 1868. It must be said that Irish historians have yet to exploit most of this potential. Comparison between Ireland and other countries forming part of the British Empire – India has particular potential in this regard – has been more prolific, even if it also falls far short of the potential. Comparative examination of constituent parts of the Empire tends to fall into two categories: that in the empirical mode favoured by most historians; and that in a Cultural Studies mode dominated by colonial theory.

If the nineteenth century is now a happy hunting ground for historians and other students of the Irish past, it was scarcely in its time a golden age of Irish historiography. There were substantial achievements, and the groundwork was laid for critical historiography, but no Macaulay-style national narrative emerged that could elide differences. W. E. H. Lecky (1838–1903) was a liberal who came close to bridging the historiographical gap. However, as a rentier, he was repelled by the anti-landlord nationalism of the Land League and became embroiled like most of his contemporaries in the divisive politics of Home Rulers versus Unionists that bedevilled history writing as so many other aspects of the country's life.

As conventional scholarly writing of the history of Ireland was establishing itself from the 1890s through to the 1930s, study of the medieval and early modern eras predominated. By the 1960s emphasis had switched to the nineteenth century, with a focus on political movements and personalities, and especially on Parnell and the Land War. This concentration on the manifestations of political nationalism was in line with the established preoccupations of mainstream historiography in most other countries. Other areas of history were, however, catching on, as was illustrated by the appearance in 1973 of *Irish Economic and Social History*, the journal of the Economic and Social History Society of Ireland. *A New History of Ireland* as devised and planned in the 1960s, while prioritising a predominantly political narrative, provided extensive treatment of other aspects of the nineteenth (and other) centuries, including: economy, law, language and literature, administration, education, emigration, the Irish abroad, music and the visual arts.

In the course of the past twenty years the period from 1918 onwards has superseded the preceding century as the most popular area of research for Irish history postgraduates. Nonetheless, the nineteenth century has a constant stream of new devotees in history departments. At the same time, the Society for the Study of Nineteenth-Century Ireland has prospered, endowing scholarship in the period with twelve volumes of conference proceedings since 1996. These involve historians with a wide range of interests and also specialists from a series of other disciplines, all drawn to the abundance and accessibility of what is the most richly recorded epoch of the history of Ireland in terms of estate and personal papers, governmental and cadastral publications, cartography, periodical press, popular literature, and visual images.

Notes

1   W. E. Vaughan (ed.), *Ireland Under the Union, 1:1801–70*, vol. 5 (Oxford, 1989); ibid., *Ireland Under the Union, 2:1870–1921*, vol. 6 (Oxford, 1996).

CHAPTER 2

Gustave de Beaumont

Ireland's Alexis de Tocqueville

Tom Garvin and Andreas Hess

Alexis de Tocqueville and Gustave de Beaumont were, during their lives, inextricably associated with each other both in their own minds and in the perceptions of their French countrymen. Both were very well known social commentators, and Tocqueville's fame has long outlived him. American studies and his *De la démocratie en Amerique (Democracy in America)* are almost automatically associated together in people's minds; this classic work in the sociology of politics set the internal and international debate on American politics and society so decisively that a century and a half later it still is the intellectual fulcrum of much academic argument about the United States. The same cannot be said about Beaumont, nineteenth-century France's other sociologically minded explorer of the Anglophone world. Beaumont was the author of an equally classic work about a very different country, pre-famine Ireland, published in 1839, more or less at the same time as *Democracy in America. L'Irlande – sociale, politique, et religieuse* was published almost simultaneously in French and in English translation in 1839.[1]

Gustave de Beaumont (1802–66) was, with his friend and lifelong co-worker Alexis de Tocqueville (1805–59), one of the best-known social and political commentators in the world during the period 1830 to 1865. Both men had French gentry backgrounds, and were best described as democratic liberals in the French Catholic tradition; both lived in a France whose old feudal upper class had lost power and which was apparently destined to adopt democratic institutions in the near future as the ideas of the French Revolution, the English and Scottish Enlightenments, and those of the American Republic's founding fathers worked their way into French intellectual and popular culture. Both men did their most important work during the reign of Louis-Philippe (1830–48), both tending towards legitimism and democracy and therefore being somewhat at odds with the Orleanist regime. Tocqueville is best known for his monumental two-volume treatise on the

United States, published in French and almost simultaneously in English translation, between 1835 and 1840. The book, an instant classic, has never been out of print and has become a proverbial key work for the analysis of American society, political culture and the historical significance of the United States as a new, non-European, world power. Beaumont was, and is, less well known, and it is often not fully realised how closely they worked together – proof reading, rewriting and commenting on each other's work-in-progress. The two Frenchmen were passionate admirers of Anglo-American representative institutions and constitutional traditions, being both in the intellectual tradition of Montesquieu. Montesquieu's *Spirit of the Laws* (1749) argued that an idealised version of the English constitution, providing for government by good laws and a separation of powers, was superior to government by good men. Even good powerful men were not immune to the temptations of arbitrary, despotic government, as Lord Acton famously observed. Tocqueville and Beaumont in their turn believed that the English in America, in particular, had evolved and put into practical use an English-derived constitutional system involving semi-democratic participation and the exercise of human rights to an extent unparalleled in the world of the early nineteenth century. They admired this liberal democratic system despite such evidently scandalous features as race-based slavery and the often-ruthless exploitation and even expropriation of native populations. Both men saw this Anglo-Saxon democratic liberalism as ahead of its time and as a model of the political future of a mainland Europe that was still by and large monarchic and aristocratic. The two anglophiles had an informal division of labour: despite much overlap, Beaumont did his most important work on Britain and Ireland, while Tocqueville's most mature achievement was about America's political experiment. It is interesting that both men saw an intellectual and political comrade in the Catholic Irish liberal leader Daniel O'Connell: democrat, anti-slaver and philosemite as he was.

Heinrich Heine, in exile in Paris, found it difficult to warm to Alexis de Tocqueville. He felt that Tocqueville had an aristocratic arrogance and an intellectual certainty, which ill-became an academic scholar. By way of contrast, he found Tocqueville's friend Beaumont to be an attractive and warm person. Even today Tocqueville is still celebrated as the political prophet, the time traveller, the man who predicted an inevitable long-term tendency towards democratisation in conjunction with the creation of modern mass societies, the emergence of the United States and Russia as superpowers in the twentieth century, and the dangers of racism in some possible and shadowly imagined united Germany. Beaumont, on the other hand, is usually sidelined as the rather obscure travel companion of modern democracy's intellectual seer.

However, a rather different picture emerges on further investigation. It is obvious that the two men were almost inseparable throughout most of their adult lives; they shared their observations and research and debated every aspect of any intellectual conversation either of them might have had with any third party; in effect, they constituted a two-man department of political sociology in a platonic university. They discussed every scholarly line either of them had written with each other, whether these lines had been written together or separately. It is often difficult to say whose ideas are whose. The history of social ideas in Europe knows very few examples of such an intimate intellectual companionship. Benjamin Constant and Madame de Stael, Marx and Engels, and Adorno and Horkheimer come to mind; but even these examples do not parallel in any real way the extraordinarily intimate intellectual friendship between Tocqueville and Beaumont.

Seymour Drescher has pointed out that the two figures must be studied together; this admonition is very well taken. However, we wish to do justice in this essay to Beaumont's own significant intellectual achievements, achievements that his friend's work has tended to overshadow; students of Tocqueville have often paid lip service to Beaumont's *oeuvre* but it is seldom given any real appreciation.[2] In what follows a short account of Beaumont's life is given in which his friendship with Tocqueville and his political and early intellectual career is outlined. To anticipate, the initial success of his first two books, *The Penitentiary System of the United States* (1833) and *Marie, or Slavery in the United States* (1835) is seen as providing a major breakthrough for his literary and academic reputation. The second part discusses Beaumont's most successful, and arguably most important book, *L'Irlande*, his pioneering 1839 study of pre-famine Ireland, in context. Here it is argued that, although the Irish study was one of the first sociological bestsellers in France and has become an important source for Irish and other historians working on nineteenth century Ireland, it remains an almost forgotten classic in the wider academic world, deserving rediscovery and appreciation. What is even less well known is that in 1862–3 Beaumont wrote a new longer introduction to the seventh edition of *L'Irlande*, giving a brilliant, impassioned and moving description of the Great Irish Famine, its catastrophic progress, the frantic efforts of the often reviled London government to assuage its impact, its monstrous aftermath in the form of starvation, disease, death on a huge scale, emigration to the United States and the British colonies and the catastrophe's devastating long-term effects on Irish and Irish-American society, literary culture and politics.[3]

INTERTWINED LIVES: GUSTAVE DE BEAUMONT
AND ALEXIS DE TOCQUEVILLE

Gustave de Beaumont de Bonninière was born on the sixth of February 1802, at Beaumont-la-Chartre in the Sarthe. Beaumont's parents and family were both of French aristocratic background and the family had always been linked to the more enlightened circles of the French upper class. The Marquis de Lafayette, the famous aristocratic soldier who had fought alongside Washington against the British during the American War of Independence was Beaumont's grandfather. Lafayette represents an intriguing early American family connection. Not much is known of how Beaumont spent his childhood. His first appearance on the historical record as an adult is as *juge auditeur* and then as a deputy public prosecutor at the court of Versailles. It was also at Versailles that Beaumont first met Alexis de Tocqueville, a fellow student who had been pursuing a similar legal career. The two men shared more than just the fact that both came from similar aristocratic backgrounds and were aspirant lawyers. They took to each other personally, intellectually and politically; a friendship soon developed between Alexis and Gustave and in the following years the two developed their habit of reading and studying together. Both had an interest in political economy and were particularly taken by the theories of Jean-Baptiste Say. Again, both of them attended the lectures of François Guizot, a well-known liberal historian. They were particularly influenced by Guizot's arguments concerning the history and course of French civilisation.

The July Revolution (1830) brought an end to the reign of Charles X, and both young men were faced with difficult decisions. They had been forced to take an oath of loyalty to the new regime of Louis-Philippe; after much soul searching the two friends finally decided to take the oath so as to protect their legal careers. Since Tocqueville and Beaumont were deeply worried about the possible intentions of the new regime they also began to make contingency plans. Part of their plan was, quite simply, to take some time out by getting away from France. Beaumont had already written a short study of the French prison system. In this pilot study he had adumbrated a further, more detailed, investigation into prison systems from a comparative perspective.

To their astonishment the two friends actually received funding for their project; perhaps someone wanted to get rid of them or, alternatively, was throwing the two bright young fellows a much needed political and financial lifebelt. The pair were commissioned to travel together to America with the purpose of investigating the new prison systems of the United States to find out to what extent they resembled the French system and whether there were any innovations which the French authorities might profitably study. In April 1831 the two friends left Le Havre for America where they were to stay until February 1832.[4] They first arrived in New York and spent the first few weeks in the city and its environs (May–June). From New York they went to Boston, Philadelphia, Baltimore and Washington before returning again to New York. Two further excursions were also part of the trip, one to the Old Northwest and Canada, and another down the Mississippi river to New Orleans.

The trip turned out to be a success in more than one respect. The two friends managed to gather plenty of information about prisons and the American penitentiary systems. However, the most important result of their journey was the discovery that the comparison of prison systems also provided the key to a new, democratic 'philosophy'. They argued that the way a penitentiary system treats its prisoners reveals how a regime treats its individual citizens or subjects in general. American prisons apparently attempted at that time to turn criminals into good citizens rather than simply mete out retribution or vengeance; times may have changed in the intervening centuries. This enlightened American approach was a true revelation to the two Frenchmen: American institutions, American *mores* and attitudes, a new democratic and egalitarian approach to social relations which had evolved in the young United States, showed France and the rest of mainland Europe the future the two men hoped for.

On their return to France in the spring of 1832 Beaumont immediately started writing their joint report. Tocqueville at first found himself unable to put his own thoughts into writing; however, he contributed to the final stages of the draft and supplied statistics and useful collections of other data. In the meantime the news had spread to their joint boss, the French state, that Tocqueville and Beaumont were suffering from an apparently incurable new spiritual disease: love of democracy. Both found themselves peremptorily dismissed from their duties as public prosecutors. However, since both remained registered at the bar, this decision did not seem to have threatened their career prospects in any major way. As it turned out, the dismissal actually did the pair no harm at all.

Early in 1833 their report was finally published. *The Penitentiary System of the United States and its Application to France* proved to be an immediate success.[5] The study was widely discussed and was awarded the prestigious Montyon prize. Second and third editions followed in 1836 and 1844. Furthermore, the book soon appeared in translations; it was particularly widely read and appreciated in America and Germany. Beaumont embarked on a new project, a novel about the more tragic aspects of their American experiences while Tocqueville was writing his *magnum opus*, his monumental book on American democracy.

In retrospect it seems that in 1835 their ship really came in. In the summer of 1833 Tocqueville travelled to England for the first time.[6] He had hoped that England, the mother country of America, would provide further insight and perhaps provide some kind of intellectual key to an understanding of how the young American republic had been shaped. To his disappointment, no clear clues emerged during his first trip across the Channel. Furthermore, he was apparently treated like a nobody. However, two years later, Tocqueville was received very differently; the first part of *Democracy in America* had finally appeared in France and a translation had been published in England.[7] The book caused a sensation. In London the two friends met the translator of *Democracy*, Henry Reeve. Other contacts proved to be equally crucial for getting to know English society and its political system; in particular the help and advice of two eminent political economists, John Stuart Mill and Nassau William Senior, were central.[8]

Tocqueville and Beaumont continued their travels as far as Ireland, where they toured for six weeks.[9] The two friends used Dublin as a base, staying in the city for a few days before starting for a round trip that would bring them first to the south-east (Carlow, Waterford, Kilkenny), the south-west (Cork, Killarney, Limerick), the west (Ennis, Galway, Castlebar) and then back to Dublin via the midlands (Longford). They seem to have skipped the North of Ireland. At the end of their stay in Ireland Tocqueville and Beaumont also attended a meeting of the British Association for the Advancement of Science at Trinity College, Dublin.[10] While travelling together, they also talked about their publication plans for the future. They agreed on two things. Firstly they established that they would respect each other's publication plans and individual research interests. Beaumont would write on the unfulfilled promises of American democracy, the plight of African Americans and Native Americans, and the colonial relationship between England and Ireland, while Tocqueville would focus mainly on America's political system, French political development and the prospects for both American and European democracy. Secondly, to prevent possible misunderstandings, overlapping of research effort or any intellectual turf war, they agreed to show each other their work before publication.

The year 1835 not only saw Tocqueville's publication of the first volume of *Democracy in America* but also the publication of Beaumont's novel *Marie, or Slavery in the United States*.[11] While *Democracy* looked mainly at America's political system, *Marie* was an attempt to take a closer look at the seamier side of American society. The two books have to be read as companion volumes in order to make complete sense of America, or rather to grasp the two men's joint understanding of the country. *Marie*, like *Democracy in America*, was a huge success and was reprinted numerous times in French over the following decades. However, *Marie* remained a local French success and was almost unknown in America for over a century; American slavery was apparently a more popular topic in Europe and, to put it mildly, the book did not harmonise well with any American tendencies toward self-congratulation. The two books paid off in career terms; Tocqueville got himself elected to the French Academy of Moral and Political Sciences, thus emulating Beaumont's Montyon prize. Their publishing triumphs were also accompanied by personal fulfilment; Beaumont married his cousin Clementine de Lafayette, the granddaughter of General Lafayette, while Tocqueville married an Englishwoman, Mary Motley. The two friends also made a promising start to their political careers by being elected to the French Parliament.

During the summer of 1837 Beaumont travelled a second time to England and Ireland, this time on his own, to gather material for his Ireland project. Two years later *L'Irlande* finally appeared as a two-volume study.[12] An English translation of the book was published later that year.[13] It turned out to be an intellectual *tour de force* and proved to be even more of a hit than his first two studies. During the author's own lifetime the book saw seven French reprints; once again he was awarded the Montyon prize. He also became a member of the French Academy of Moral and Political Sciences. However, the commercial and academic success of the book was again mainly confined to France; the English-language translation, while respectfully received, only had one edition in 1839.

Quite apart from their publishing record and their political and academic achievements, Tocqueville and Beaumont remained liberals dedicated to social reform. Unlike many other liberals, however, they also remained internationalist; their opinions were not confined to internal French issues and they argued publicly, for example, against the excesses and abuses of an emergent French colonialism. By now the two friends had perfected their division of labour. Thus, for example, Tocqueville presented a report on the abolition of slavery to Parliament while Beaumont simultaneously presented a petition to the Chamber on behalf of the French Abolitionist Society. In 1841 they both travelled to Algeria, again an experience that would lead to both looking for more coherent and humane French policies in North Africa. Tocqueville and Beaumont were later to become members of the parliamentary commission on Algeria and they always remained interested in the subject as long as their political careers lasted.

The Revolution of 1848 ushered in the Second Republic. They both became members of the new National Assembly and both were selected to join the Constitutional Commission. In the following year Beaumont was appointed Special Ambassador to the United Kingdom and went to London while Tocqueville became France's Minister for Foreign Affairs. Yet this improvement in terms of political status and achievement didn't last long. In 1851, after Louis Napoleon seized power and declared himself emperor, both men were simultaneously forced to resign. They were arrested and imprisoned for opposing Louis Napoleon's coup d'état against the Second Republic.

The arrests (and almost comically prompt releases) marked their withdrawal from public affairs and the end of two remarkable political careers.

Tocqueville retreated to his home in the countryside and continued his intellectual reflections, *Souvenirs* (written 1850–1, published posthumously in 1893)[14] and *L'Ancien Régime* (1856)[15] being the results. Beaumont was in a way less fortunate and found that he could not devote all his time to writing. He had to attend to financial matters out of economic necessity connected with a legally encumbered inheritance from his father-in-law, Georges de Lafayette; this unpleasant experience seems to have informed his quite strong grasp of Irish land law, the plight of Irish encumbered estates and the malign social consequences of the interaction of land law and indebtedness, as is illustrated vividly in his 1863 introduction to the seventh edition of *L'Irlande*, looked at in the next paragraph of this essay. Occasionally, Beaumont managed to surface from his retreat. In 1854 he presented a longer meditation entitled *La Russie et les États-Unis* to the Academy of Moral and Political Science – once again the paper seems to have been in part the result of a long discussion with Alexis.

After Tocqueville's death in January 1859, Gustave began editing his friend's published and unpublished writings. Six volumes appeared between 1861 and 1866.[16] Preoccupied as he was with these editorial efforts Beaumont seems to have found less time to voice his concern for the oppressed and the excluded. Only once more would he succeed in making this concern public. Shocked and disappointed about British attitudes to the Irish tragedy after the famine, he presented the Irish case *(Notice sur l'état present de L'Irlande)* to the Academy of Moral and Political Science in 1863 and a longer version of this presentation became the preface or introduction to the seventh edition of *L'Irlande* in the same year.[17] The *Notice* is an old man's impassioned protest at the plight of Ireland combined with an optimism derived from, as ever, his rather uncritical admiration for the English constitution. As far as is known, this was Beaumont's last major public utterance before his death on 22 February 1866 in Paris.

ENTWINED LIVES, DIFFERENT INTELLECTUAL PASSIONS

We hope we have made it clear that the two men were pretty much intellectual equals; only history and circumstance have occluded Beaumont's very real intellectual eminence. Back in 1835, sometime in the summer on their joint travels in England and Ireland, Tocqueville and Beaumont had carved out their respective intellectual territories and also reached an agreement concerning their respective future publication plans. As we have seen, Tocqueville was to address the political systems and the development of modern democracies in France and the United States, while Beaumont was to investigate the less attractive side of the process, in particular by looking at America, Britain and Ireland. In the case of the United States this meant the maltreatment of slaves and Indians; in relation to the British Isles it involved dissecting the peculiar political arrangements and links of superordination and subordination that England had with Ireland. It is exactly this joint agreement, which throws light on the different political and intellectual preoccupations of the two friends. As demonstrated by the first publication on the American and French penitentiary systems (for which, despite a notional common authorship, Beaumont had mainly been responsible), Beaumont was clearly more interested in the downside of modern democracy and the plight of the underdog while Tocqueville was equally obviously fascinated by the possibly larger question of the future of democracy. The comparative study demonstrated that Beaumont understood himself as a liberal, but as also an advocate of the wretched of the earth: those who had either been omitted from, or who had been marginalised by, the democratic process. In *Marie*, a strange mixture of romantic narrative and critical political and sociological reflection, Beaumont had addressed the negative side of American society in particular. This concern with the victims of democratic or semi-democratic societies is perhaps what most clearly distinguishes Gustave intellectually and emotionally from Alexis. A similar sensitivity towards the weak occasionally shows through in Tocqueville's *Democracy* but is never the main thrust of his discourse. In *Marie* Beaumont persistently emphasises the normative content of the Declaration of Independence, the Constitution and the Bill of Rights in the sense that all these founding documents had either presupposed or promised political equality. He was shocked by the contrast between their high aspirations and the rather grubby or even evil realities of American politics; he noted bluntly that the documents remained mere rhetoric when it came to the systematic dispossession of the Indians and the equally systematic mass enslavement of black people. Thus, it should not come as a complete surprise that the American edition of *Marie* took more than 120 years to appear in print (1958 to be precise), its re-publication coinciding, probably not by accident, with the emerging anti-segregation movement of that time in the United States.[18] It is also only around the same time that it finally dawned on some that *Marie* and *Democracy* actually had to be regarded as companion volumes and needed to be studied together.

Of course, the American critics and reviewers who belatedly welcomed Beaumont's sociological novel had a point: *Marie* had to be interpreted as the much-needed corrective to Tocqueville's omissions in his *Democracy*. However, such late and posthumous success came at a price: while American critics praised Beaumont's book as a classic and as a forerunner to the emerging civil rights movement, they seemed quite unaware of the success his work on British rule in Ireland had enjoyed in Europe during his lifetime. *Marie* had been celebrated in France when it first appeared there. Viewed retrospectively, however, it was clearly inferior to the book on Ireland. Unlike *Marie*, the book on Ireland was not only awarded the prestigious Prix Montyon and reprinted many times up to 1914; it also brought Beaumont membership of the French Academy for Moral and Political Sciences.

The reason for this success is easily explained: while *Marie* had shed light on the problematic aspects of American democracy, *L'Irlande* had an obvious European context. The book made it starkly and unpleasantly obvious that even the 'oldest democracy in the world', the United Kingdom, had, to put it extremely mildly, a negative side. Of course it could be argued, more or less *ad hominem* and quite unfairly, that Beaumont's study and its reception were mainly an expression of French national pride. It could even be argued that, by their enthusiasm for his study of the plight of the Irish, his French readers were showing an ancient antipathy toward *L'Albion perfide*; after all, it wasn't all that long since Waterloo. However, nothing could be further from the author's intentions. As we have seen, like Alexis and like their common intellectual predecessor Montesquieu, Beaumont showed a deep but perhaps somewhat uncritical admiration for the English Constitution. Indeed, it is exactly this admiration that helps to explain the immediate success of his book on Ireland. In *L'Irlande*, Beaumont hits all the emotional registers, he weighs all the pros and cons, he appears to be the advocate of the British Government and uses all available arguments for the defence of its policies in Ireland, but finally he gives up and concludes sadly and reluctantly that Ireland was to the United Kingdom what slavery was to the United States; Ireland was that ironic entity, a persecuted martyr nation in the midst of a free polity. In particular, his instinct for the underdog drove his impassioned preface of 1863. In fact, he has been accused of exaggerating the pre-famine poverty of the Irish; while the potato was free of blight, the Irish were actually unusually well fed, it has been argued, and the famine came like a bolt from the blue. However, there had been earlier failure, and 1847 followed two years of partial failure; the British Government had had some warnings from Mother Nature, *pace* Joel Mokyr.[19]

Beaumont pursues two lines of argument in *L'Irlande*. In the first part he outlines the history of the island since the Norman invasion of 1169 and the subsequent development of a hybrid Gaelic and Anglo-Norman mediaeval society. He then recounts the bloody reconquest of Ireland by the nascent Tudor English state in the sixteenth century, followed by the dispossession of the Catholic landholders of Ireland by Protestant undertakers in the seventeenth century. He explains how over the course of nearly two centuries the English conquerors and the Protestant Anglo-Irish aristocracy ('the Ascendancy') that took over the island never quite legitimated themselves. Naturally, this tiny and fantastically privileged minority were going to be resented by the mainly Catholic aboriginal inhabitants of Gaelic and Anglo-Norman descent and even by people of lower status who were Protestant by religion. However, this privileged minority attempted to constitute itself as the Irish nation *toute courte* in the eighteenth century, ignoring the teeming millions of men and women of no property below it with their covertly expressed collective ideology of dispossession and sullen dreams of *revanchisme*, commonly expressed in Gaelic prose, poetry and verse.[20] The Ascendancy essentially drifted between two extreme poles: social, political and religious indifference to the dispossessed native Irish on the one hand and a passionate wish to exterminate Irish popery by a policy of proselytism on the other.[21] Thus, the English Ascendancy in the conquered island was never really capable of conceiving of a majoritarian project which might have made it possible to assimilate the Catholic majority to its colonial polity, whether during the Cromwellian period, during the Restoration, after the great land grab of the early eighteenth century, during the period of Grattan's Parliament (1782–1800) or even during the period that was, as it turned out, the time of the Irish Ascendancy's last chance: the early years of the parliamentary union of Britain and Ireland after 1800. Catholicism remained politically illegitimate and the religion of foreign enemies in the eyes of the joint British-Irish state. Property, and particularly landed property, remained mainly in the hands of Protestant proprietors. Catholics were forced by law to finance the upkeep of the Protestant Church in Ireland. Edmund Burke's famous pleas for religious tolerance fell on deaf ears, as did the more pragmatic private warnings of the Duke of Wellington. As a consequence of this stubbornness, any chance of a reconciliation between aristocracy and people in Ireland was stillborn. Two generations later, William Butler Yeats was to mourn, in one of the central themes of that great Irish poet, the passing of a great opportunity: a nationalist Catholic Ireland led by a mainly Protestant, but tolerant, Anglo-Irish nobility. Furthermore, while the aristocracy in England was open to the industrialisation of Britain, in Ireland the landed Anglo-Irish aristocracy seems to have been reluctant or unable to get involved in such enterprise, with the usual exception of the north-eastern part of the island, where a true cross-class Protestant community containing a significant Presbyterian tradition had grown up and developed a preoccupation with British-style modernisation and industrialisation. On top of this, pre-industrial Ireland's cottage artisanate was wiped out by British manufactured goods under the free trade regime of the time between 1815 and 1850. Furthermore, the mainly Scottish-derived plantation in Ulster did not have much impact on Irish society outside the northeast.

In the second part of his Irish study Beaumont describes the political and social constellations that arose from this seemingly irresolvable dilemma. Again and again he stresses that, through English colonisation, Ireland had also been given all the constitutional tools to free herself from colonial oppression. Daniel O'Connell had grasped that fact intellectually as a young man and had, for thirty years between 1815 and 1845, wrested concessions from an unwilling Protestant ascendancy in both islands by means of a lethal, very Irish and brilliant blend of mass popular agitation, loyalty to the Catholic faith, liberal political principles and constitutional argument; like the Irish poor, Beaumont admired the beloved Dan, King of the Beggars and the charismatic leader of the emergent Irish democracy. However, in the end Beaumont remained sceptical about the prospect of any real sea change in the powerful landed aristocracy of Ireland. It seemed to be too out of touch, too arrogant and too unwilling to learn from past mistakes; like the Bourbons, it learned nothing and forgot nothing.

Much as Tocqueville had pointed to central aspects of American social and political culture, Beaumont gave a thoroughgoing and vividly written diagnosis of the Irish disease. Despite his admiration for Anglo-Saxon constitutionalism, his book could have been legitimately entitled, following Tocqueville's famous title *De la démocratie en Amérique, De la tyrannie en Irlande*. The country was agrarian, the land was controlled by what he repeatedly termed a 'bad aristocracy', an aristocracy hampered by being derived from a recent and remembered conquest, alien in nationality, language, religion and culture from the vast bulk of the underlying population. As Beaumont spotted in 1839, the landlords despised the lower orders and the lower orders returned the compliment with a ferocious blend of covert contempt and hatred masked by an apparently genial subservience; Somerville and Ross miss this covert hatred completely in their affectionate contemporary portrayal, from an aristocratic point of view, of the late Victorian peasantry of the country.[22] This arrogant aristocratic tyranny used the law and the soldiery to enforce its exploitation of the vast majority, who defended themselves in the only way they could: by collective solidarity, secret combination, threats, assassination and mass agitation. This discredited ruling class, pathetically dependent on British support, was, by the time of the Great Famine, politically illegitimate. It was also incompetent and helpless because of the vicious stalemate that dominated Irish property relations, a stalemate brilliantly described by Beaumont, particularly in his 1863 introduction.

Like most of Tocqueville's prophecies concerning American democracy, most, but not all, of Beaumont's prophecies concerning Ireland came to pass. The Irish famine of the 1840s radicalised the Catholic majority further. It also caused the British government to write off the Irish Ascendancy finally. After 1850 Westminster tried to change horses in Ireland and side with the vast peasant-cum-farmer majority against the landlords. Following on O'Connell's precedent, a series of mass movements, agitating for land reform and a native government ('Home Rule') emerged. Beaumont foresaw the land reform, and prophesied the emergence of an Ireland of small owner-occupier farmers, as duly happened in the period 1880–1903. However, he also expected the Irish to settle down after land reform as part of a British-Irish constitutional democracy. Strangely enough, even as an old man he did not foresee the rise of a large, successful and vengeful Irish-American community in the United States that willingly encouraged and financed Irish militant insurgents from 1865 on. Irish veterans of the Union Army led the Fenian rising of 1867, which attempted to transform Ireland into an independent republic; these ex-soldiers were referred to respectfully in Ireland as 'the men in the square-toed [GI] boots'. A covert, and later overt, hatred of the British government continued to flourish in Ireland as well as in Irish-America; the famine had partially delegitimated the British state in Ireland. It was fatally easy to represent British rule in Ireland as consisting of the rule of a group of complacent men watching the Irish poor starve to death. Beaumont never fully appreciated this cultural fact, but of course he could not have foreseen the general European calamity of 1914.

Because of the First World War, which destabilised most of Europe, Ireland descended, with much of the rest of the continent, into revolution, civil war and sectarian pogrom after 1918. Eventually an Irish independent democratic state emerged in 1922 as a result of a violent democratic revolution, but it was shorn of the northeastern counties with their very different culture and social structure. This new country rapidly evolved into a republican democracy of yeoman farmers with institutions heavily influenced by both British and American prototypes. The landed ascendancy died out, leaving behind a formidable cultural heritage; the great houses of the aristocracy were burned down, turned into convents, used as schools or, eventually, converted into hotels, spas and golf clubs. Despite many back-slidings, most of twentieth-century Ireland had achieved an ambivalent freedom, or, as Michael Collins, the Irish revolutionary leader, famously put it in a presumably unconscious echoing of Beaumont, the freedom to achieve freedom. Collins was in the strange position of a revolutionary leader trying to sell electoral democracy to a population going through a period of hyper-nationalist enthusiasm; he succeeded in most of Ireland.

However, the sectarian curse and static politics of old Ireland lived on in Northern Ireland and has yet to be clearly lifted from Ulster society. Still, in both parts of Ireland equal rights and liberty for all citizens were no longer revolutionary demands but had gradually become practical achievements, starting in the south in the 1920s and in the north forty years later. Versions of the English constitution worked in interestingly different ways in the two

Irish political entities to enable a gradual liberalisation and equalisation of society to be engineered over the generations.

It could be argued that *L'Irlande* does not quite measure up intellectually to *Démocratie*. After all, Tocqueville's masterpiece has influenced the entire course of democratic political theory since the 1830s; it also predicted the rise of a superpower. Poor old Ireland had no such destiny ahead of her. We think that Beaumont set himself a far more difficult task; he had to time travel like his famous friend, but Tocqueville only had to travel into the luminous future of the United States; Beaumont had to travel into both the murky future of Ireland and into the unfortunate country's deep past to get to the historical roots of Ireland's strange, ancient, slow moving and secret civil war. It is not for nothing that the great English novelist, Evelyn Waugh, once remarked that for the Irish there were only two realities: Hell and the United States.

Gustave's task in Ireland is more difficult and complex than that of Alexis in America. What took the form of an early constitutional promise in America, to be realised only over generations and after a huge civil war and a century of racial discrimination and political struggle, was fought for as bitterly and over a far longer time in a European country that had to build democracy in the face of the stubborn resistance of an ancient entrenched agrarian aristocracy with great social, cultural and intellectual power; in the terms of Yeats, the Irish aristocracy was no petty people, and everyone knew that the old ascendancy constituted the people of Irish patriotism as well as the people of Beaumont's collective tyranny. They were the people of patriotic and liberating leaders such as Burke, Swift, Grattan and Parnell as well as being the people of tyrannical figures such as Saurin and Castlereagh.[23] Again, quite apart from the political claims of a brilliant if illegitimate aristocracy, democracy had, as in many other European countries, to contend with a peasant communal culture of solidarity which was ambivalent about the essentially individualist liberalism characteristic of representative democracy.

However, Gustave de Beaumont, Ireland's Alexis de Tocqueville, has given us what is in effect a classic account of the painful birth pangs of an Irish democracy in the womb of the British polity, Ireland providing in miniature a precursor and pre-enactment of the tragic but ultimately successful struggle for democracy in a Balkanising Europe. Ireland also served as a role model or prototype for many other post-feudal and post-imperial nations in Europe and elsewhere; India, Cyprus and Israel are prime examples of countries that looked to both revolutionary and constitutional precedents first experimented with in Ireland. Even Canada and Australia watched with great interest the Irish constitutional manoeuvrings by which total legal independence was achieved in the decades after 1922. Beaumont did not foresee Irish independence, but he did foresee Irish constitutional self-realisation. His work on Ireland deserves to be rediscovered and given intellectual recognition by the English-speaking world; after all, he could easily be termed the father of Irish sociology, and certainly a father of the sociology of politics in Ireland. More widely, he can also be plausibly looked upon as one of the founders of the sociology of the oppressed.

Notes

1 A drastically truncated version of this essay serves as the Preface to a new English-language edition of *L'Irlande* (2006) published by Belknap Press of Harvard University Press. We wish to thank Seymour Drescher for his comments on an early draft. A slightly different version of this text – with a focus on the role of Beaumont (and Tocqueville) as public intellectuals *avant la lettre* – appeared as 'Tocqueville's dark shadow: Gustave de Beaumont', in Christian Fleck, Andreas Hess and E. Stina Lyon (eds), *Intellectuals and their Publics: Perspectives from the Social Sciences* (Aldershot: Ashgate, 2009).

2 Up to the present day there is not one study, PhD dissertation or biography available that analyses Beaumont's work in any comprehensive way. At present, the best studies containing material on Beaumont are: S. Drescher, *Tocqueville and England* (Cambridge, Mass.: Harvard University Press, 1964); from the same author 'Tocqueville and Beaumont: a rationale for collective study', in S. Drescher (ed.), *Tocqueville and Beaumont on Social Reform* (New York: Harper and Row, 1968), 201–17; and G. W. Pierson, *Tocqueville in America* (Baltimore: Johns Hopkins University Press, 1996 [1st edn 1938]). Pierson has also published an essay which tries to portray Beaumont: 'Gustave de Beaumont: liberal', in *Franco-American Review*, 1 (1936–7), 307–16. Further helpful information is contained in H. Brogan, *Alexis de Tocqueville* (London: Profile Books, 2006), and in A. Jardin, *Tocqueville – A Biography* (Baltimore: Johns Hopkins University Press, 1988). Jardin also edited the three-volume set of the *Correspondance d'Alexis de Tocqueville et de Gustave de Beaumont* (Paris: Gallimard, 1967). The new Harvard University Press edition of Beaumont's *Ireland* has triggered a new wave of reception – see particularly two longer review essays by Michael Drolet in *History of European Ideas*, 33 (2007), 504–24 and in the *European Journal of Political Theory*, 7: 2 (2008), 241–53, and the essay by Andreas Hess, 'Gustave de Beaumont: Tocqueville's darker shadow?', *Journal of Classical Sociology*, 9: 1 (Feb. 2009), 67–78. A more thorough study, particularly using the Tocqueville and Beaumont material that is available in the Yale Beinecke Library, is called for; the present text cannot, of course, be a substitute for such a study.

3 Tom Garvin has translated the 1863 introduction for publication in the new edition of the complete book in English (Beaumont 2006).

4 A primary source is Pierson's (1996 [1st edn 1938]) almost day-by-day reconstruction of the trip in his study *Tocqueville in America*. Particularly interesting in Pierson's book is the list of acquaintances and contacts, among them John Quincy Adams and Daniel Webster. They also had one meeting with the then president, Andrew Jackson.

5   G. de Beaumont and A. de Tocqueville, *On the Penitentiary System of the United States and its Application to France* (Carbondale: Southern Illinois University Press (reprint), 1964 [1st edn 1833]). Francis Lieber, whom Tocqueville and Beaumont had met on their American trip, had translated the American edition.

6   The notes and diaries from the two trips to the British Isles have been published posthumously in: Alexis de Tocqueville, *Journeys to England and Ireland*, J. P. Mayer (ed.), (New Brunswick: Transaction, 1988).

7   For more details see Seymour Drescher's account (1964) *Tocqueville in England*.

8   For a more detailed account on the various intellectual influences (not all of them British) see Michael Drolet's excellent study *Tocqueville, Democracy and Social Reform* (Houndmills: Palgrave-Macmillan, 2003).

9   A detailed reconstruction of this trip can be found in Emmet Larkin, *Alexis de Tocqueville's Journey to Ireland* (Dublin: Wolfhound Press, 1990) and in S. Drescher, *Tocqueville and England* (1964).

10   Although it cannot be confirmed by any records it is probable that Beaumont met his future translator William Taylor at this academic gathering. William Cooke Taylor (1800–49) was a writer and economist. Taylor had been educated at Trinity College, Dublin but later moved to London where he became a contributor to the whig–liberal, reform-oriented weekly *Athenaeum*. Throughout his life he remained supportive of the Irish cause, following a liberal and reformist agenda and being particularly keen on furthering Irish higher education. He is also known as the founder of the Dublin Society for Statistical and Social Inquiry, a learned society which still exists. Two of his books dealt particularly with Ireland: *History of the Civil Wars in Ireland* (Edinburgh: Constable, 1831); *Reminiscences of Daniel O'Connell by a Munster Farmer* (London, 1847). His *magnum opus* was *The Natural History of Society in the Barbarous and Civilised* State (London: Longman, 1840), in which he argued that mankind was created by God to be civilised and that savagery is not a natural condition but rather the product of ignorance.

11   There are now a few modern translations available. Particularly good ones are Alexis de Tocqueville, *Democracy in America*, translated by George Lawrence, J. P. Mayer (ed.), (London: Fontana Press, 1994); and Alexis de Tocqueville, *Democracy in America*, translated by Gerald E. Bevan; edited and introduced by Isaac Kramnick (London: Penguin, 2003). Gustave de Beaumont's slavery book has been re-issued recently in English: Gustave de Beaumont, *Marie, or Slavery in the United States* (Baltimore: Johns Hopkins University Press, (1999 [1st edn 1958]).

12   G. de Beaumont, *L'Irlande – social, politique, et religieuse* (Paris: Michel Lévy Frères, 1839).

13   G. de Beaumont (ed. W. C. Taylor), *Ireland – social, political, and religious* (London: Richard Bentley, 1839).

14   The first American edition is: Alexis de Tocqueville, J. P. Mayer and A. P. Kerr (eds), *Recollections* (New York: Doubleday, 1970); as pointed out above, *Souvenirs* was first published in 1893 and is now vol. 12 of the Collected Works of the Gallimard edition, edited by J. P. Mayer (1964).

15 The first American edition is Alexis de Tocqueville, *The Old Regime and the French Revolution* (New York: Doubleday, 1969); the book was first published in Paris in 1856 (Michel Lévy Frères).

16 Alexis de Tocqueville, Gustave de Beaumont (ed.), *Oeuvres completes D'Alexis de Tocqueville* (Paris: Michel Lévy Frères, 1860–6).

17 G. de Beaumont, *L'Irlande – sociale, politique, et religieuse* (Paris: Michel Lévy Frères, (1863, 7th edition), I–LXXXIV.

18 On American self-criticism and intermittent angry awareness of the lack of congruence between American political ideals and the sometimes squalid and brutal realities of American life, see in particular Samuel P. Huntington, *American Politics: the Promise of Disharmony* (Cambridge MA: Belknap/Harvard, 1981).

19 Joel Mokyr, *Why Ireland Starved* (London: Allen and Unwin, 1985), 6–29.

20 See Breandán Ó Buachalla, *Aisling Ghéar: na Stíobhartaigh agus an tAos Léinn, 1603– 1788* (Baile Átha Cliath: Clóchomhar, 1996) [*Sharp Vision: The Stuarts and the Intellectuals, 1603–1788* (Dublin: Clóchomhar, 1996)], on both old Catholic aristocratic and popular Irish-speaking attitudes toward the English Hanoverian and Protestant regime; essentially these attitudes were rather dreamy, but clearly Jacobite or separatist, and eventually there was a drift toward separatism and republicanism in the late eighteenth century once the bankruptcy of the Catholic Stuart tradition was understood; the 'King across the Water' became the descendant, mythically speaking, not of James II, the legitimate Catholic monarch of the Three Kingdoms, but *Seamus Cachach*, or 'Shitty Jimmy', the alleged coward of the Boyne Water.

21 For a vivid illustration of English proselytism and hatred of Catholicism in Ireland in the early nineteenth century see Charlotte Elizabeth Tonna, *Irish Recollections* (Dublin: UCD Press, 2004), first published as *Personal Recollections* (London, 1841).

22 E. O. Somerville and Martin Ross, *The World of the Irish R. M.* (London: Lewis, Gifford, 1989).

23 See Donald R. Pearce (ed.), *The Senate Speeches of W. B. Yeats* (London: Prendeville, 2001), 88.

Bibliography

Beaumont, G. de and A. de Tocqueville, 1964 [1833]. *On the Penitentiary System of the United States and its Application to France*. Carbondale: Southern Illinois University Press (reprint).

Beaumont, G. de, 1839. *Ireland – social, political and religious*, W. C. Taylor (ed.), London: Richard Bentley.

Beaumont, G. de, 1839. *L'Irlande – sociale, politique, et religieuse*. Paris: Michel Lévy Frères.

Beaumont, G. de, 1999 [1958]. *Marie, or Slavery in the United States*. Baltimore: Johns Hopkins University Press.

Beaumont, G. de, 2006. *Ireland*, edited and newly introduced by Tom Garvin and Andreas Hess, Cambridge, Mass.: Belknap Press of Harvard University Press.

Brogan, Hugh, 2006. *Alexis de Tocqueville*. London: Profile Books.

Drescher, S., 1964. *Tocqueville and England*. Cambridge, Mass.: Harvard University Press.

Drescher, S., 1968. 'Tocqueville and Beaumont: a rationale for collective study', in S. Drescher (ed.), *Tocqueville and Beaumont on Social Reform*. New York: Harper and Row, 201–17.

Drolet, M., 2003. *Tocqueville, Democracy and Social Reform*. Houndmills: Palgrave-Macmillan.

Drolet, M., 2007. 'Failed states and modern empires: Gustave de Beaumont's Ireland and French Algeria ' (Review essay), *History of European Ideas*, 33, 504–24.

Drolet, M., 2008. 'A morality tale, or tyranny in Ireland' (Review essay), *European Journal of Political Theory*, 7: 2, 241–53.

Hess, A., 2009. 'Gustave de Beaumont: Tocqueville's darker shadow?', *Journal of Classical Sociology*, 9: 1, 67–78.

Huntington, Samuel P., 1981. *American Politics: the Promise of Disharmony*. Cambridge Mass.: Belknap/Harvard.

Jardin, A. (ed.), 1967. *Correspondance d'Alexis de Tocqueville et de Gustave de Beaumont*. 3 vols. Paris: Gallimard.

Jardin, A., 1988. *Tocqueville – A Biography*. Baltimore: Johns Hopkins University Press.

Larkin, E., 1990. *Alexis de Tocqueville's Journey to Ireland*. Dublin: Wolfhound Press.

Mokyr, J., 1985. *Why Ireland Starved*. London: Allen and Unwin.

Ó Buachalla, B., 1996. *Aisling Ghéar: na Stiobhartaigh agus an tAos Léinn, 1603–1788*. Baile Átha Cliath: Clóchomhar.

Pearce, D. R. (ed.), 2001. *The Senate Speeches of W. B. Yeats*. London: Prendeville.

Pierson, G. W., 1936–7. 'Gustave de Beaumont: liberal', *Franco-American Review*, 1, 307–16.

Pierson, G. W., 1996 [1938] *Tocqueville in America*. Baltimore: Johns Hopkins University Press.

Somerville, E. O. and Martin Ross, 1989. *The World of the Irish R. M.* London: Lewis, Gifford.

Tocqueville, Alexis de, 1860–1866. *Oeuvres completes D'Alexis de Tocqueville*, Gustave de Beaumont (ed.), Paris: Michel Lévy Frères.

Tocqueville, A. de, 1964 [1893]. *Souvenirs*. vol. 12, Collected Works, J. P. Mayer (ed.), Paris: Gallimard.

Tocqueville, A. de, 1969. *The Old Regime and the French Revolution*. New York: Doubleday.

Tocqueville, A. de, 1970. *Recollections*, J. P. Mayer and A. P. Kerr (eds), New York: Doubleday.

Tocqueville, A. de, 1988. *Journeys to England and Ireland*, J. P. Mayer (ed.), New Brunswick: Transaction.

Tocqueville, A. de, 1994. *Democracy in America*, translated by George Lawrence, edited by J. P. Mayer, London: Fontana Press.

Tocqueville, A. de, 2003. *Democracy in America*, translated by Gerald E. Bevan, edited and introduced by Isaac Kramnick, London: Penguin.

Tonna, C. E., 2004. *Irish Recollections*. Dublin: UCD Press (first published as *Personal Recollections*, 1841).

CHAPTER 3

John Stuart Mill and Ireland

Graham Finlay

John Stuart Mill's engagement with Ireland ranged over his entire writing life, from a long analysis of Parliamentary wranglings over Catholic Emancipation, written when Mill was nineteen, to the incendiary pamphlet of 1868, 'England and Ireland', a few years before his death. The views expressed in these various writings vary almost exactly with Mill's development as a thinker. Focusing as they do on questions of justice, nationality and reform, they give a good indication of the radical position he occupied at the end of his life and the reasons he was driven to it. Far from being occasional pieces, Ireland seized Mill's entire attention at various times and has a claim, with India, to be one of the great fields on which his entire social science and his capacity for political action were displayed. Although he has been criticised from various quarters for being inconsistent, for being slow to learn about conditions in Ireland or for being an imperialist, Mill's treatment of Irish matters exhibits a great deal more consideration and sophistication than these criticisms allow. In what follows, I argue both that his writings on Ireland illuminate better-known aspects of Mill's work and that the case of Ireland is a crucial companion to the case of India for understanding the practical implications of Mill's thought. Given Mill's long occupation as a top servant of the East India Company and his wider reputation as the greatest economist of his time, Ireland serves, for him, as the near and European social experiment that complements the remote and Asian one.

Every recent commentator bemoans the lack of scholarship on this subject. There is one book-length study by Bruce Kinzer,[1] several articles by economists and economic historians, mostly exploring his relation to the Land Question,[2] and Lynn Zastoupil's short discussion of how the case of Ireland figures in Mill's moral and political thought with a particular emphasis on his writings about the famine (Zastoupil 1983), as well as short discussions in a number of books about Mill. Perhaps the most interesting aspect of these latter accounts is the recent tendency for post-colonial critics of Mill, like Uday Singh Mehta and Jennifer Pitts, to criticise his relation to Ireland in the broader context of his relationship to empire in general and to India in particular.[3] I will particularly urge that this tendency to elide the cases of Ireland and India, encouraged by some passages of Mill's, seriously mis-represents the distinctive recommendations Mill had for Ireland and ignores the significant differences between the two cases. A different accusation, and in many ways an opposing one, is that Mill wants to 'absorb' Ireland into the British nation, as the Bretons and Scottish highlanders have been absorbed into France and Britain respectively. I am equally critical, in this essay, of the 'assimilationist' interpretation of Mill's late thought about Ireland. Ireland is, in many ways, a special case for Mill and his thoughts on Ireland repre-sent a sophisticated response to both the practicalities and moral aspects of conflicts of nationality and religion.

Space does not permit more than a cursory survey of all of Mill's writings on Ireland. His first publication, listed as 'Ireland' in the *Collected Works*, is an orthodox Benthamite analysis of the debates surrounding Catholic Emancipation. In it Mill exposes, at considerable length, the fallacious argu-ments of various speakers in the House of Commons as had been demanded of him by the editor of the *Parliamentary History and Review*, the journal in which it appeared.[4] There Mill argues that 'sinister interests' have led to the Irish people being victimised by their landlords but, given the presence of landlords on both sides of the House of Commons, both parties have seized upon Catholic Emancipation as a way of avoiding dealing with the genuine problems of Ireland (Mill 1982a: 68). In the 1830s, Mill treats Irish politics in the context of his plans for developing a radical party capable of forming a government, adjusting his responses to suit the political advancement of this cause. At the same time, he was experiencing his spiritual crisis and its resolution: from the publication of the 'Spirit of the Age' in 1831 through the publication of 'Bentham' and 'Coleridge' in 1840, Mill was fleeing from the Benthamism of his father towards the revelatory conservatism of Carlyle and Coleridge and the social philosophy of the Saint-Simonians and Comte, both groups possessing a considerable authoritarian streak. It is at this point that he writes, in a letter to John Pringle Nichol, that his preferred policy toward Ireland was 'for a good stout Despotism – for governing Ireland like India', a policy that 'cannot be done', since the 'spirit of Democracy has got too much head there, too prematurely'.[5] This unguarded comparison of the task of governing Ireland with the practice of English rule in India is one of the bases for the 'post-colonial' reading of Mill on Ireland, despite being a throwaway line in a long letter on other subjects. Soon after, Mill's views changed again, leaving behind whatever he thought was excessive in his reaction against his father's thought and assuming, with the publication of the *System of Logic* and, more important for this essay, his *Principles of Political Economy*, the increasingly stable and well-refined view that constitutes his mature thought and the basis on which he increasingly evaluated political questions.

Just as he was finishing the *Principles of Political Economy* in 1846, Mill took six months out to write forty-three articles in the *Morning Chronicle*, urging the acquisition of millions of acres of waste lands in Ireland for the purpose of improving them and converting them into peasant proprietorships.[6] Unlike cottier tenancy where competition bids up rents and the benefits of improvements do not go to the tenant, this secure form of proprietorship would, Mill thought, improve the character of the tenants in terms of industry and lead them to make reproductive choices that discourage overpopulation because the benefits of improvements and the harms of overpopulation would fall directly on these new peasant proprietors. He vehemently opposes two responses to the famine proposed by the *Times* and other newspapers, relief through outdoor public works and a new poor law for Ireland, claiming that both proposals encourage the opposing vices and further overpopulation. In this, he found himself engaged in a debate with another friend of Ireland, the political economist and member of Parliament, George Poulett Scrope. Scrope had predated Mill in advocating the cultivation of the waste lands, but thought that a 'new' more extensive poor law for Ireland was necessary for the successful reclamation of those lands, especially while they were being reclaimed.[7] Unlike the existing Poor Law in Ireland, itself only passed in 1838, under Scrope's proposal the able-bodied poor would have a right to relief and that relief could come in the form of work outside the workhouse and specifically on reclaiming the waste lands.[8] Mill was opposed to this form of relief because of his emphasis on peasant proprietorships as an instrument for long-term moral reform. Any direct relief, especially a guaranteed one, would work against a radical reform of the land system and, more importantly, would remove the incentive for peasant proprietors to improve their land.[9] Despite all of Mill's efforts and the good will of the Prime Minister, Lord Russell, towards the reclamation project, Mill's arguments did not succeed. A new poor law providing for public-works relief for the able bodied and a bill providing direct relief through soup kitchens was adopted, while proposals for reclaiming the waste lands were dropped in the face of parliamentary resistance.[10]

Mill's hostility to cottier tenancy and his advocacy of peasant proprietorships would play a significant role in the *Principles of Political Economy*, even though his outrage would subside through later editions because he thought that Ireland had become more prosperous, famine and emigration having removed the pressure of population and the Encumbered Estates Act having gone some way to reducing the number of cottiers.[11] The *Principles'* discussion of Ireland is otherwise notable for Mill's outrage at the extent of emigration. Mill thunders,

> The land of Ireland, the land of every country, belongs to the people of that country. The individuals called landowners have no right, in morality and justice, to anything but the rent, or compensation for its saleable value. With regard to the land itself, the paramount consideration is, by what mode of appropriation and of cultivation it can be made most useful to the collective body of its inhabitants. To the owners of the rent it may be very convenient that the bulk of the inhabitants, despairing of justice in the country where they and their ancestors have lived and suffered, should seek on another continent that property in land, which is denied them at home. But the legislature of the empire ought to regard with other eyes the forced expatriation of millions of people. When the inhabitants of a country quit the country *en masse* because the government will not make it a place fit for them to live in, the Government is judged and condemned. (Mill 1965: 326)

This passage, with its hostility to absolute conceptions of property, the appeal to general utility and the moral outrage with which Mill viewed questions of government and empire, sums up Mill's position and foreshadows his views in 'England and Ireland'.

For his knowledge of conditions in Ireland, Mill was strongly indebted to John Elliot Cairnes, the Irish political economist. There is some scholarly controversy about the extent of Cairnes's influence on Mill. T. A. Boylan and T. P. Foley see Cairnes as more radical than Mill and quicker to adopt the radically critical attitude to the English idea of absolute property in land embodied in the passage above, whereas Steele describes him as 'deferential', and Kinzer largely agrees with Steele.[12] Cairnes's initial approach to Mill is unquestionably deferential in tone[13] and he continuously invokes positions that Mill already holds on various economic subjects as the basis for his own views. The claim that serves as the basis for both Mill's and Cairnes's eventual commitment to considerable interference in property in land is that this is an unwarranted extension of a peculiar local English custom to a different economic and cultural environment, under the pretence of a commitment to absolute property in land as a universal law of political economy. Mill had held these views long before he ever met Cairnes.[14]

Cairnes was not, however, nearly so ready to defer to Mill in his discussion of another Irish question in which Mill was involved, the Irish University Question. In 1865 Mill was elected to parliament for Westminster. He had been encouraged before to run for an Irish seat by the Tenant League, but had been prevented by his official position within the East India Company (Mill 1981: 272). As Kinzer shows, Mill consistently avoided using his influence either as a writer or an MP to fight a measure Cairnes detested, the proposal to allow Catholics to receive degrees from the Queen's universities without having attended these non-denominational colleges. Such a move would require alteration of the Queen's universities' charters and would extend the power of the Catholic Church in Ireland, because students of the seminary in Maynooth and the newly founded Catholic University (now University College Dublin) would constitute the bulk of the applicants for the accrediting examinations (Kinzer 2001: chapter 4). As Kinzer shows, Mill's interest in protecting Gladstone's administration was more important to him than fighting for principles that he acknowledged to be worthwhile in the abstract, the importance of secular education and of reducing the influence of the Catholic Church (Kinzer 2001: 159–160). Although Mill wanted to protect Gladstone because he was likely to promote political reform and expansion of the franchise, Mill's final position on university education is worth quoting:

> a really national university for any country, but especially for a country divided between different religions, would be a university in which instead of only one professor of history, of ethics, or of metaphysics, there should be several of each, so that as long as there are subjects on which interested people differ, they might be taught from different points of view; & the pupils might either choose their professor, or attend more professors than one in order to choose their doctrine, examinations & prizes being made accessible to all.[15]

With this in mind, Mill proposes that Trinity College be reorganised along these lines, adding: 'Considering moreover how very noxious the higher instruction given by the Catholic prelates is sure to be, I think it right to avoid by every means consistent with principle the subsidising it in any shape or to any extent.'(Mill 1972b: 1893) As Kinzer notes, because Cairnes had an even greater antipathy to the Catholic Church, this would not have been his solution (Kinzer 2001: 162). It is, however, an important passage for understanding Mill's mature thoughts about governing divided societies, an aspect of Mill's thought that I will return to at the end of this essay. In the event, the intransigence of the various sides meant that none of the envisaged changes to Irish higher education were made in Mill's lifetime (Kinzer 2001: 160–1).

In 1868, while still a member of parliament, Mill brought out his most famous publication on Irish questions, 'England and Ireland'. Although this pamphlet was his principal literary response to the Fenians' activities, Mill had already responded as a politician, leading a delegation of MPs intent on persuading Lord Derby to spare Thomas Burke's life and giving several speeches to the same end.[16] 'England and Ireland' startled English popular opinion and the press and, to some extent, has equally surprised recent commentators on Mill's thought. In it Mill, who was sanguine about the progress of Ireland and the removal of grievances against England on Ireland's part in both the *Considerations on Representative Government* and the editions of the *Principles of Political Economy* published just before 'England and Ireland', declares that unless England is prepared to give the mass of the Irish people what they want, i.e. control over Irish land, then England's union with Ireland will be jeopardised and will be unjust. Mill advocates a 'judicial inquiry', in the form of a commission, which would have the power to compel landlords to convert their tenancies from a variable to a fixed rent (Mill 1982c: 527). This would provide each landlord with the 'rent he now receives (provided that rent be not excessive)' and landlords would have the option of receiving this rent directly from the state, a guarantee that Mill hoped would lead to a reduction of the influence of absentee landlords, uninterested in the condition of Ireland (Mill 1982c: 527). This change in his economic proposals has been viewed as a radical alteration in Mill's thought, but it should be acknowledged that his original goal remains in force, the improvement of the Irish people, to which he adds the goal of preserving the Union, an arrangement he thinks is very much in the interest of both England and Ireland. The argument for this economic reform is also the same: the different understandings of property in England and Ireland (Mill 1982c: 512–13). The shift is only in terms of the type of economic solution offered: once, Mill says, the conversion of waste lands into peasant properties would have been enough but now, with the real danger of a nationalist revolution, only a wholesale conversion of the conditions of tenants will do (Mill 1982c: 518–19). The preservation of the Union, Mill thinks, is important for both the strategic interests and moral concerns of both England and Ireland. An independent Ireland would pose a standing threat to England and would impoverish itself politically, whereas a failure to deal justly with Ireland would leave England condemned in the eyes of the world (Mill 1982c: 520–1).

In the ensuing debates surrounding the Irish question Mill's pamphlet was roundly attacked in the press and the House as a call for the 'spoliation' of all property, and Mill was compelled to defend it. In a speech on 12 March 1868 Mill argued that many landlords need not fear his proposal, since many tenants did not pay the full rent.[17] As he remarked to Cairnes, 'England and Ireland' was an attempt to put forward a radical proposal in the hopes that it would make less radical proposals politically feasible.[18] Mill accordingly gave himself a great deal of credit for the Land Act of 1870 (Mill 1981: 280). Subsequently, Mill served as chairman of the launching committee of the Land Tenure Reform Association and advocated its work in speeches and in print (Kinzer 2001: 208). He was struck from the committee of the Cobden Club just before his death for his membership of the

Association and for these heretical views on land tenure (Collini 1991: 323) and long after his death in 1873 his step-daughter, Helen Taylor, continued to receive letters from various persons, including Michael Davitt and Anna Parnell, remembering him as a friend of Ireland.[19] Kinzer notes the importance of Mill's views to the land agitation of the 1870s and 1880s.[20] Having had slight influence on the actions of English politicians concerning Ireland, Mill had a greater posthumous influence on Irish politicians in Ireland.

Mill's thought on Ireland, as a whole, exhibits greater continuity than change and the views he held on Ireland towards the end of his life provide new insights into Mill's work through its application to a concrete case. To some extent, Mill inherits from Bentham and his father a tendency to develop an economic explanation for all things, particularly in terms of the interest of the parties concerned. This form of explanation, crudely Benthamite in his first writing on 'Ireland', becomes a centrepiece of his moral theory in his advocacy of peasant proprietorships. The later Mill is more concerned about finding the mechanisms for moral improvement, but this moral improvement has a material base that is not always noticed in Mill scholarship.[21] In his writings on the Irish character and Irish prospects, Mill emphasises the radically plastic character of human beings and the formative power of circumstances. So, if people in Ireland appear to be morally degraded, or lazy, or incapable of self-government it is not the fault of some essential traits of the Celtic character, but the product of unjust economic relations, lack of incentive to improve their holdings or to limit the size of their families and Irish tenants' despair of the willingness of English politicians to redress their grievances. Mill says,

> Is it not, then, a bitter satire on the mode in which opinions are formed on the most important problems of human nature and life, to find public instructors of the greatest pretension imputing the backwardness of Irish industry, and the want of energy of the Irish people in improving their condition, to a peculiar indolence and *insouciance* in the Celtic race? Of all vulgar modes of escaping from the consideration of the effect of social and moral influences on the human mind, the most vulgar is that of attributing the diversities of conduct and character to inherent natural differences. What race would not be indolent and insouciant when things are so arranged, that they derive no advantage from forethought or exertion?'[22]

Although Mill goes on to attribute some national character to the Irish – 'a pleasure-loving and sensitively organized people' – he claims that they are 'not less fitted for ['steady routine labour'] than their Celtic brethren the French,[23] nor less so than the Tuscans, or the ancient Greeks' (Mill 1965: 319). In these passages, Mill dispenses with biologised, racial accounts of group difference, all the while affirming a contingent material and psychological understanding of 'national character'.[24] Once Irish emigrants have the benefits of American opportunities, American education and American land, in twenty or thirty years 'they are not mentally distinguishable from other Americans' (Mill 1965: 334).

It is following this discussion of the Irish character that Mill enters into his most sophisticated discussion of the relation between Ireland and India. Ireland and India share the same history of the misapplication of English, class-based institutions. In India, this took the form of the promotion of the *zemindars* who, instead of becoming English magistrates, became Irish landlords (Mill 1965: 321). In the recent administration of India, that of James and John Stuart Mill, this economic error has been corrected, with the result that the principal landlord is the government, with the rent paid directly by the 'immediate cultivator' who holds the land on a long lease (Mill 1965: 322). This, of course, is the same solution that Mill was to advocate for Ireland twenty years later, with the most radical government intervention he was prepared to envisage. In this way, the rule of India is better than that of Ireland and Mill's conviction on this score, in 'England and Ireland', is explained. Mill's hope for a more enlightened administration of Ireland explains away what has been seen as a simple-minded equivalence, on his part, between the characters of Irish and Indian people. Mill actually says, in 'England and Ireland':

Englishmen are not always incapable of shaking off insular prejudices, and governing another country according to its wants, and not according to common English habits and notions. It is what they have had to do with India; and those Englishmen who know something of India, are even now those who understand Ireland best. Persons, who know both countries, have remarked many points of resemblance between the Irish and the Hindoo character; there certainly are many between the agricultural economy of Ireland and of India. But, by a fortunate accident, the business of ruling India in the name of England did not rest with the Houses of Parliament or the offices at Westminster; it devolved on men who passed their lives in India, and made Indian interests their professional occupation. There was also the advantage that the task was laid upon England after nations had begun to have a conscience, and not while they were sunk in the reckless savagery of the Middle Ages. The English rulers, accordingly, reconciled themselves to the idea that their business was not to sweep away the rights they found established . . . but to ascertain what they were; having ascertained them, to abolish those only which were absolutely mischievous, otherwise to protect them, and use them as a starting point for further steps in improvement. This work of stripping off their preconceived English ideas was at first done clumsily and imperfectly, and at the cost of many mistakes; but as they honestly meant to do it, they in time succeeded, and India is now governed, if with a large share of the ordinary imperfections of rulers, yet with a full perception and recognition of its differences from England. What has been done for India must now be done for Ireland; and as we should have deserved to be turned out of the one, had we not proved equal to the need, so shall we to lose the other. (Mill 1982c: 519)

This is not the claim that Irish and 'Hindoo' characters are the same, but that their land systems are similar. Notably, in this very late passage in his writing life, Mill envisages for both India and Ireland the prospect of separation if the English do not fulfil their moral role. Mill's willingness to end the rule of the empire if it fails to live up to its responsibilities is a leap of imagination that Mill's post-colonial critics continually praise in Edmund Burke, but fail to acknowledge in John Stuart Mill.[25] In terms of Mill's economic remedy and in terms of his willingness to consider separation, Mill's views on Ireland are similar to his views on India, and the continuity of his thought, right through 'England and Ireland', is apparent.

But, of course, Ireland and India are also different. Although Indians and Irish people are alike subjects of the Empire, Irish people are, by the Act of Union, subjects on an equal legal basis with English subjects, especially once the religious tests had been removed. Much has been made of the preference Mill expresses for a 'good stout Despotism – for governing Ireland like India' in his letter to John Pringle Nichol, but even in 1837, soon after the 'highwater mark' of his reaction against Benthamite and James Millian democracy, he recognises that such a course is impossible (Mill 1963: 365). India lacks, according to Mill, the institutions of an independent state, whereas Ireland has the political institutions of the British state. It is worth noting, then, that half of 'England and Ireland' is devoted to arguing for the desirability of the continuation of the Union, although this argument has been neglected in the vigorous debate surrounding his proposals for land reform. Mill argues that there are good strategic and geo-political reasons why both England and Ireland would be better off under a political Union if the necessary economic reforms of Irish land tenure could be made. Not only would holding Ireland despotically lead to universal moral condemnation by the other world powers, but 'if separate, they would be a standing menace to one another (Mill 1982c: 521). Ireland would have to arm itself against England, and it is not clear that the people want to bear this tax burden. Alternatively, rather than becoming independent, Ireland might join France or America. Even if Ireland remained independent of these former rivals of England, England would still have to occupy Ireland at 'every commencement of hostilities' to prevent it from being used as a base by some other power' (Mill 1982c: 522). Further, the despotic control of Ireland would bring to Ireland's aid all the liberal powers of the world, including the United States: 'Neither Europe nor America would now bear the sight of a Poland across the Irish Channel' (Mill 1982c: 520).

The relevant writing for this discussion is clearly Mill's discussion of foreign policy and the independence of sovereign states in 'A few words on non-intervention'. Mill's considerations there act as an important supplement to the prevailing discussion in the secondary literature, where Mill's chapter on 'Nationality' in the *Considerations on Representative Government* receives almost exclusive attention. In his discussion of independence in 'A few words on non-intervention', Mill emphasises that a willingness to struggle for popular government is the chief criterion for aiding nations in their pursuit of self-government and so, presumably, for providing them with self-government. Mill says: 'The only test possessing any real value, of a people's having become fit for popular institutions, is that they, or a sufficient portion of them to prevail in the contest, are willing to brave labour and danger for their liberation' (Mill 1984a: 122). That these legitimate struggles for self-government are actually struggles for popular government indicates Mill's view about purely 'nationalist' revolutions. Mill explicitly compares the suggestion that Ireland be governed by brute force to the oppression of the nationalities that fired the Romantic imagination in the nineteenth century. Mill says:

> It is not consistent with self-respect, in a nation any more than in an individual, to wait till it is compelled by uncontrollable circumstances to resign that which it cannot in conscience hold . . . If England is unable to learn what has to be learnt, and unlearn what has to be unlearnt, in order to make her rule willingly accepted by the Irish people; or, to look at the hypothesis on its other side, if the Irish are incapable of being taught the superiority of English notions about the way in which they ought to be governed, and obstinately persist in preferring their own; if this supposition . . . is true, are we the power which, according to the general fitness of things and the rules of morality, ought to govern Ireland? If so, what are we dreaming of, when we give our sympathy to the Poles, the Italians, the Hungarians, the Servians, the Greeks and I know not how many other oppressed nationalities? On what principle did we act when we renounced the government of the Ionian Islands? (Mill 1982c: 519–520)

All of these peoples, with the exception of the Ionian Islands, suffered under undemocratic regimes. This is why it is important for Mill to emphasise that the legal barriers to political participation by Catholics have almost all been removed, since exclusion from political participation forms part of the justification for the rebellion of these nationalities (Mill 1982c: 507–8). This also informs Mill's comparison of the Irish with the Hungarians and his dismissal of the suggestion that the recently established 'equal union' between Austria and Hungary was a viable solution for England and Ireland (Mill 1982c: 525). E. D. Steele has argued, with some heat, that Mill viewed the

Irish as less civilised than the Hungarians and, accordingly, as lacking the 'necessary attributes' for self-government.[26] But consideration of Mill's actual claims shows that it is a difference in the qualities of the political violence in the two cases that is crucial. The Hungarians had fought a proper revolution, in Mill's eyes, of the kind with which he sympathised. It was general, it was popular, and it was for popular self-government, not merely the feeling of nationality, or, as Mill puts it, the mere 'satisfaction, which she [Ireland] is thought to prize, of being governed solely by Irishmen – that is, almost always by men with a strong party animosity against some part of her population' (Mill 1982c: 524). Mill thinks that the Irish people are not yet hell bent on this satisfaction and that the Fenians do not yet constitute a polit-ical class that represents the real strivings of the Irish people, unlike the leaders of the Hungarian revolution, nor have the Fenians proved themselves capable of serving as the leaders of an independent country.[27] 'England and Ireland' is a desperate plea for England to undertake the necessary economic reforms that will avert the rise of this narrowly nationalist revolution.

Seeing the Fenian rebellion as a merely nationalist one is itself a mistake that English politicians are making, a mistake calculated to assuage their consciences: if the rebellion is merely for the idea of nationality, then it does not stem from long-standing economic abuses that might have been removed (Mill 1982c: 509). But this scorn for ideas for concrete economic reforms is a further mistake: 'Rebellions are never really unconquerable until they have become rebellions for an idea' (Mill 1982c: 509). This analysis of the Fenian rebellion is connected with Mill's other discussions of revolu-tions, principally French ones. Mill admired the revolutionaries of 1789 and of February 1848 in France, because the former was the first 'popular revolution' and the second was the first revolution for an 'idea', crucially, for Mill's view, the economic idea of cooperation.[28] Mill takes pains to connect developments in France and Ireland. He points out that only bad weather prevented the French General Hoche from landing in Ireland during the war against revolutionary France and connects this with his proposals for econ-omic reform. All Ireland wants is what Hoche would have given it: fixity of tenure (Mill 1982c: 518). If this had happened, the Irish peasant would have become, through peasant proprietorship, as developed and industrious as the French peasant, who had benefited in this way through the redistribu-tion of property following the revolution of 1789.[29] What is needed now is to

give the Irish peasant all that he could gain by a revolution – permanent posses-sion of the land, subject to fixed burthens. Such a change may be revolutionary; but revolutionary measures are the thing now required. It is not necessary that the revolution should be violent, still less that it should be unjust. It may and it ought to respect existing pecuniary interests, which have the sanction of law. An equivalent ought to be given for the bare pecuniary value of all mischievous rights which landlords or any others are required to part with. But no mercy ought to be shown to the mischievous rights themselves; no scruples of purely English birth ought to stay our hands from effecting, since it has come to that, a real revolution in the economical and social constitution of Ireland. In the completeness of the revolution will lie its safety. (Mill 1982c: 518–9)

It is not political self-determination that the people of Ireland want or lack; it is economic self-determination.

What, then, is the relation between Mill's hopes for the Union and his theory of nationality? Steele and Lebow claim that Mill advocates the 'absorption' of the Irish into the British polity along the lines of absorption of the Bretons into the French polity (Steele 1970b: 432; Lebow 1979: 10). In doing so, however, they ignore some of the nuances of Mill's treatment of Irish nationality in his famous chapter on the subject in *Considerations on Representative Government*. Mill's discussion of the absorption of 'inferior and more backward portion[s] of the human race' into more civilised peoples refers to the Bretons and Basques, the Scottish Highlanders and the Welsh, but not to the Irish (Mill 1976b: 549–50). When he returns to the subject of nationalities mixed in the same state, the case of Ireland appears as somewhat different from that of the Bretons:

When the nationality which succeeds in overpowering the other is both the most numerous and the most improved; and especially if the subdued nationality is small, and has no hope of reasserting its independence; then if it is governed with any tolerable justice, and if the members of the more powerful nationality are not made odious by being invested with exclusive privileges, the smaller nationality is gradually reconciled to its position, and becomes amalgamated with the larger. No Bas-Breton, nor even any Alsatian, has the smallest wish at the present day to be separated from France. If all Irishmen have not yet arrived at the same disposition towards England, it is partly because they are sufficiently numerous to be capable of constituting a respectable nationality by themselves; but princi-pally because, until of late years, they have been so atrociously governed, that all their best feelings combined with their bad ones in rousing bitter resentment against the Saxon rule. This disgrace to England, and calamity to the whole empire, has, it may be truly said, completely ceased for nearly a generation. No Irishman is now less free than an Anglo-Saxon, nor has a less share of every benefit either to his country or to his individual fortunes, than if he were sprung from any other portion of the British dominions. The only remaining real grievance of Ireland, that of the State Church is one which half, or nearly half, the people of the larger island have in common with them. There is now next to nothing, except the memory of the past, and the difference in the predominant religion, to keep apart two races, perhaps the most fitted of any two in the world to be the completing counterpart of one another. The consciousness of being at last treated not only with equal justice but with equal consideration, is making such rapid way in the Irish nation, as to be wearing off all feelings that could make them insensible to the benefits which the less numerous and less wealthy people must necessarily derive, from being fellow-citizens instead of foreigners to those who are not only their nearest neighbours, but the wealthiest, and one of the freest, as well as most civilized and powerful, nations of the earth. (Mill 1976b: 550–1)

Although this long passage conveys the radical difference between the *Considerations on Representative Government* and 'England and Ireland' regarding the state of Irish resentment, Mill's description of the Irish people is considerably different from that of the Bretons. Unlike the Bretons, the Irish have sufficient numbers to make up a 'respectable nationality'. Even though Mill's previous description of the 'absorption' of the Bretons is less assimilation than the breeding of a new nationality, in which cultural 'types' are not 'extinguished', but contribute to a new and improved form of polity, even this fate is not reserved for Ireland.[30] Rather they will serve as the 'completing counterpart' of the English – which I interpret as something less than 'absorption' – with whom they will live as 'fellow citizens', benefiting from the English not principally in terms of civilisation, but in terms of their markets, industry and power ('numbers') and wealth. All of the emphasis in 'England and Ireland' is on Ireland's *difference*, particularly the Irish people's different sentiments about property.[31] The Union can only be saved if this difference is acknowledged. If I may add a speculation based on Mill's rhetoric, the relation seems to be similar to the relation of 'perfect equality' that Mill hopes will characterise marriages between men and women.[32]

Within the country, Mill also proposes institutions that belie many interpretations of *On Liberty*, which interpret it in a strictly individualist fashion. Mill's hostility to the Catholic Church pervades his writings, from 'Ireland' to 'England and Ireland', including *On Liberty*.[33] For Mill, the Catholic Church is intolerant and reactionary in both its national and international policies and has a sinister interest in controlling the people through fear of hellfire. Nevertheless, his eventual recommendation regarding the Irish University Question shows the flexibility of his view. Mill's recommendations in *On Liberty* frequently describe the 'experiments in living' that ought to be protected as practices, not just as individual eccentricities. For example, Hindus and Muslims in India and Mormons in Utah should be allowed to practise their religions under the shield of the liberty principle, despite an hostility on Mill's part to some of their practices – like the polygamy of the Mormons – which is as great as his antipathy to the Catholic Church (Mill 1976a: 284–5, 290). Mill's solution to the University Question –

that individuals should be able to choose from multiple professors – is in harmony with this practice-based aspect of *On Liberty* and with his larger educational recommendations. In a divided society, the goal is to keep up a diverse set of practices so that individuals have real choices. If those practices require state sanction and support, then Mill is prepared to endorse that, even in a sector as important to him as education. In an area like university education, where state regulation and control is unavoidable, Mill insists that diversity within institutions must be maintained, because the greatest danger is that schools and universities will become instruments of indoctrination if they are under the exclusive governance of any interested group, including the state.[34] Further, the notion of looking at things from another group's point of view is essential to his educational practice. In his Rector's speech at St Andrew's, Mill says:

> Improvement consists in bringing our opinions into nearer agreement with facts; and we shall not be likely to do this while we look at facts only through glasses coloured by those very opinions. But since we cannot divest ourselves of preconceived notions, there is no known means of eliminating their influence but by frequently using the differently coloured glasses of other people: and those of other nations, as the most different, are the best. (Mill 1984b: 227)

This is, I argue, one reason why Mill was prepared to make the compromise he did regarding university education in Ireland. Beyond allowing him to support Gladstone, the way had been paved by his philosophy of diversity itself. Such a view reinforces the importance of the peculiar Irish case of national difference. To have a majority Catholic society incorporated, politically, with England's Protestant society forced upon legislators a crucial element of diversity, and the practical and moral obligation to create a set of institutions that provided real alternatives for Irish students.

All of these aspects of John Stuart Mill's mature position concerning Ireland show the importance of Ireland as a crucial test for his mature social and political thought in its entirety. Ireland was neither a faraway colony nor a mere region of the mother country, neither an independent nation in waiting nor an integral part of British culture. It was a field for political action, but not a clear field on which anything might be erected. Hundreds of years of misgovernment and the resentment and division that that injustice had caused meant that the House of Commons of the Union, and English reformers generally, must adopt economic and social measures adapted to Ireland's peculiar situation. It is the specificity and complexity of the Irish situation that makes Mill's recommendations on this subject so individual and specific, not some momentary or aberrant deviation from his settled philosophical and political views.

Notes

1   Kinzer, 2001. As will be obvious from what follows, I am tremendously indebted to Professor Kinzer for his illumination of many aspects of Mill's thoughts on Ireland, including chronology, sources and avenues of inquiry. I am also grateful for his kind comments on a draft of this chapter.

2   Collison Black, 1953; Steele, 1970a and 1970b; Lebow, 1979; Boylan and Foley, 1983.

3   Mehta 1999: 4 and Pitts 2005. I am very grateful to Jennifer Pitts for showing me advance copies of some chapters of her book, including chapter 3 'Edmund Burke's Peculiar Universalism' and chapter 5, 'James and John Stuart Mill: The Development of Liberal Imperialism in Britain'. For the claim that Mill sees India and Ireland as 'less civilised', see Pitts 2005: 284, although Pitts is sensitive to the ways in which this claim is belied by his later position on Ireland. Steele also strongly criticises Mill as an imperialist in Steele 1970b.

4   Mill 1982a. On the expectations of Mill's editor, see Kinzer, 2001: 13.

5   Mill 1963: 365. Cited in many places, including Kinzer, 2001: 35 and Zastoupil, 1983: 714.

6   These articles, all titled 'The condition of Ireland', are found in volume XXIV of Mill's *Collected Works*. For the amount of acres to be converted, see Mill, 1986a: 898–9.

7   Mill notes that his waste lands proposal had been anticipated by various authors, including Scrope, W. T. Thornton (see Thornton 1971) and William Blacker, for which see Mill 1986e.

8   This summary of Scrope's views is drawn from Kinzer 2001: 68–70.

9   Scrope wrote several letters to the *Morning Chronicle* responding to Mill's attack on his proposal. Mill replies to Scrope in Mill 1986c and Mill 1986d, among other places.

10   See Kinzer 2001: 78–81. Peter Gray discusses the debate between Mill and Scrope in Gray 1999: 56–7, with particular reference to emigration.

11   For the successive changes between the 1852, 1856 and later editions, see *Principles of Political Economy* (Mill 1965: 324–36), where Mill gives his own account of changes in Irish economic life.

12   See Boylan and Foley 1983: 104–6. For the passage they are criticising, see Steele 1970a: 232. Kinzer claims that Boylan and Foley's case is overstated, Kinzer 2001: 6.

13   Their correspondence, including Cairnes's 'Notes on the state of Ireland' have been reproduced as Appendix H of the *Collected Works* edition of the *Principles* (Mill 1965).

14   For Cairnes, see Boylan and Foley 1983: 104–6, where they cite Cairnes's articles in the *Economist*, from 9 Sept. to 4 Nov., 1865. For Mill, see Mill 1965: 228–32. The same claims about landed property are found in his *Morning Chronicle* writings, e.g., Mill 1986b: 904–7, written before Mill met Cairnes at the Political Economy Club in 1859. For the date of their meeting, see Boylan and Foley 1983: 98. The general notion of the error of English political economists mistaking local conditions for universal laws was a hobby-horse of Mill's. For a particularly early example, see 'Miss Martineau's summary of political economy' [1834], Mill 1967: 225–6.

15   Mill 1972b: 1,892–3. Cited in Kinzer 2001: 162.

16 See Mill 1981: 276, where he takes credit for saving Burke's life. Mill's speech at the delegation to Lord Derby can be found as 'The Fenian convicts', 25 May, 1867, in Mill 1989: 165–7. Further speeches in the House of Commons and at a large Reform meeting touched on this issue. See, variously, Mill 1989 [25 May, 1867]: 171–4, [14 June, 1867]: 188–190, [21 July, 1868]: 315–6. On Mill's response to Fenianism, see Kinzer 2001: 167–8.

17 See 'The state of Ireland', in Mill 1989 [12 Mar., 1868]: 254–5. On this speech, see Steele 1970b: 446–7 and Kinzer 2001: 193–9.

18 'To John Elliott Cairnes', Mill 1972a [10 Mar., 1868, Letter No. 1,204]: 1,373. See also Mill 1981: 280.

19 See Item 195: Helen Taylor from Michael Davitt, 12 Nov. 1885, ff. 63–4, and Items 73–84: Helen Taylor from Anna Parnell, 1881–1889, ff. 165–187, Volume 18 Mill–Taylor Collection, British Library of Political and Economic Science, Archives, London School of Economics.

20 Kinzer 2001: 213. I am especially indebted to Kinzer's work for the above chronological discussion of Mill's writings on Ireland.

21 Mill says 'the substitution of long leases for tenancy at will, and of any tolerable system of tenancy whatever for the wretched cottier system; above all, the acquisition of a permanent interest in the soil by the cultivators of it; all these things are as real, and some of them as great, improvements in production, as the invention of the spinning-jenny or the steam engine'. Mill 1965: 183.

22 Mill 1965: 319. For Mill's continued hostility to 'essentialist' explanations, see 'England and Ireland', Mill 1982c: 507. In fairness, and given the importance of Celticism to this volume, the following quotation should be noted. This quotation is from a period in which Mill's thought is, perhaps, not entirely early or late and demonstrates the extent to which Mill's anti-essentialism about race developed over the course of his late period. After complaining about the incompetence with which issues of race are handled in Britain (and bearing in mind that 'race' largely stood at this time as a marker of cultural difference), Mill says:

> As far as history, and social circumstances generally, are concerned how little resemblance can be traced between the French and the Irish – in national character how much! The same ready excitability; the same impetuosity when excited, yet the same readiness under excitement to submit to the severest discipline – a quality which at first might seem to contradict impetuosity, but which arises from that very vehemence of character with which it appears to conflict, and is equally conspicuous in Revolutions of Three Days, temperance movements, and meetings on the Hill of Tara. The same sociability and demonstrativeness – the same natural refinement of manners, down to the lowest rank – in both, the characteristic weakness an inordinate vanity, their more serious moral deficiency the absence of a sensitive regard for truth. Their ready susceptibility to influences, while it makes them less steady in right, makes them also less pertinacious in wrong, and renders them, under favourable circumstances of culture, reclaimable and improvable . . . in a degree to which the more obstinate races are

strangers. To what, except their Gaelic blood, can we ascribe this similarity between populations the whole course of whose history has been so different? We say Gaelic, not Celtic, because the Kymri of Wales and Bretagne, though also called Celts, and notwithstanding a close affinity in language, have evinced throughout history . . . an opposite type of character; more like the Spanish Iberians than either the French or Irish: individual instead of gregarious, tough and obstinate instead of irrepressible – instead of the most disciplinable, one of the most intractable Races among mankind.

'Michelet's history of France' [1844], Mill 1985b: 235.

23 And it is worth remembering here Mill's admiration for the French, fascination with French affairs and discussion of French nationality, of which more below.

24 On the complexities of Mill's treatment of national character, Ireland, race and Celticism, see Varouxakis 2002.

25 A partial exception to this is Jennifer Pitts, who claims that Mill is prepared to envisage separation between England and Ireland, but not England and India. See Pitts 2005: 288. For another passage in which Mill envisions the separation of England and India, see Mill 1976b: 577.

26 Steele 1970b: 431–2. For a good reply, see Zastoupil 1983: 714–15.

27 That it is not merely a matter of relative civilisation is indicated by the relevant quotation, from Mill 1982c: 526:

It may be added, that the Hungarian population, which has so nobly achieved its independence, has been trained of old in the management of the details of its affairs, and has shown, in very trying circumstances, a measure of the qualities which fit a people for self-government, greater than has yet been evinced by Continental nations in many other respects far more advanced. The democracy of Ireland, and those who are likely to be its first leaders, have, at all events, yet to prove their possession of qualities at all similar.

28 For the former, see Mill 1985a: 58. For the latter, see Mill 1965: 775.

29 Mill makes this point even more strongly in an unpublished manuscript, dated by the editors of the *Collected Works* to 1848, 'What is to be done with Ireland?', Mill 1982d: 503.

30 For this prior statement regarding 'absorption', see Mill 1976b: 549–50.

31 Mill says,

If suitability to the opinions, the feelings, and historical antecedents of those who live under them is the best recommendation of institutions, it ought to have been remembered, that the opinions, feelings, and historical antecedents of the Irish people are totally different from, and in many respects contrary to those of the English; and that things which in England find their chief justification in their being liked, cannot admit of the same justification in a country where they are detested.

Mill 1982c: 511–12. As for property in land, Mill says, 'In the moral feelings of the Irish people, the right to hold the land goes, as it did in the beginning, with the right to till it.' Mill 1982c: 513.

32 Mill does describe the choice facing a country that has conquered a smaller, less advanced one as one between 'perfect equality' and 'despotism' in his 'Notes on the newspapers' of 25 Apr., 1834 on the proposed 'Repeal of the Union', see Mill 1982b: 216, cited in Kinzer 2001: 34. In this article, Mill also compares the rule of Ireland and India at some length and blames Britain for choosing neither course, but a 'middle course' in which England placed her military at the disposal of 'an indigenous oligarchy'.

33 See e.g., Mill 1982a: 84, Mill 1982c: 523. In 'On liberty', Mill describes the Catholic Church as 'the most intolerant of churches', before going on to praise the institution of the 'devil's advocate'. See Mill 1976a: 232.

34 For Mill's views on education, see Mill 1976a: 302–3.

Bibliography

Boylan, T. A. and T. P. Foley, 1983. 'John Elliot Cairnes, John Stuart Mill and Ireland: some problems for political economy', *Hermathena*, 135, 96–119.

Collini, Stefan, 1991. *Public Moralists*. Oxford: Clarendon Press.

Collison Black, R. D., 1953. 'The classical economists and the Irish problem', *Oxford Economic Papers*, v.

Gray, Peter, 1999. '"Shovelling out your paupers": The British State and Irish famine migration 1846–50', *Patterns of Prejudice*, 33.

Kinzer, Bruce L., 2001. *England's Disgrace? J. S. Mill and the Irish Question*. Toronto: University of Toronto Press.

Lebow, R. N., 1979. 'J. S. Mill and the Irish land question', in R. N. Lebow (ed.), *John Stuart Mill on Ireland*. Philadelphia: Institute for the Study of Human Issues.

Mehta, Uday Singh, 1999. *Liberalism and Empire*. Chicago: University of Chicago Press.

Mill, John Stuart, 1963. 'Letter to John Pringle Nichol', 21 Dec., 1837, 228, in *Early Letters, Collected Works*, XII. Toronto: University of Toronto Press.

Mill, John Stuart, 1965. *Principles of Political Economy* [7th edn, 1871, first published 1848] *Collected Works*, II and III. Toronto: University of Toronto Press.

Mill, John Stuart, 1967. 'Miss Martineau's summary of political economy' [1834], in *Essays on Economics and Society, Collected Works*, IV. Toronto: University of Toronto Press.

Mill, John Stuart, 1972a. 'To John Elliott Cairnes, 10 Mar., 1868, Letter No. 1,204, *The Later Letters, Collected Works*, XVI. Toronto: University of Toronto Press.

Mill, John Stuart, 1972b. 'To John Morley', 11 May, 1872, Letter No. 1,732, *The Later Letters, Collected Works*, XVII. Toronto: University of Toronto Press.

Mill, John Stuart, 1976a. 'On liberty' [4th edn, 1869, first published 1859], in *Essays on Politics and Society, Collected Works*, XVIII. Toronto: University of Toronto Press.

Mill, John Stuart, 1976b. 'Considerations on representative government' [3rd ed, 1865, first published 1861], in *Essays on Politics and Society, Collected Works*, XIX. Toronto: University of Toronto Press.

Mill, John Stuart, 1981. 'Autobiography' [1873], in *Autobiography and Literary Essays, Collected Works*, IV. Toronto: University of Toronto Press.

Mill, John Stuart, 1982a. 'Ireland' [1825], in *Essays on England, Ireland, and the Empire, Collected Works*, VI. Toronto: University of Toronto Press.

Mill, John Stuart, 1982b. 'Notes on the newspapers', 25 Apr., 1834, in *Essays on England, Ireland, and the Empire, Collected Works*, VI. Toronto: University of Toronto Press.

Mill, John Stuart, 1982c. 'England and Ireland' [5th edn, 1869, first published 1868], in *Essays on England, Ireland, and the Empire, Collected Works*, VI. Toronto: University of Toronto Press.

Mill, John Stuart, 1982d. 'What is to be done with Ireland?' [1848?, not published], in *Essays on England, Ireland, and the Empire, Collected Works*, VI. Toronto: University of Toronto Press.

Mill, John Stuart, 1984a. 'A few words on non-intervention' [1867, first published 1859], in *Essays on Equality, Law and Education, Collected Works*, XXI. Toronto: University of Toronto Press.

Mill, John Stuart, 1984b. 'Inaugural address at St Andrew's' [2nd edn, 1867, first published 1867], in *Essays on Equality, Law and Education, Collected Works*, XXI. Toronto: University of Toronto Press.

Mill, John Stuart, 1985a. 'Scott's life of Napoleon' [1828], in *Essays on French History and Historians, Collected Works*, XX. Toronto: University of Toronto Press.

Mill, John Stuart, 1985b. 'Michelet's history of France' [1844], in *Essays on French History and Historians, Collected Works*, XX. Toronto: University of Toronto Press.

Mill, John Stuart, 1986a. 'The condition of Ireland', *Morning Chronicle*, 15 Oct., 1846, in *Newspaper Writings, Collected Works*, XXIV. Toronto: University of Toronto Press.

Mill, John Stuart, 1986b. 'The condition of Ireland', *Morning Chronicle*, 21 Oct., 1846, in *Newspaper Writings, Collected Works*, XXIV. Toronto: University of Toronto Press.

Mill, John Stuart, 1986c. 'Poulett Scrope on the poor laws', *Morning Chronicle*, 31 Oct., 1846, in *Newspaper Writings, Collected Works*, XXIV. Toronto: University of Toronto Press.

Mill, John Stuart, 1986d. 'The condition of Ireland', *Morning Chronicle*, 1 Nov., 1846, in *Newspaper Writings, Collected Works*, XXIV. Toronto: University of Toronto Press.

Mill, John Stuart, 1986e. 'The condition of Ireland', *Morning Chronicle*, 2 Nov., 1846, in *Newspaper Writings, Collected Works*, XXIV. Toronto: University of Toronto Press.

Mill, John Stuart, 1989. *Public and Parliamentary Speeches, Collected Works*, XXVIII Toronto: University of Toronto Press.

Pitts, Jennifer, 2005. *A Turn to Empire*. Princeton: Princeton University Press.

Steele, E. D., 1970a. 'J. S. Mill and the Irish question: the principles of political economy, 1848–1865', *Historical Journal*, 13 (1970), 216–36.

Steele, E. D., 1970b. 'J. S. Mill and the Irish question: reform and the integrity of the empire, 1865–1870', *Historical Journal*, 13 (1970), 419–50.

Thornton, William T., 1971. *Over-Population and Its Remedy.* [1846] Shannon: Irish University Press.

Varouxakis, Georgios, 2002. *Mill on Nationality.* London: Routledge.

Zastoupil, Lynn, 1983. 'Moral government: J. S. Mill on Ireland', *Historical Journal*, 26, 707–17.

CHAPTER 4

Harriet Martineau and Ireland

Brian Conway and Michael R. Hill

INTRODUCTION

The Victorian sociologist–novelist Harriet Martineau visited Ireland on two different occasions, first in 1832 and again, twenty years later, in 1852, just six years after the Great Famine of 1846, when the country was still very much visibly affected by that event. Her latter journey covered some 1,200 miles and encompassed all four provinces that make up the island of Ireland, north and south. Martineau was not the first foreign visitor to nineteenth-century Ireland, of course, but she provided one of the few genuinely socio-logical interpretations during this time period. This chapter, then, examines Martineau's Irish writings and her contribution to our sociological under-standing of nineteenth-century Ireland.

The chapter takes the following structure. We begin by offering a brief biographical introduction to Harriet Martineau in which Martineau's sociological credentials are delineated. Following this we comment on the methodological orientation that guided Martineau's sociological investiga-tions of Ireland. We then briefly outline the spatial organisation of her travels and the socio-historical context in which she wrote, and go on to discuss her work under the headings of religious divisions and class/gender relations. We chose to focus on these two domains of social life because of their pro-minence in her work and the insightfulness of her observations with respect to them. Two of Martineau's texts on Ireland – *Ireland* (1832), a didactic novel in her massive *Illustrations of Political Economy*, and her non-fiction *Letters from Ireland* (1852) – provide the focus for the chapter. The *Illustrations* employs fiction to demonstrate and explore the application of economic principles in concrete settings, an approach that John Stuart Mill initially opposed but later recanted in light of Martineau's wildly successful treatment (Martineau 1877, II: 1; Hill 2004; Logan 2004). Martineau's later work, though described as 'letters' from Ireland, took the character of impressionistic day-to-day field reports written for publication at the invitation of Frederick Knight Hunt, editor of the *Daily News* (Martineau 1877, II: 405–7). Her Irish accounts were composed in various settings ranging from 'a quiet chamber at a friend's house, or amidst a host of tourists, and to the sound of the harp, in a *salon* at Killarney' (Martineau 1877, II: 407). She considered writing the letters anonymously but in the end chose to write them under her own name. Taken together, they provide a survey account of the country. The final section of the essay examines the civil reform programme proposed by Martineau for the economic improvement of Irish society. Throughout we include excerpts from Martineau's original work to give the reader a sense of her writing style and abilities and to communicate her ideas directly.

The abiding impression one gets from reading even a selection of Martineau's work is that she feels Ireland is a country performing well below its potential and that, despite the signs of 'barbarism' evident, there also exist many indications of 'civilisation'.[1] A good example of this comes from her Galway letters:

> as to the aspect of Galway, the place seems to have been furnished with a vast apparatus for various social action, for which there is no scope. Here is the railroad, with, as yet, very little traffic. Here is this canal, with, as yet, no trade. Here is a nobly situated port, with, at present, no article of export. (Martineau 1852: 87)

As she prepared to leave Ireland at the end of her sojourn and took a 'rear view mirror' look at it, Martineau eloquently contrasts contemporary times with the distant past:

> in casting back a last look upon Ireland as her shores recede, the traveller naturally thinks of that remarkable island as she once was, in contrast with what she has been since, and with what she is now. There was a time when Ireland gave light – intellectual and moral – to the nations of northern Europe; when she was the centre of the Christian faith, whence apostles went forth to teach it, and where disciples of many nations came to learn it. She had a reputation for scholarship and sanctity before England and Scotland were distinctly heard of. Few nations then stood so high as the Irish; and few have ever sunk so low as she has since sunk. (Martineau 1852: 212)

Yet for all this, her writings are imbued with a strong sense of hope that the fortunes of the country will improve. Convinced of the country's wealth of natural resources and its underachievement as a nation, she feels that the Irish people have only to make a go of it if they want to see their country prosper into the future. The topics she took up in her writings were as varied as the places she visited – the Ulster linen industry, the Derry–Coleraine railway line, the Bog of Allen in Leinster, and west of Ireland emigrants. Covering gender relations, tenant–landlord relations, social stratification, law, organisations, and work, and institutions such as the family, education and religion, one can say that 'all human life' is here.

Unlike other nineteenth-century travel writers, Martineau did not write with the intention of enticing people to come to Ireland (Hooper and Young 2004) in a 'Let's Go Ireland' manner. Rather her focus is documenting and analysing its economic exigencies and conditions. To this end, Martineau felt that Ireland's economic prosperity could be better secured within rather than outside the union with Britain. She also took the view that the ills of Ireland were primarily economic rather than political in nature, writing early on in her work that 'though it is my business to treat of the permanent rather than of the transient cause of the distress of Ireland, – of her economy rather than her politics, – I have been perplexed by some of the difficulties which at present beset all who would communicate with the public on her behalf' (Martineau 1832: i). But, in claiming this, she arguably understated the long-term entanglements between political and economic issues and problems as played out in the specifically Irish context. Politics are not completely disavowed, however, and one finds frequent mentions of it throughout her work.

A BRIEF BIOGRAPHY OF HARRIET MARTINEAU (1802–76)

Harriet Martineau was born in Norwich, Norfolk, England, on 12 June 1802. She had multiple identities as a novelist, sociologist, and public intellectual. She was socialised into a Unitarian religious tradition and both her parents – Thomas and Elizabeth Rankin Martineau – were devout Unitarians. Her parents sent her to a co-educational private school in Norwich (where the family lived) for two years, followed by 15 months at a boarding school in Bristol, though she was largely home-schooled and self-schooled and her formal private schooling amounted to only slightly more than three years. In the main her early life was unremarkable except for the fact that her father died when she was 24 years of age and this, together with the sudden death of her fiancé, meant that she began early adulthood as an independent woman. The years 1832 to 1834 marked an important period in her life; during this time her first major work appeared – *Illustrations of Political Economy* – witnessing the launch of a remarkable sociological journey (Hill 1989, 1991; Hill and Hoecker-Drysdale 2001; Hoecker-Drysdale 1992).

In 1834 she embarked on an ambitious tour of the United States and wrote a landmark ethnography and comparative study, *Society in America* (1837), based on her observations. While in America she travelled widely and consulted with both cultural elites like Ralph Waldo Emerson and William Ellery Channing as well as ordinary people. Her work on America was guided by the methodological principles later set down in *How to Observe Morals and Manners* (1838), the first systematic treatise on socio-logical methods (Hill 1989). Interestingly, Martineau was a contemporary of Alexis de Tocqueville, the subject of comment in another essay in this collection, and her American work received much less attention, undeser-vedly, than his (Hill 2001). One of her especially significant sociological achievements was a translation/condensation in 1853 of Auguste Comte's *Cours de philosophie positive*. A move to the English Lake District in 1845, prompted by failing health, led her to turn her attention to the English north and culminated in her *Complete Guide to the English Lakes* (1855). Between her two visits to Ireland, she overcame a major illness (Martineau 1844, 1877, II: 145–174) and showed a strong resolve by coming back to Ireland a second time (Hill 2004). Martineau died in Cumbria in 1876; among the hills and lakes she dearly loved (Hill 2004), leaving a prodigious record of published and unpublished work (Logan 2002a, b; 2007; Rivlin 1947). In sum, by the time Martineau visited Ireland for the second and last time, she was an accomplished sociologist, political economist, and well-known writer and world traveller. The *Illustrations* and subsequent works attracted a wide, often appreciative and sometimes critical, audience.

MARTINEAU'S IRISH ITINERARY

Travel in nineteenth-century Ireland was a difficult endeavour. Little is known about Martineau's first visit in 1832, but her 1852 trip is thoroughly outlined. Though suffering from a hearing disability, Martineau travelled around the country by means of railway and post-car (a horse-drawn one) and mostly with a travelling friend, her niece (Hooper 2001: 6). She didn't find the going easy and in her autobiography indicated her belief that her failing health at the time was the beginnings of a 'fatal malady' (Martineau 1877, II: 407). Her self-diagnosis was overly pessimistic, however. The Irish trip was obviously less fatal than Martineau surmised, as she lived and worked productively for nearly a quarter century after her visit to Ireland. Surprisingly, her Irish observations do not receive as much attention in her autobiography as one might expect. Like any visitor to a strange new country, Martineau's experiences were a mixture of serendipitous encounters, unexpected difficulties, and confirmed expectations. The beauty of the country struck her very much and time and again we find references in her letters to the Irish landscape. Of Connemara, she writes that 'there are few things in the world more delightful than a drive at sunset, in a bright autumn evening, among the mountains and lakes of Connemara . . . the air here, on such an evening, is like breathing cream' (Martineau 1852: 92).

Most visitors to modern-day Ireland come first through Dublin but Martineau entered Ireland via Lough Foyle. Her earlier letters have to do with Northern Ireland and she has a good deal to say about Donegal and Derry and settler–native relations. From the northern part of the island, she travelled down to Dundalk and then on to Dublin and from the capital city travelled across to Galway on the west coast taking in midland counties Kildare and Queen's County (now County Laois) along the way. Extensive references in her letters to the Bog of Allen, which Martineau refers to as 'the Irish California' (Martineau 1852: 77), stretching through most of Leinster, reveals the interest she took in bogs both for their quiet and tranquil beauty and capacity to function as a source of economic betterment. But it also points to the fact that she may well have considered America as a frame of reference for her work on Ireland.

Along the west coast she travelled through counties Mayo (stopping in Ballina, Westport, Newport and Castlebar and travelling to Achill Island), Galway and Clare (stopping in Clifden, Ballyvaughan and Ennistymon) and then on to Kerry (stopping in Cahirciveen, Kenmare, Valencia Island, and the Dingle Peninsula), Cork, eastwards to Tipperary towns such as Clonmel, and further east to Waterford and Wexford where the visitor was impressed by the signs of industry. Islands, long attracting the attention of foreign observers of Ireland, also caught Martineau's attention and she visited three islands along the west coast – Aran, Valencia and Achill.

METHODOLOGICAL ORIENTATIONS

Martineau was methodologically ready for her work in Ireland. Guided by the principles elaborated in *How to Observe Morals and Manners*, she paid great attention to what she terms the 'observation of things' by which she meant all manner of observable behaviours and artifacts, including archival material and documentary sources. Within this framework, discourse (i.e. face-to-face interview data) was important, but secondary (Hill 1989; Martineau 1838: 63, 222–30). She notes the rarity of finding 'information given by anybody' being validated by the 'independent testimony of anybody else' (Martineau 1852: 214) and thus questions the independent reliability of interview data.

As part of her preparations for her countrywide tour of Ireland, Martineau drew on the work of the Dublin Statistical Society and the Belfast Social Inquiry Society, two early sociological organisations, to provide her with sensitising concepts before she set out to make her own observations and inquiries. She was especially influenced by Professor William Hancock, a key figure in the Dublin Statistical Society and met with him in Dublin to discuss her work (Martineau 1852: iv). Hancock was professor of political economy at Trinity College Dublin, author of *Impediments to Prosperity in Ireland* (1850),[2] and a disciple of Adam Smith's *laissez-faire* approach. Through his work with the Dublin Statistical Society, Hancock sought to bring the insights of political economy to bear in ameliorating Ireland's social problems. Martineau's work reflected this emphasis on social improvement and sought to draw attention to the constraints and barriers to Ireland's future economic betterment.

Another feature of Martineau's methodological approach is her use of demographic data which she supplies on various towns and villages encountered in her journeys. This data comes from the 1841 Census, the first comprehensive national census carried out in Ireland (Bourke 1999: 32), and, in itself (along with the earlier Ordnance Survey mapping of the country in 1836), a major example of early sociological work on the part of the state to map the demography of the island (Gray 2005).

During her journeys she kept detailed notes in a travel journal and she was careful to do this as soon as possible after leaving the field. She also consulted local key informants and a variety of sources including census data, historical studies, and government reports. Beyond acquainting herself with this documentary material, Martineau was convinced of the need to do on-the-ground empirical sociology and this meant actually going into the field for extended periods of time, immersing herself in people's everyday lives and seeking to understand the social world from their standpoint. To be sure, sometimes this could generate unsettling feelings in the researcher as Martineau explains in a letter of 21 September 1852: 'a few days of observation of how the people live, merely by our going to see them, are sad enough to incline one to turn away, and never come again' (Martineau 1852: 150). Collectively, though, such data sources provided the basis for a rich description of Irish social life and lent to her writings a strong and powerful sense of immediacy and realism well captured in her early fictionalised account of poultry keeping:

> The fowls and pigs disappeared at the same time; and to all the hubbub which disturbed the morning hours, the deep curses of Sullivan, the angry screams of his wife, the cackling of the alarmed poultry, the squealing of the pigs, and the creaking of the crazy cars, there succeeded a hush, which was only interrupted by the whirring of Dora's wheel. (Martineau 1832: 20)

It is, of course, a long intellectual journey from Martineau's fact-based fictional account of 1832 to her direct observational report of 1852, but her attention to detail and empirical veracity show clearly throughout her writings.

SOCIO-HISTORICAL CONTEXTS

Nineteenth-century Ireland was a very poor society. Pre-famine Ireland was marked by a number of important economic, demographic and political features (Ó Tuathaigh 2007). Economically, Ireland was an agricultural-based society with little or no industrial base, with the exception of Belfast, and an even weaker market economy. And, as Martineau observes, it was a society with some class distinctions:

> Between the policy and the operation of the penal laws about religious matters, there was created a great gap in Irish society where there should have been a middle class . . . Even now, it is a curious spectacle to the English traveller, – the attempts of the Irish to sell food to each another. (Martineau 1853: 37)

The potato crop was the mainstay of the farming economy, aided by a favourable climate and soil for production, and consumption of the food cut across class lines (Ó Gráda 2000). Subdivision of land meant that many peasants farmed on very small holdings, a practice that proved disastrous when the potato famine struck.

In the post-famine period, although the population was now drastically reduced through death and outmigration, Ireland remained an agriculturally-based society. Production of the potato reduced significantly after the famine (Ó Gráda 2000). Agricultural labourers still comprised a substantial section of the population. Most lived in miserable cottages and cows and poultry were the major kinds of livestock (Bourke 1999). In Ulster, flax growing was more common and generated an important linen-making industry which exported its goods to Belfast and beyond to neighbouring Britain, representing, according to Jane Gray, a form of 'capitalism before the factory' in which women (and children) were to the forefront (Gray 2005: 3). Family life in post-famine Ireland was marked by low rates of marriage but within marriage by high rates of fertility. The subdivision of land, which was common before the famine, gave way to a new practice of passing on the farm to a single inheriting son, usually the eldest, who, with land in hand, made an attractive match for a dowried partner. The other non-inheriting siblings were faced with the choice of either emigrating or staying on the farm as relatives assisting (Ó Tuathaigh 2007; Ryan 1965). Thus, inheritance customs crucially shaped marriage and fertility patterns in Irish society and resulted in an unusual pattern of late marriage and high fertility within marriage.

The post-famine period was also marked by the intensification of the Poor Law, administered in each local area by Poor Law unions, and designed to alleviate the poverty and destitution of labourers. On her journey around the island, Martineau visited a number of workhouses, the Ennistymon workhouse in County Clare for example, and wrote warmly, for the most part, about the condition of these buildings representing state authority. She writes, 'the visitor . . . enters the workhouse gates without that painful mingling of disgust and compassion in his mind which is one of the most disagreeable feelings in the world' (Martineau 1852: 158).

The many villages that Martineau visited would have taken a simple form with the chapel or church at their centres and surrounded by a public house, post office, and a small bundle of houses. The chapel, usually in gothic style, was the hub of the village and was marked out from other buildings by iron railings (Bourke 1999).

Culturally, an old world of folk beliefs and practices such as those centred on wakes was giving way, in the post-famine period, to a new world based on standardisation and regularity (Bourke 1999). At one point in the *Illustrations* Martineau mentions the Irish custom of wakes, the traditional cultural practice of paying homage to the dead, which, she opines, 'rank so high among social obligations in Ireland' (Martineau 1832: 70). Such is the importance of funerals in Irish social life that it has sometimes been described as a funerary culture (Bourke 1999: 131). Describing the character of Dan, Martineau writes:

> He gave notice, at the same time, to his captain and comrades, that when a blaze should be seen on the cliff, and the funeral lament heard, all would be ready for their reception at the wake: – the burning of the bed of his deceased before the door, and the utterance of the death cry, being the customary mode of invitation to the wakes of the Irish poor. (Martineau 1832: 70)

Wakes, as Gibbons reminds us, tended to be associated with story-telling, dancing, drinking and sexual adventure, and for these reasons, often provoked the ire of clergy (Gibbons, 2002, p. 69). At another point Martineau mentions fairies, another key feature of this old world. On her visit to Achill Island her account reveals that 'it was by mere accident that we discovered that, of all the population of the Catholic village of Keel, there are no adults who dare go out after nightfall, *for fear of the fairies*' (Martineau 1852: 123, our emphasis). Storytelling too, around a fire or more likely in a public house, was very common for socialising and educating the next generation (Bourke 1999), as this account from Martineau suggests: 'many a laughing party may be seen round a huge pile of smoking potatoes, in a dirty cabin' (Martineau 1852: 128). But these cultural practices – story-telling, wakes and belief in the fairies – were declining as the world of the railway, mechanised agriculture, and print culture (Bourke 1999) become more and more important.

So when Martineau returned to Ireland in the mid-1800s she came to a society in transition. She did not come under the aegis of a government or funding agency and funded her travel expenses from her own personal resources. This intellectual freedom allowed her to focus on people's everyday concerns and to detail the small print of Irish people's social worlds. Above all, she saw herself as a liberal and a 'lady of very superior qualifications' (Martineau 1877: 4) who could bring the insights of the then hegemonic political economy perspective to bear wherever she ventured – America, the Middle East or Ireland. In what follows we examine her insights and observations in two specific domains – religious divisions and class/gender relations – and, following this, offer an assessment of Martineau's contribution to our understanding of nineteenth-century Ireland.

The first thing that should be noted about Martineau's orientation to Ireland was her sympathetic attitude towards its people. In the preface to her work on the 'Green Island', for instance, she announces a strong sympathy with the plight of the Irish poor (Martineau 1832). She visited the country, as she puts it herself, as an 'indignant witness of her wrongs' and proceeds to document and discuss these in a way that would 'most serve the cause of the Irish poor' (Martineau 1832: ii), revealing early on, from her vantage point as a foreign stranger, the practical import of her work (Hill and Hoecker-Drysdale 2001). The bold assertion that 'Ireland has been and is misgoverned' leaves no room for ambiguity (Martineau 1832: iii), though the blame seems to lie more on the Irish than the English side. She is even more explicit about her intentions in another part of the opening section of her work:

> the purpose of my title is to direct the work into the hands of those whom it most concerns; and my personages are few because it is my object to show, in a confined space, how long a series of evils may befall individuals in a society conducted like that of Ireland, and by what a repetition of grievances its members are driven into disaffection and violence. (Martineau 1832: ii)

Only by knowing about the grievances of the poor, according to Martineau, could one understand their consequences in rebellious acts of various kinds that have marked Irish history and, in turn, motivate and inspire government action to redress these grievances. Not all people were positively disposed to her work, though, and one reviewer in the Scottish periodical, *Edinburgh Review*, while seeing some merit in Martineau's account, overall finds it deficient:

> In this tract are to be found many of the characteristics of Miss Martineau's other publications; – an adherence to her general principles, carried, perhaps, too far, – great distinctness and power in enunciating them . . . Still, though this tale is

very able, yet, taken on the whole, it is not attractive. It appears to us to deal too much in shadows; and where a light is thrown in, it is rather that of a torch, or of an explosion, than of the noonday sun. (*Edinburgh Review* 1833: 252)

RELIGIOUS DIVISIONS

One of the features of nineteenth-century Ireland that attracted noteworthy attention from Martineau was religion and specifically the role in Irish society and culture of both the Catholic Church and the Church of Ireland. She was particularly drawn to what she terms the 'theological strifes of Ireland' (Martineau 1852: 152). While she recognises the important role of the church in social life, she clearly implicates it in Ireland's underdevelopment:

> The world sees, and Ireland feels, that all her peace and progress (and it is not premature to speak of peace and progress now) are owing to influences quite apart from both Churches; while the obstacles, the discouragements, the dissensions with which she has to contend, are owing to the faults of the one or the other Church, or their mutual strife. (Martineau 1852: 220)

This line of argument, in which religion as ideology stands in the way of economic progress and modernisation, is difficult to square, however, with the emphasis Martineau places on education, largely provided in and through the Catholic Church, as a mechanism for bettering the island: 'we must look for hope and help to that power which will never disappoint us – to education. Of all the new features of Irish life, this is the most important . . . It is a *leading out of*. Education will lead the Irish people out of their woes; and it will lead them up to the threshold of a better destiny' (Martineau 1852: 211). She notes the 'eagerness for learning' among the Irish poor (schools were then funded by the state, under the National School Act of 1831, but were run and controlled by the Catholic Church) but commented how little use this human capital was put to in terms of improving the material conditions of the land and generating badly needed economic capital.

Regional variation in religious cleavages surprised her and she seemed puzzled by the apparently friendly Catholic–Protestant relations in Dublin and the seemingly strong religious cleavages animating life along the west of Ireland Atlantic coast. Competition for the hearts and minds of the island people of Achill, County Mayo, between the newly established Protestant mission, on the one hand, and the Catholic Church, on the other, led by the formidable Dr John McHale, then Archbishop of Tuam, or the 'Lion of the West' as he came to be known,[3] is a good example of this inter-religious rivalry between Gael and Gall. Faced with strong Protestant proselytising,

Archbishop McHale consecrated a new Catholic chapel on the island to help energise the devotional life of the Catholic faithful (Martineau 1852: 121). On her journey from Dublin to Galway, Martineau offers this short account of the national seminary at Maynooth, the training ground of the priesthood she frequently takes issue with: 'the college at Maynooth appears to be surrounded by gardens and thriving plantations; and some old trees hang about the neighbouring ruins of the ancient castle of the Fitzgeralds of Leinster, and clothe the entrance to the estate of the Duke of Leinster' (Martineau 1852: 75).

In this poverty-ridden society, Martineau notes the religious fervour of its people and the esteem and symbolic power of priests within it even if she is critical of their role as moral entrepreneurs (Cohen 1980).[4] A good example of the great respect for clergy is given in this fictionalised passage about a home visitation of Fr Glenny:

> Dora came curtseying to the door to invite him to repose himself on the turf seat within; her mother rose feebly to pay her reverence as he entered, and hoped he would be pleased to remain till her husband and Dan returned. (Martineau 1832: 37–38)

Beyond the national seminary at Maynooth, her letters are peppered with references to various chapels and cathedrals encountered on her journeys. In the Lough Foyle region, we are told 'we find a Company building a handsome Catholic chapel', the term chapel being more widely used than church in nineteenth-century Ireland and around which whole villages tended to grow (Bourke 1999: 5). The Irish poor looked to the Catholic priest as much for advice on worldly matters, such as making enough money to preserve their livelihood, as they looked to him for the receipt of the sacraments:

> After more words of exhortation and comfort, the priest gave Dora a small present of money, and expressed his hope of seeing them all at mass in the morning, after which he would converse further with them on their affairs. (Martineau 1832: 43)

Adherence to church norms about the regular use of the confessional as the source of absolution from one's sins was a key feature of the Irish Catholic habitus (Inglis 1998). In Martineau's narrative, non-confessed sins and worries about her husband's Whiteboy activism weighed heavily on Dora's conscience, so much so that she felt the need to turn to Fr Glenny, who alone could bring relief to her anguish. This passage reveals the strong influence of the church in the moral lives of ordinary people:[5]

Again and again, in her solitude, she had meditated a night's expedition to Father Glenny's dwelling . . . she was more than ever distressed at her own spiritual state . . . her conscience so burdened with an accumulation of sins. (Martineau 1832: 81)

In the main, Martineau characterises Catholic priests negatively and their influence as malevolent, seeing them as an impediment to the quest for reviving a central place for truthfulness in Irish life – contrasting this with the role of the National School system – (Martineau 1852: 215) and as thwarting the ability of Irish peasants to gain 'knowledge and independence' (Martineau 1852: 216). She attributes the 'fear and hatred' of the Irish to the dominance of the Catholic Church and 'a priesthood as theirs for their moral guides' (Martineau 1852: 214). Looking to the future, she predicts the demise of the Church's power and confidently claims 'that priesthood is obviously destined to decline. It may become more noisy and quarrelsome as it declines, but its power for mischief would soon be over' (Martineau 1852: 219).

CLASS AND GENDER RELATIONS

Martineau's letters from Ireland provide an important and rare insight into a society convulsed by a massively traumatic event, the Great Famine of 1846, or 'Black Famine' as it has come to be known (Ó Gráda 2000). Her earlier letters do not give us a good sense of these events because they provide accounts of the Ulster experience, which was less affected by the famine than the western coastal regions. Early on, the picture that emerges from the letters is of a relatively prosperous and industrious country, but this story changes radically as Martineau's journey takes her to the west of Ireland speckled with 'rows of deserted cottages' and 'wrecks of habitations', stark and visible reminders of the horrors of the 1846 Famine (Martineau 1852: 77). At the same time, ruins of castles, monasteries and churches in places like Athenry register and summon up an earlier 'land of saints and scholars' Ireland.

Her account begins with the Lough Foyle region, near present-day Derry, and reveals how class relations were given spatial form. Catholics tended to live on poorer mountain land, from which they undoubtedly had a great view of the world around them, while Protestants, or more precisely, Scottish Presbyterians descended from Ulster planters, tended to live on land more favourable for tillage and farming. Property relations between the Anglo-Irish landowners and native Irish tenants loom large in *Illustrations*. Irish tenants found it difficult to raise enough income from meagre crop and potato production and the sale of animals to pay their landlords, and sometimes resorted to using child labour to generate additional monies. Overcrowding among tenants and eviction were common grievances also. Some peasants joined the ranks of secret agrarian societies like the Whiteboys to challenge the landlord system that impoverished them. Societies such as these operated in a clandestine manner and used the methods of terrorism to challenge the colonial hegemony of the Anglo-Irish gentry (Murphy 2001). In Martineau's narrative, Dora's desire to conceal the whereabouts of her husband and especially his membership of the Whiteboys, after intensive interrogation from English soldiers, reveals Ireland as a society of secrecy and hidden truths (Murphy 2001) and helps to explain why the ruling Protestant elite kept tenants under constant close observation:

> She was next questioned about the shipwreck: and here she was safe. She knew nothing of the matter but by hearsay, and could not answer a single question. Then came inquiries whither her husband had gone. She did not know; from place to place, she supposed, as he did before he married (p. 84) . . . The officer was not so sure of this when he saw how earnestly she glanced from time to time towards some particular spot in an opposite direction from the alder bush. It was an artifice; for Dora now began to be cunning, and to wish an end to this visit, lest her husband should appear from the beach . . . A soldier was left to guard her till their return. (Martineau 1832: 84, 88)

The other soldiers, though, set off to negotiate their way through the hazardous bog, a metaphor, as Trumpener points out, of Anglo-Irish attitudes towards the Irish – as a hard to understand, recalcitrant people (Murphy 2001: 148). For Trumpener, the bog, at once a mnemonic device and a constantly shifting landscape, stands as an 'emblem for Ireland's intractable national character' (Trumpener 1997: 47).

Martineau's account of Dora's romantic plans reveals the importance of instrumental things like land as much as expressive factors like love in the making of a marriage match in nineteenth-century Ireland:

> (Dan) had been long in love with Dora, and would have married her out of hand, if he had had so much as half an acre of ground to marry upon. (Martineau 1832: 7)

Inheritance of the family farm allowed a newly married couple to raise a family but, without it, marriage was either postponed or abandoned altogether.

Martineau seems to suggest that unequal class relations influenced people's orientations to the law. Irish hostility to legal codes came under criticism from Martineau and she seemed to be disappointed by the low respect for the law among the people, observing that:

We have had frequent occasion to regret the high walls which surround all the pretty places in the neighbourhood of the towns we have last visited ... we have been told the reason – that the people have so little idea of the law being instituted for just and mutually protective purposes ... we should like much more to see the people learning that the law is meant to be every honest man's friend, and guarding it accordingly. (Martineau 1852: 215)

Irish antipathy to law, as Gibbons notes, was a common target of attack by nineteenth-century civil reformers, both Irish and English (Gibbons 2002: 15), and to the extent that this is true Martineau was in step with opinion at the time. Against wretched circumstances of dire poverty and destitution, it is not surprising that some peasants took to stealing to meet basic subsistence needs, justified on the basis that it was necessary to provide for one's family dependants, and that a minority seized upon violent means to effect political change (Martineau 1832: 62). Martineau mentions the violence of the secret agrarian group, the Whiteboys, at various points in the *Illustrations*. In an account of their plundering of a ship marooned at night along a barely visible but highly dangerous and rugged west coast, she notes that the aggressive actions of the Whiteboys did not find a receptive audience in county Mayo towns like Ballina and Killala. This description of the travels of survivors of the shipwreck points to a strong rural–urban cleavage with respect to indignation about agrarian violence in nineteenth-century Ireland and the limits of 'popular' support for rural agitation:

As they went along the road, and through small villages, they met with little sympathy in any of their complaints against whiteboys; but the townspeople were of a different temper, and Ballina and Killala soon rang with the tidings of the horrible outrage, which had been committed on the coast. (Martineau 1832: 74)

Interestingly, sites of popular culture such as wakes and weddings were often attended by the recruiting sergeants of the Whiteboys, infusing these rituals with a strong political meaning (Gibbons 1998).[6]

In addition to class relations, Martineau was also interested in the status of women and their social relations with men. The industriousness of Irish women impressed her a good deal and she noted that it was 'the industry of the women which is in great part sustaining the country' (Martineau 1852: 65) and that 'the employment of the least in the place of the most able-bodied is one of the peculiarities which marks the anomalous condition of Ireland' (Martineau 1852: 65–6). The range of women's work, extending far beyond the private sphere of the household, also surprised her: 'we observe women working almost everywhere. In the flax-fields there are more women than men pulling and steeping. In the potato fields it is often the women who are saving the remnant of the crop' (Martineau 1852: 69). Martineau also makes reference to the keeping of poultry, an important economic activity in nineteenth-century Ireland, and an especially important source of income for women (Bourke 1999).

Her next destination point, Galway, is described as a strange place, owing to the practice of using seaweed as a form of manure. A visit to the village of Claddagh in Galway is vividly recalled by Martineau with forensic-like detail and makes some reference to Irish mothers, mentioning their practice – unsavoury in Martineau's eyes – of removing lice from the heads of their children:

> The cottages are in rows; and there are streets or alleys, where grass springs between the stones, or moss tuffs them, and where a stunted elder-bush, or other tree, affords a strange little patch of verdure in the dreary place . . . nettles, docks, and grass grow to the height of two feet, and the thistle and ragwort shed their seeds into the thatch . . . but infinitely worse is the inside. Some have no windows at all. Voices are heard from the interior of one where there was no window, and where the door was shut . . . elsewhere we saw a litter of pigs wallowing in the mud close by the head of the bed. Many mothers in the street, and even in the fish-market, were performing that operation on their daughter's heads or on their own persons, which is apt to turn English stomachs in Naples or Lisbon. (Martineau 1852: 84–5)

Martineau's observations on Irish bogs reveal her concern for bettering Irish society. The bogs, she feels, represent an enormous economic asset that could transform the country's fortunes, if only they were speedily reclaimed for agricultural use: 'if it were probable that the substance which occupies nearly 3,000,000 of acres of the surface of Ireland could be turned into wealth, the fact would be of such incalculable importance to the whole people – and to our whole empire – that no degree of earnestness could be ridiculous or misplaced' (Martineau 1852: 78).

Although Martineau demonstrates in her writings a great eye for empirical detail, she goes beyond mere description by attempting to explain why things are as they are in Ireland. In her account of Galway, for example, she attempts to explain the lowly position of the city, in terms of 'the absence of a middle class of society' (Martineau 1852: 89). Commenting on class location in the city, she observes that two groups make up the aristocracy – old families, on the one hand, and college professors and officials, on the other (Martineau 1852: 89) – with a missing population in between. It is this absence of a stable middle class that Martineau feels prevents the city, with many infrastructural advantages such as transport links, from realising its potential as an economic hub.

MARTINEAU'S IRISH CIVIL REFORM PROGRAMME

Schooling, religious belief and practice, family inheritance, the subdivision of land, tenant–landlord relations, absentee landlordism, and agrarian violence in nineteenth-century Ireland, were all topics that attracted Martineau's interest and sociological comment and constituted her empirical concerns. But she was as much interested in changing the way people organised their everyday lives as in understanding them; and, as a way out of Ireland's economic ills, she comes down, in the final analysis, to endorsing education and capital development as viable solutions to Ireland's miseries and as key to reconfiguring Anglo-Irish relationships. The emphasis on education was understandable given that the ability to read and write was crucial to participation in the newly emerging modern world (Bourke 1999). But not everyone could take advantage of education and Martineau endorses emigration as a safety valve for a population whose needs ran ahead of its resources – 'the clearance of the land by a method which secures the maintenance of the inhabitants seems to us a very great good' (Martineau 1852: 205) – allowing those that remain behind to sustain a livelihood that they would not be able to do otherwise, thus stabilising social and economic relations.

She tells us 'of the Irishman's passion for land' as being explainable in terms of the symbolic meaning of land as a source of 'power, independence, and dignity' (Martineau 1852: 217). But Martineau sees this as a constraint on the country's ability to modernise and prosper. For her, this preoccupation with land led to 'habits of slovenly cultivation, of dependence on the potato, and of consequent idleness' (Martineau 1852: 216), all traits that did not fit well with a modernising agenda. For this reason, Martineau advocated a more rational organisation of economic life; Ireland's economy more than its politics being her key concern, centred around 'regular and punctual labour' and greater 'observance of hours and rules' (Martineau 1852: 217). In this view, Ireland stands at a critical switch point in her economic trajectory – one road leading to modernisation through agricultural improvement, the other to a pastoral society of continued stagnation and decline. In this view, the world of oral culture, of encapsulating knowledge about geography, moral codes, and sources of danger in story and myth, is viewed as backward and regressive, standing in stark contrast to the orderly world represented by censuses, maps, and written records.[7]

This analysis of Ireland's situation might be interpreted by some scholars as representing a crude caricature of the Irish as lazy and feckless and incapable of showing any signs of industry and commerce or of a capacity to govern themselves. But Martineau is full of praise for the Irish character, reminding us of its globally recognised 'fine qualities'. Towards the end of her letters she offers an extended and highly complimentary assessment of the Irish people:

there is nothing the matter with the original structure of the country. The land is good enough: the sea is fruitful enough . . . there is nothing the matter with the country. And there is nothing the matter with the men in it . . . employ them at task-work – at secure work and they soon show themselves as industrious as anybody. (Martineau 1852: 213–14)

But she singles out the lack of respect for law and truthfulness, thrown into sharp relief in the country's court system, as a major vice of the people and as 'the natural product of the fear and hatred in which the people have lived for centuries, with such a priesthood as theirs for their moral guides' (Martineau 1852: 214). This is a good example of Martineau's curious tendency (a Martineaunian 'set piece' perhaps), evident at different points in her writings, to lavish praise on the subjects of her analysis and, almost in the same breath, to put forward a very strong critique.

CONCLUSION

Through her wide-ranging and discerning writings, Harriet Martineau offers the reader a rare sociological and important insight into Irish society and culture. The author's objective of carrying out a 'good study of the Paddies' (Martineau 1852: 2) is indeed realised. Crucially, her work bears on pre- as well as post-famine Ireland and for this reason we get a unique 'before' and 'after' account of what it was like to live in Ireland during these two important periods in nineteenth-century Irish history. She feels this event is assured a place in Irish collective memory by reminding us that 'the people cannot be expected to forget what they have seen in ghastly years just over' (Martineau 1852: 213). Of all the issues that Martineau engages with, it is perhaps the land question that looms the largest, which, she claims, helps to explain certain features of the Irish character, the chief ones being economy with the truth, a tendency towards idleness, potato dependency, and poor agricultural techniques. Though at times this comes close to a 'nothing-good-can-come-out-of-the-Irish' position common among foreign observers imbued with the myth of Ireland (Ryan 1965: 77), Martineau exhorts the Irish people to turn to the modern world – associated with such things as waged labour – to lift them out of their current impoverished social condition.

Though here not expressly comparative, Martineau's earlier work on America provided a comparative and international frame of reference for her Irish writings. She sometimes mentions, for example, and draws a comparison between the conditions of the Irish landed poor and indentured black slaves in America. But she is struck by how much better things would be if the landed poor took to waged 'work on some social labour which requires an observance of hours and rules' rather than the unwaged, unsystematic labour on the land.

Now, Martineau is increasingly mentioned in sociology theory textbooks and other writings as an early pioneer in the discipline and the first female sociologist (Hill 1989, 1991; Hill and Hoecker-Drysdale 2001; Hoecker-Drysdale 1992). In nineteenth-century studies too, her contribution is increasingly noticed and commented upon. Less well known and recognised is the important contribution she made to nineteenth-century Irish studies, though she was recently mentioned as an early pioneer of Irish sociology (Conway 2006; Share, Tovey and Corcoran, 2007: 6–7). We hope this chapter helps to introduce the person and her work to Irish sociologists and to a wider audience. While many may well take issue with her diagnosis of Ireland's ills as having to do largely with 'economical and religious causes' and her marginalisation of a sharp political analysis, she is no doubt eloquent and provocative in putting forward her analysis. Towards the end of her work, her description of Ireland as a 'country which has begun to taste of peace and progress' was accurate in its thrust if not in its timing. More broadly, the text from the *Illustrations* and *Letters from Ireland*, the focus of this chapter, exemplify the general features of Martineaunian sociology: concern with everyday social life, direct empirical observation, a desire to make sociology socially useful, a strong commitment to bettering society, and independence of thought (Hill 2005) – all important traits with continuing relevance to and topicality in contemporary social science.

Notes

We thank Séamas Ó Síocháin for inviting us to contribute to this collection. An earlier version of this essay was presented at the Harriet Martineau Sociological Society, 4th International Working Seminar, National University of Ireland Maynooth, County Kildare, 21–23 May 2007, and in a classical social theory course (SO 201) taught in Maynooth in autumn 2007.

1 It should be pointed out that Martineau's use of words such as barbarism and civilisation, and the word 'Paddy' to denote the Irish, suggest a colonial world view. Words like barbarism and Paddy were in common currency among nineteenth-century political elites and were frequently seized upon in descriptions of colonised subjects like the Irish, contrasting with the 'civilisation' of the colonial centre (de Nie 2004).

2 We owe this point to Eamonn Slater.

3 For an interesting biography of Dr John McHale, Catholic Archbishop of Tuam, see Andrews (2001).

4 The concept of moral entrepreneur comes from the work of Stanley Cohen (see Cohen 1980).

5   For a discussion of declining Catholic Church influence in Irish society from the nineteenth-century golden age of Irish Catholicism to the contemporary era, see Inglis's case study of the 'Kerry Babies' (2003).

6   Gibbons notes that the use by the Whiteboys of wakes and other social gatherings of ordinary people to recruit and organise pointed to the 'integration of rituals of resistance into the everyday rounds and folk customs of rural life' in nineteenth-century Ireland (Gibbons 1998: 41).

7   See William Smyth's monumental study, from the perspective of a cultural geographer, of how map-making was a key element of the English colonial programme (Smyth 2006).

Bibliography

Andrews, H., 2001. *The Lion of the West: A Biography of John McHale*. Dublin: Veritas.

Bourke, A., 1999. *The Burning of Bridget Cleary: A True Story*. London: Pimlico.

Cohen, S., 1980. *Folk Devils and Moral Panics: The Creation of the Mods and Rockers*. Oxford: Basil Blackwell.

Conway, B., 2006. 'Foreigners, faith and fatherland: the historical origins, development and present status of Irish Sociology', *Sociological Origins*, 5: 1, Special Supplement, 5–35.

de Nie, M., 2004. *The Eternal Paddy: Irish Identity and the British Press, 1798–1882*. Madison: University of Wisconsin Press.

Edinburgh Review, 1833. Review of Harriet Martineau's *Ireland, A Tale*. 57, 249–79.

Gibbons, L., 1998. 'Between Captain Rock and a hard place: art and agrarian insurgency', in T. Foley and S. Ryder (eds), *Ideology and Ireland in the Nineteenth Century*. Dublin: Four Courts Press, 23–44.

Gibbons, L., 2002. *The Quiet Man*. Cork: Cork University Press.

Gray, J., 2005. *Spinning the Threads of Uneven Development: Gender and Industrialization in Ireland During the Long Eighteenth Century*. Lanham: Lexington Books.

Hill, M. R., 1989. 'Empiricism and reason in Harriet Martineau's Sociology', in H. Martineau, *How To Observe Morals and Manners* [Sesquicentennial edn]. New Brunswick, NJ: Transaction, xv–lx.

Hill, M. R., 1991. 'Harriet Martineau', in M. J. Deegan (ed.), *Women in Sociology: A Bio-Bibliographical Sourcebook*. New York: Greenwood, 289–96.

Hill, M. R., 2001. 'A methodological comparison of Harriet Martineau's *Society in America* (1837) and Alexis De Tocqueville's *Democracy in America* (1835–1850)', in M. R. Hill and S. Hoecker-Drysdale (eds), *Harriet Martineau: Theoretical and Methodological Perspectives*. New York: Routledge: 59–74.

Hill, M. R. (ed.), 2004. *An Independent Woman's Lake District Writings: Harriet Martineau*. Amherst, New York: Humanity Books.

Hill, M. R., 2005. 'Sociological thought experiments: five examples from the history of Sociology', *Sociological Origins*, 3: 2, Special Supplement, 3–19.

Hill, M. R. and S. Hoecker-Drysdale (eds), 2001. *Harriet Martineau: Theoretical and Methodological Perspectives*. London: Routledge.

Hoecker-Drysdale, S., 1992. *Harriet Martineau: First Woman Sociologist*. Oxford: Berg.

Hooper, G. (ed.), 2001. *Letters from Ireland: Harriet Martineau*. Dublin: Irish Academic Press.

Hooper, G. and T. Young (eds), 2004. *Perspectives on Travel Writing*. Aldershot: Ashgate.

Inglis. T., 1998. *Moral Monopoly: The Rise and Fall of the Catholic Church in Modern Ireland* (2nd edn). Dublin: UCD Press.

Inglis, T., 2003. *Truth, Power and Lies: Irish Society and the Case of the Kerry Babies*. Dublin: UCD Press.

Logan, D. A., 2002a. *The Hour and the Woman: Harriet Martineau's 'somewhat remarkable' Life*. DeKalb, IL: Northern Illinois University Press.

Logan, D. A. (ed.), 2002b. *Writings on Slavery and the American Civil War*, by Harriet Martineau. DeKalb, IL: Northern Illinois University Press.

Logan, D. A. (ed.), 2004. *Illustrations of Political Economy: Selected Tales*, by Harriet Martineau. Peterborough (Canada): Broadview.

Logan, D. A. (ed.), 2007. *The Collected Letters of Harriet Martineau*. 5 vols. London: Pickering & Chatto.

Martineau, H., 1832. *Ireland. (Illustrations of Political Economy*, 9). London: Charles Fox.

Martineau, H., 1837. *Society in America*. 3 vols. London: Saunders and Otley.

Martineau, H., 1838. *How To Observe Morals and Manners*. London: Charles Fox.

Martineau, H., 1844. *Life in the Sick-Room*. Boston: Bowles and Crosby.

Martineau, H., 1852. *Letters from Ireland*. (Reprinted from the *Daily News*). London: John Chapman.

Martineau, H., 1853. 'Condition and prospects of Ireland', *The Westminster Review* 3, 35–62.

Martineau, H., 1877. *Harriet Martineau's Autobiography*, with *Memorials* by Maria Weston Chapman. 3 vols. London: Smith, Elder, & Co.

Murphy, W., 2001. 'The almost hidden Ireland: secrecy and the Irish novel, 1800–1829', PhD Dissertation, Department of English, University of Notre Dame, Indiana, USA.

Ó Gráda, C., 2000. *Black '47 and Beyond: The Great Irish Famine in History, Economy, and Memory*. Princeton: Princeton University Press.

Ó Tuathaigh, G., 2007. *Ireland Before the Famine 1798–1848* (3rd edn). Dublin: Gill & Macmillan.

Rivlin, J. B., 1947. *Harriet Martineau: A Bibliography of Her Separately Published Books*. New York: The New York Public Library.

Ryan, L., 1965. 'Sociologists look at the Irish family', *Rural Ireland*, 77–83.

Share, P., H. Tovey and M. P. Corcoran, 2007. *A Sociology of Ireland* (3rd edn). Dublin: Gill and Macmillan.

Smyth, W. J., 2006. *Map-making, Landscapes and Memory: A Geography of Colonial and Early Modern Ireland*. Notre Dame: University of Notre Dame Press.

Trumpener, K., 1997. *Bardic Nationalism: The Romantic Novel and the British Empire*. Princeton: Princeton University Press.

CHAPTER 5

Sir Henry Maine and the
Survival of the Fittest

Séamas Ó Síocháin

INTRODUCTION

The career of Sir Henry Maine (1822–88) was distinguished if unexciting. From a modest middle-class background, he was a talented student, a regular winner of prizes and scholarships. After undergraduate studies in Pembroke College, Cambridge, he was in 1847 appointed regius professor of civil law at Trinity Hall, Cambridge, still in his mid-twenties. In 1852 he became first reader on Roman law and jurisprudence at the Inns of Court in London. In 1861, not yet forty, came the book which was to establish his reputation and which still stands as his most important work, *Ancient Law*. In addition to his legal work, Maine had a deep interest in public affairs and as early as 1850 he had begun a lifelong practice of journalism, most of it anonymous, written for quality periodicals, such as the *Saturday Review*.[1] It was this combination that led to his next appointment, in 1862, as legal member of the Viceroy's council in India, a post he held for seven years. On his return to England in 1869 he was appointed to the Corpus professorship of jurisprudence in Oxford and was awarded a knighthood in 1871. After his Indian career, he produced four further books. In 1871 came *Village Communities*, in which, drawing on his widened Indian experience, he compared village communities there with early village communities in Europe. In 1875 he produced *Early History of Institutions*, which included detailed discussion of the early Irish (brehon) laws, gained during a visit to Ireland in the summer of 1873. In the same year he was appointed to a seat on the Indian Council in London. Two years later, he was elected Master of Trinity Hall. In 1883 *Dissertations on Early Law and Custom* appeared and in 1885 his last book, *Popular Government*. In 1887 he was appointed Whewell Professor of International Law, Cambridge, and he died in Cannes in the following year, on 3 February 1888. A few years prior to the publication of *Popular Government*, from May 1880 to December 1881, Maine had written a series of unsigned articles on issues of the day in the newly established evening paper, the *St James's Gazette*; many of these articles or leaders were concerned with events in Ireland, then experiencing the turmoil of the Land War period. These virtually unknown essays reveal a great deal about Maine's thoughts on society, but must be read both in the context of his general approach to social evolution, as set out in *Ancient Law*, and in that of his ideas on the political system of his day, as presented in *Popular Government*.

According to his friend, Lord Acton, Maine was 'one of the finest intellects of his generation', while Professor Harold Laski, referring to *Ancient Law*, wrote: 'If I had to name a book to tempt the outsider into a sense that jurisprudence was a great subject, I think I should ask him to read Maine, and then deny greatness at his peril' (quoted in Feaver: xv). A more recent assessment holds:

> The extent and profundity of Maine's influence among the intellectual class would be hard to exaggerate: he set the terms of debate not only for legal historians but for a generation of writers on the place of custom in the development of political institutions or the growth of forms of property, whether in medieval Europe or nineteenth-century India; writers who could not easily or exclusively be classified as historians, political theorists or economists. (Collini et al.: ii, 210)

And, the anthropologist Alan Macfarlane claims that

> Maine survives all his detractors with that quality which makes him, like Montesquieu or de Tocqueville or Hobbes, immortal: the ability to speak to us directly and still to contribute strikingly to the intellectual puzzles which face historians and anthropologists. (Diamond: 112)

ANCIENT LAW (1861)

It has been suggested by Maine's biographer, George Feaver, that, from the moment *Ancient Law* appeared, lawyers and historians of his own generation viewed it 'with much the same sort of enthusiasm as natural scientists had received Darwin's *Origin of Species*' (Feaver: 45). Reacting against the abstract reasoning of the utilitarian jurists, Bentham and Austin, Maine argued (as summarised by Cocks: 52) 'that their notion of law was not of universal application but related almost exclusively to industrial societies where, for example, sovereign power could be clearly identified'. In *Ancient Law* he hoped 'to demonstrate that a greater appreciation of the social basis of all legal institutions would be achieved when lawyers used the techniques of the historian to trace the implications, for all present systems of law, of the full course of legal development in the ancient world'. His work, then, was one of empirical history, but within a theoretical framework explaining the general evolution of legal systems (Feaver: 45, 46).

Maine traces the development of law (and society) through a number of evolutionary stages and identifies a number of mechanisms for legal change (fictions, equality, legislation). He is best remembered for a number of polar contrasts between early society and modern progressive society. The most famous of these contrasts is the movement from relations based on status to those based on contract. In his own words:

> The movement of the progressive societies has been uniform in one respect. Through all its course it has been distinguished by the gradual dissolution of family dependency, and the growth of individual obligation in its place. The Individual is steadily substituted for the Family, as the unit of which civil laws take account . . . The word Status may be usefully employed to construct a formula expressing the law of progress thus indicated . . . If then we employ Status, agreeably with the usage of the best writers . . . we may say that the movement of the progressive societies has hitherto been a movement from Status to Contract. (Ancient Law: 149–51)

The change came about only slowly; according to Feaver (49), Maine '. . . held that only slowly did the sense of mental obligation basic to advanced notions of contract become disentangled from the originally more important ceremonial technicalities, and finally surmount them as the sole ingredient of the contract'.

In addition to the posited transitions from status to contract and from family to individual, other related ones formulated by Maine were those from kinship to territory, from joint or communal ownership of property to private property, and from a stage when civil and criminal law were not distinguished to one where certain injuries involved individuals while others were crimes against the whole society (see Harris: 191–2).

Strictly speaking, Maine's formulations only applied to what he termed the 'Aryan' peoples, but at times he did appear to make universal claims about early society. Within the Indo-European area, he suggested that a separation took place between western and eastern branches: in the west belief in the sacred powers of kings eventually declined, leading to domination by military and political aristocracies and, later, to modern progressive society; while, in the east, such a transition did not take place – power continued to be shared between kings and priestly elites, and society remained stagnant (Feaver: 46).

For Maine, the progression to civilisation had been a precarious one and the civilised state was vulnerable – in this regard his use of the term 'hitherto' in his status to contract formula has been noted. John Burrow comments:

The effect of stressing, as Maine was so often to do, the normality of the 'unprogressive' condition of mankind, the implacable conservatism and custom-bound rigidity of most human societies, was to make progress seem not so much a self-generating, ultimately invincible process . . . but rather a rare and fortunate mutation, dependent on a certain set of conditions and vulnerable to their displacement. (Burrow 1991: 60)

In Maine's own words:

the rigidity of primitive law, arising chiefly from its early association and identification with religion, has chained down the mass of the human race to those views of life and conduct which they entertained at the time when their usages were first consolidated into a systematic form. There were one or two races exempted by a marvellous fate from this calamity, and grafts from these stocks have fertilised a few modern societies. (*Ancient Law*, ch. 4, 68)

Maine was unclear about the precise mechanism driving progress. He wrote: 'The difference between the stationary and progressive societies is . . . one of the great secrets which inquiry has yet to penetrate . . . no one is likely to succeed in the investigation who does not clearly realise that the stationary condition of the human race is the rule, the progressive the exception.' (*Ancient Law*, ch. 2, 21)[2]

Finally, the term progress had for Maine not only a descriptive connotation; it was a moral term. As Raymond Cocks (61) puts it:

He believed that a society based on contract was a society in which, of necessity, individuals had come to adopt high moral standards, and these standards, he believed, enabled them to trust each other in the course of commercial and other dealings.[3]

POPULAR GOVERNMENT (1885)

Maine's *Popular Government* was published in 1885, three years before his death. The book was, effectively, a long discourse on the dangers of what Maine termed 'extreme democracy'.[4] When it appeared its direct political character surprised many as it seemed of a different order from Maine's earlier work; more recently, however, the ideas expressed in *Popular Government* have been judged to be consistent with those expressed in his apparently more detached publications, including *Ancient Law*. It received some negative reviews at the time, especially from Radical Liberals; indeed its anti-Radical tone was marked. Yet his fears were widely shared in his day.

'Despite its "mixed" critical reception,' writes William Coxall, *'Popular Government* was a considerable commercial success, going through nine editions and exerting influence on interpretative works and democratic theory and on the British Constitution down to the First World War.' One authority, Norman Pilling, described the book as 'the major work of analytical conservatism written in the 19th century' (Coxall: 165, 25).

Maine's position on democracy has been characterised as broadly Whiggish. William Coxall (38) interprets his writings of the 1880s as:

> the product of a mind overwhelmed by a sense of constitutional crisis. His work should therefore be seen mainly as a defence of the British system of parliamentary government, as it existed between 1832 and 1867, during his own youth and middle age, with its supportive Whig–Liberal political values, against what he perceived as the imminent, destructive advent of democracy.

The mid-Victorian Constitution that Maine valued comprised a regime of parliamentary representative government resting on a very narrow franchise and still dominated by an aristocracy which received periodic infusions from the middle class. His Whiggism involved a preference for institutions that had grown with time over those which were prefabricated ('usefulness proved by experience'). The ideal was for limited, moderate Government and for firm leadership combined with responsiveness to public opinion. It located decision-making in parliament and did not depend for effective operation on popular understanding of public affairs. It involved the idea of government for the good of the community as opposed to government by the community itself, i.e. by numerical majority.

Maine was a Liberal elitist; he saw progress as being linked with key individuals – minorities, especially intellectual minorities. He found support for this in the Darwinian notion of natural selection: 'A privileged class arises because it is stronger and wiser than others.' On the one hand, he had an admiration for traditional aristocracy – fitness to rule was handed on in a hereditary system, and rule by aristocrats granted independence from electoral pressures. On the other hand, a middle-class elite of knowledge drew not on its class origins but on its characteristics: knowledge, experience, intelligence, intellectual integrity, self-control, and willingness to compromise.[5]

Maine worried about the effect of 'democratic legislation' on human motives. He worried, for example, that legislation to re-divide wealth would destroy the imperative to work. Social inequality was necessary for the continuation of material progress.

> The motives, which at present impel mankind to the labour and pain which produce the resuscitation of wealth in ever-increasing quantities, are such as

infallibly to entail inequality in the distribution of wealth. They are the springs of action called into activity by the strenuous and never-ending struggle for existence, the beneficent private war which makes one man strive to climb on the shoulder of another and remain there through the law of the survival of the fittest. (*Popular Government*, 50)

Following a Malthusian line he argued that economic legislation to benefit the working class would be self-defeating; it would lead to a short-term increase in living standards, which, in turn, would lead to higher reproduction, then a greater imbalance between food and population, and eventual crisis again.

Part of the book's originality was to locate 'democracy' in a long-scale historical perspective; in other words, Maine applied to it his historical method (*Popular Government*, v–vi). Democracy was effectively new: after the experience of the Greek and Roman republics, it had been replaced by monarchies for seventeen centuries. Historically, then, monarchy was much more common, more 'popular'. In modern times, democracy was found in only a few small political entities (Swiss cantons, the Netherlands) and then in a number of large states (French Jacobin democracy; U.S. representative democracy). From the eighteenth century onwards, there had been a slow revival of the early 'tribal freedom', which owed more to British political experience than to Continental theories.[6] Part of Maine's purpose was to point out that modern democracy was not inevitable but the result of a series of accidents. He sought to persuade public men that the advent of democracy was not inevitable, contrary to prevailing evolutionary ideas that tended to see it as an inevitable and progressive stage. He felt that what was being taken as an irresistible stream was not so and might be turned back by an energetic group. For him democracy was simply 'a form of government', as were aristocracy and monarchy; it was to be judged as to how it contributed to the effectiveness of government functions, such as the preservation of the state and the maintenance of order.

Democracy he deemed 'a leaderless form of government by a numerical majority', and his fears for the direction in which the British political system was moving are captured in his frequent use of terms such as 'anarchy', 'revolution', 'despotism', 'dictatorship', and 'socialist democracy'. The extension of the franchise was one of the changes causing concern to Maine; the vote, he believed, would be weakened or diluted by the numbers casting it. He opposed, for example, the extension of suffrage to agricultural labourers. His fear was that, once labourers and artisans sensed power, they would use it for their own ends. He also feared that there would be no guiding force between government and public opinion, which would be a fickle, ignorant, superficial force, foisted on the mass by the crafty few ('submerged and menacing interest of the lowest classes').[7]

Democracy, he held, would not bring innovation and therefore progress, because the masses were conservative; the natural condition of man was not progressive but stagnant; democracy would produce 'a mischievous form of Conservatism' (*Popular Government*, 350). Maine cited India to prove his point: the Indian village community 'was stagnant, resistant to change & socialist. For it was based on co-proprietorship. Backwardness and socialism were therefore, argued Maine, combined' (Coxall: 138, and see *Popular Government*, 133).

He was an advocate of minimal government interference, especially on economic issues. Legislation was important, but it should be subordinate. And it was vital that legislation leave property and contract untouched, indeed they were the very agencies ensuring the material improvement of the entire community. He warned of the new evil: the 'process of legislating away the property of one class and transferring it to another' (*Popular Government*, 106).

While Maine made criticisms of the political system in the United States (it was the home of corruption, of wirepulling, and a 'spoils system'), more broadly he saw it as a free society, which included constitutional safeguards against the power of the sovereign people. Its major virtue was its conservatism; it was, in reality, a version of the British constitution. One of the attractions for him of the constitutional system of the United States was its approach to economic matters. In economic policy it was a neo-Darwinism, *laissez-faire*, free enterprise, individualist paradise . . . democracy was merely 'political', was only skin deep – there was no attempt to legislate for an egalitarian society, or even to palliate the grosser social evils. 'There has hardly ever before been a community in which the weak has been pushed so pitilessly to the wall, in which those who have succeeded have so uniformly been the strong, and in which in so short a time there has arisen so great an inequality of private fortune and domestic luxury.' (Coxall: 145, and *Popular Government*, 51)

MAINE'S JOURNALISTIC TREATMENT OF IRELAND:
THE ST JAMES'S GAZETTE

While *Popular Government* was published in 1885, its component chapters had appeared in the *Quarterly Review* between 1883 and 1885. And while there is hardly a reference to Ireland in *Popular Government* events there had clearly dominated his thinking shortly before he formulated the political ideas in his book. For not long before, from May of 1880 to December 1881, Maine had contributed a series of unsigned articles to the newly established *St James's Gazette* in which Ireland loomed large.[8] The appearance of the *Gazette* and the beginning of this phase of Maine's journalism coincided with the start of the second Gladstone government and with the Irish Land War. Events in Ireland were clearly of great concern to Maine, as some 58 out of a total of 135 articles dealt with affairs there; during the months of November 1880 to January 1881 Ireland was almost the only topic he dealt with. But where the arguments in *Popular Government* were to be presented in analytic scholarly vein, those in the *St James's Gazette* pulsed with emotion and specific reference.

All of the issues which were to be of concern to Maine in *Popular Government* had been reflected in his fears concerning Ireland in his *St James's Gazette* articles or leaders. There is the threat to property and contract; fear for the constitution through obstructionism; fear of democratic numbers; fear of the dangers of socialistic legislation and of anarchy, of barbarism at the gates; and the Malthusian theme of the survival of the fittest or of the unfittest. Though brought to public attention in Feaver's 1969 biography, Maine's articles on Ireland have been virtually ignored to date; there is scarcely a reference to them in recent works on Maine.[9]

The Land War dominated Irish public life in the years 1879–81. The 1870s had been years of agricultural depression; increasing international competition led to falling prices not only in Ireland but in England and Scotland, thereby removing also the seasonal migratory labour option for Irish farmers and labourers. Added to this, bad weather and three years of poor to disastrous harvests, including the failure of two successive potato crops, made starvation a real possibility, with conditions worst in the west of the country. Inability to pay rents led to a jump in the number of evictions; emotions were inflamed and retaliatory actions increased in number. 'Agrarian outrages' ranged from the maiming of cattle, the burning of farm buildings to attacks on landlords and their agents.

In response to the worsening agricultural situation, the National Land League was formed in 1879 and, on a platform of 'the land of Ireland for the people of Ireland', it organised opposition to landlords, as well as aid for farmers. The Land War that followed has been described as 'the greatest mass movement of modern Ireland'. The two most prominent leaders of the public agitation were Michael Davitt and Charles Stewart Parnell, the new leader of the Irish Parliamentary Party, whose policy included obstructionism in the House of Commons. Gladstone returned to power in April 1881 and his government responded with a mixture of coercion and agrarian reform. The latter took the form of the Land Act of 1881 and the former of two coercion bills. Davitt was arrested in February 1881 and, later, all the principal leaders, including Parnell. Ultimately, a compromise solution was reached and the leaders released. In October 1881 the Land League was suppressed.

DISTRESS IN IRELAND: DIAGNOSES AND REMEDIES

Alarm at events in Ireland and at the response of the Gladstone government permeated Maine's articles through 1880 and 1881. He was willing to concede that there was some distress in Ireland; but he was more exercised by the lawlessness of the Irish and by what he took to be the threat to some of the fundamental planks of western civilisation. 'We do not for a moment deny that the distress of the agricultural classes in Ireland, so far as it exists, is a legitimate element in the question. The mode of relieving this distress, which . . . ought to take precedence of all others, is wide and liberal bestowal of the bounty of the State.'[10] But he was sceptical about the extent of distress and the danger of manipulation – Parnell, he wrote, 'of course asserted, and would still assert, that there was terrible distress'. But he pointed to the need to analyse the level of distress coolly and analytically:

> Was there distress in Ireland last winter? If so, what was its magnitude, and to what portions of the country did it extend? It is absurd to say that there is satisfactory evidence on any of these points . . . We do not certainly deny that there was some evidence of suffering; but there is evidence the other way to which no sufficient justice has been done.

He suggested the need to analyse the 'increase of deposits in the savings banks' over the period and the testimony of 'persons who resided through the winter in the afflicted counties', whose evidence went contrary 'to anything having occurred which bore out the language of the agitator and panic-monger'.[11]

The greatest threat to a cool analysis of the facts of the situation came from a too easy giving in to the emotion of sympathy. He talked of 'blind emotions like sympathy or pity' and of the need for 'unflinching legislative surgery', as shown by those who reformed the poor laws earlier in the century. 'What is manifestly wanting to English statesmanship, in its relation to Irish distress and Irish disorder, is not knowledge, but courage . . . The Liberal leaders in particular dare not offend that large mass of their followers who, when they read of a grievance anywhere, act like the man whose hand goes instinctively to his pocket as soon as he hears a beggar's whine.'[12]

Distress or not, Maine's priority was with the proper diagnosis and remedy for Ireland's problems. Frequently using the language of health and disease, he believed that the wrong diagnosis was being made and the wrong remedies applied. He talked of 'Irish distress', 'Irish disease', 'the Irish malady', 'the Irish nightmare' and of 'remedies', 'quack remedies', 'medicine' and so on.[13] At the real core of the problem for Maine, the ultimate cause of distress, lay the poverty of Irish resources.

It will not, we presume, be denied that Ireland suffers under serious natural disadvantages with which the British Government has no more to do than it has with the condition of Patagonia. The Irish climate is about the worst in Europe. The Irish soil consists to a very great extent of bog-land either uncultivable or cultivable only at heavy cost; and where it is fertile, its fertility is not of the kind to require to be assisted by a numerous population. There is scarcely any mineral wealth in Ireland . . . Ireland confined to her own resources could never have been a manufacturing country on any but the most insignificant scale . . . There is no question what Ireland would have been if she had existed always or for a long time as a country independent of Great Britain. She would have been constantly scourged by civil wars and periodically desolated by famines.[14]

Overpopulation was Ireland's second major problem. While many principles of traditional political economy were being challenged, one authority could not, Maine argued: Malthus and his 'law of population', which held that 'population had a natural tendency to outrun subsistence'. Malthusian theory 'has added to political economy the only portions of that science which are beyond question and cavil, and it has enabled the modern observer and experimentalist to unlock the secret of Nature and to reconstruct the history of organic life . . .'[15]

In a piece titled 'The survival of the unfittest', he wrote:

Now what is the most striking fact associated with the Irish race? It is fertility . . . The Irishman alone is prolific under all circumstances and everywhere . . . it certainly seems as if races who are above savagery (for savages, at all events with their present practices, are said to be very infertile), but who have not quite emerged from barbarism, are characterized by an extra-ordinary fecundity; and the influence of the Roman Catholic Church has plainly a good deal to do with the phenomenon . . . That the races which tend most to multiply and to elbow out the others under the conditions of modern society are the imperfectly civilized races, and those which have no affection for liberty either in Church or State, is a fact of importance to the enthusiast for democracy.[16]

Agrarian reform, he concluded, 'is a mere expedient for enabling the Irish multitude to live in comparative plenty for a year or two at the certain cost of falling back into a condition of starvation for which there will be no remedy, since the only sovereign cure will have probably been made impossible by erroneous treatment'.[17]

Can there . . . be a madder policy, viewed in the light of science, than that which the present Government insists on applying to Ireland? It requires a supreme admixture of dullness and impudence to deny that Ireland is over peopled, or to assert that any conceivable legislation can enable subsistence to overtake population.[18]

Emigration was a key part of a true remedy for the Irish malady: 'Emigration . . . is a real and direct remedy, and for all human purposes a practically permanent remedy.'[19] Referring to the way the Greek common-wealths swore never to redivide land and sent out colonies instead, he continued: 'There will never be a rational treatment of the Irish disease till we recover the wisdom which was a possession of the most civilized part of mankind not much short of three thousand years ago.'[20] However, not only was emigration being ineffectively opposed by the Government (it had been peripheralised in Gladstone's bill) but also, the classes that opposed it – the priest and the agitator – were too strong.[21]

IRISH HISTORY AND RELIGION

If Maine held that Gladstone's agrarian legislation misread the true causes of Ireland's problems, neither did he have any sympathy with the argument that Ireland's historic wrongs at the hands of England were the cause and needed to be redressed. Looking back at English treatment of Ireland in preceding centuries, he was not apologetic.

> The confiscations of Irish land at the end of the seventeenth century . . . were the comparatively gentle and moderate reprisals of the only powerful Protestant State left in Europe for the wholesale confiscations of the lands of Protestants which had taken place throughout the greater part of Europe during the whole of that age . . . This, then, was the story of the alleged English oppression of Ireland in the seventeenth century. It was the last chapter of the Wars of Religion. It followed an example set everywhere through the century, and was immediately provoked by a conspiracy against English liberty in which Irishmen took part, and by a dangerous rebellion conducted by Irishmen with foreign aid. It consisted of measures far milder than those adopted under similar circumstances in any other country; and the severity of these measures has been steadily and voluntarily relaxed.

He concluded: 'To the economist, all this is of course immaterial. The world was thought to have learned that questions as to the origin of property were irrelevant, and that its best chance of happiness lay in taking property as it found it.'[22]

Present day Irish problems should not be explained as a reaction to past severity of treatment and it was wrong to try to attribute current events to the reaction of the Irish to historical punishments. In the Austrian Empire, people had been dealt with far more severely, yet Bohemia was 'a land of peace and order as compared with Ireland'. But, a more accurate comparison of Ireland's condition would be with the Spanish-American republics: in these, 'too, there is no discernible Sovereign, there is small respect for property, there is no security for promises, there is general impunity for crime'. Part of the answer lay in their common Catholicism, with its leaning towards anarchy. But, more importantly, both areas had but recently emerged from barbarism. 'Ireland – and this is its great peculiarity – is the European country which remained barbarous longest. Other sections of the great race, which filled the Western world, have been forced back into barbarism by tyranny. But the Irish emerged from barbarism for the first time only, so to speak, the other day. Far the best explanation of what most other nations as well as Englishmen consider the paradoxes of Irish history is that they are the result of a substratum of barbarism continually pushing through the layer of superficial civilization above it.' It was, perhaps, a fault on England's part that 'this barbarism was not schooled into civilization in the only way in which it could be schooled'. England had learned how to do this in various parts of the world. 'We have found out that the secret of this success is to be rigidly just and inflexibly severe. First make up your mind what principles you intend to apply, and then tolerate nothing short of absolute submission to their application.' The fault of the English in Ireland was in not handling barbarism firmly enough: 'we are succumbing to a disease of modern origin which is enervating our fibre and softening our brain'; it is 'really a deadly virus: *lues philanthropica* [the plague or pestilence of philanthropy] – governing Ireland by Irish ideas'. 'Now it is one of the axioms of modern sociology that the savage, the barbarian, or the semi-barbarian is not, indeed, "lower than the Christian child," but very much on a level with it. His undevelopment is very like the undevelopment of civilized childhood.' Should one, he asked, raise children by the ideas of children?[23]

Maine thought that the historical influence of Catholicism on Ireland was baneful. He believed that the mediaeval European Church, as a softening and moralising influence on the feudal lord, had had a positive formative influence on the emergence of the modern order. But if either had been left on its own, the result would have been different. 'Left to them-selves, the feudal monarchies would have made the Western countries as submissive and motionless as China; left to itself, the Church of Rome would have produced general anarchy.' Part of Ireland's problem was that, historically, it had been subject only to strong church influence.[24]

In Ireland, two strands of ideas tended towards anarchy: those stemming from the Catholic Church (unchecked by the state) and those associated with Socialism and Communism. While obedience to the law had become second nature to the Englishman, 'in Ireland the legal penalty is everything. The Irishman has a certain number of loose notions of right and wrong which he owes to his religion; but his view of the law is that it is to be obeyed so long as it can compel obedience, and no longer. It is to such a people, with vague unanalysed impressions of justice and injustice, but with no respect for law as such, that the Irish Secretary announces his intention not to enforce the law when he thinks its application will be unjust . . .'.[25]

Observers had hoped that the disestablishment of the Anglican Church in 1869 in Ireland might have been expected to produce a Catholic Church that was conservative and a defender of order. That had not happened. The Church was silent as Irish agitators encouraged 'confiscation of property, the dismemberment of the national territory, and death as the penalty deserved by unpopular classes . . .' Why? Because she was demoralised by not being herself Established – she relied on 'voluntaryism' – on the people for support or taxation. Hence, chained to ideas popular with the peasantry, she was an ally of radicalism (especially so the young priests). British Radicals were wrong – the 1869 Act had failed miserably in its purpose. The Catholic Church, relying on the income from the people from marriages and births, therefore encouraged population growth and discouraged emigration.[26]

LAND AND LANDLORDS

Maine's reading of the Irish land system was in keeping with his wider view of Irish history. The Irish landlords of his own day were capitalist farmers, the last of three types of landowner in Irish history. Of pre-conquest Irish landowners he suggested that their 'oppression of their tenantry seemed to the Englishmen of Queen Elizabeth's time to be perfectly intolerable'. The second type 'was intended to be a fortress helping to protect the English liberties and the English religion against a general conspiracy set on foot throughout Europe by the Catholic despotic Sovereigns and by the Pope'. The last type 'is scarcely forty years old, and owes its establishment to the clear opinion of English statesmen of the last generation, and particularly of Sir Robert Peel, that Ireland would be regenerated if large estates burdened by a century of improvidence were thrown into the market, purchased by capitalists, and left to the operation of economical forces'.[27]

He believed the English record in Ireland in the nineteenth century to be a positive one. 'We venture to assert that the conduct of England to Ireland, during the period to which historical investigations are properly confined for practical purposes, has been not only justifiable, but exemplary.' He argued that since 1800: i) repressive laws had been removed; ii) Ireland had enjoyed a number of material benefits: a transition from poverty to comparative richness, based on the benefits of manufacturing, of migration to English cities, and of a thriving agriculture (with English capital); iii) on the moral and political levels she enjoyed freedom of speech, thought, education and so on. Other countries had endured turmoil in fighting for these. What was Ireland's response? It was to strive to return to barbarism, to a situation of multitudinous small cultivators and intellectual bondage of the Roman Catholic Church.[28]

For Maine, then, landed property in his own day was only one kind of private property, though a key one. Referring to England, he wrote:

> For all practical purposes, the English landlord is simply a capitalist whose fortune happens to be invested in a particular way. He or his predecessors have either paid for it with some form of capital or they could exchange it for another kind of property . . . The quantity of land which has been held by the same families of proprietors ever since there was what with any laxity of language can be called a feudal system in England is extremely small. There has always been plenty of land for sale in England since the Reformation . . . How did they get the land upon which their dignity has been sustained? Of course they bought it.[29]

He spoke approvingly of the many benefits that came from having large estates in England: moderation of rents, security of tenure, the security and friendliness of almost hereditary holdings. Also large English estates helped cushion agriculture from bad harvests and imports; they could sustain losses where small holders would go out of business. He was opposed to the Radical preference for cutting up estates into small patches. In England it would lead to business classes investing in land, thereby driving up rents.[30]

Referring to the case of William Bence Jones, whose book *The Life's Work in Ireland of a Landlord who Tried to do his Duty* (1880) had just appeared, Maine defended landlordism with the words: 'the system exemplified by Mr Bence Jones . . . tends directly to the survival of the fittest, to the encouragement of thrift, industry, self-helpfulness, and foresight; and it tends as undoubtedly to the conversion of the unfit into the fit by impelling him to the emigration known more or less as a resource all over Ireland'.[31] Given the current pressure on English and Scottish farmers from world markets, what was happening in Ireland? You had the (part) transferral of ownership from the intelligent landlord to the 'grossly ignorant and often recklessly improvident' Irish peasant. There might be a parallel with India, but India didn't have to compete with the United States. In the present 'industrial condition of the world', he believed, this system was doomed. The real solution was to reduce numbers, through emigration.[32]

The deepest level of Maine's opposition to Gladstone's legislative programme for Ireland lay in the threat he believed this programme posed to the principles of property and contract. These were vital to civilisation and misconceived proposals were dangerous not only for Ireland, but for Britain as a whole: 'the condition of Ireland is spreading throughout the British Empire'. What was at stake was Britain's 'material prosperity, and not simply our reputation'. He then gave a pen-picture of how the British system worked: 'What is the character of the industrial and commercial system thus threatened? . . . The system, beyond all question, is the most complex, the most artificial, the most nicely poised and adjusted in the whole world.' Britain did not produce enough food for her own population, relying on imports paid for by manufactured exports:

> The process by which the food we eat is obtained and brought to our shores consists of practically infinite stages; and there is not a single one of all these stages which does not depend for the possibility of carrying it through on the maintenance of one or both of the priceless institutions which the de facto Irish Government has set aside – property and contract . . . Now, the most elementary of all expectations are that a man shall continue to enjoy the property which he possesses, and that the promises which are made to him shall be fulfilled. The entire fabric of English society rests on the fact that this is what all Englishmen expect, and all but invariably secure. If at any time their confidence turns out to be unfounded, if any set of new ideas produces habitual disappointment instead of habitual fulfilment, the ship will not issue from the port or return to it, the coal will not leave the mine, the cotton will not be brought to the factory, and the yarn will not be carried away from it . . . With such principles as now prevail in Ireland seriously exercising influence in England, the mechanism, we will not say of British industrial and mercantile prosperity, but the British food supply, would fall utterly out of gear in a twelvemonth, and would probably cease to work in a few years. This deadly influence is, however, coming nearer and nearer.'[33]

At the core of the successful system lay the motivations and behaviour of the capitalist: 'The desire of wealth, the wish to do what you like with your own, the preference of the cheapest market for buying and of the dearest for selling, are the very motives which produce the growing national income of which the Chancellor of the Exchequer is always taking a portion. But they are also the very motives which produce the class of landlords now denounced as enemies of the Irish race.'[34]

It was this system of contract and private property that was being attacked by the Land League in Ireland. The ordinary practices of contract were being stood on their heads in landlord–tenant relations; history would show, Maine wrote,

> that the proprietors of Irish land have been most abused for their best deeds . . . If a tenant, having hired your land and bound himself to pay you rent, fails to fulfil his promise, the law of all civilized countries, at all times and under all circumstances, has hitherto compelled him, the tenant, to pay damages to you, the landlord. Mr O'Connor Power proposes to reverse the inferences hitherto drawn by civilized mankind from the institution of property. It is to be the landowner who will pay damages to the tenant whenever, having failed to pay the rent, he is requested to surrender the land in respect of which the rent is payable. And this is the principle which, within certain limits, the Chief Secretary for Ireland intends to borrow from Mr O'Connor Power.[35]

When terms such as 'solvent tenant' or 'fair rent' were being bandied about in the land reform debates, Maine related them to the issue of contract.

> They are essentially terms of the market. They relate to the process by which one man undertakes to hire another man's land; and a fair rent is the average result of bargaining in the market by persons who look after their own interests. But what do they mean under this new and transcendental order of economic ideas? What is a fair rent when there is no open market for land?[36]

Freedom of contract, he argued, must still be defended even when the contracting parties held unequal power. This position stood from the time usury laws were abolished.[37] Freedom of contract, he argued, was more fundamental than free trade. It was possible to make a case for protectionism, but not for lack of freedom of contract. The free trader needed to sell as well as manufacture; and selling rested on free contracts.[38]

The attack on property was similar to the attack on contract. The term 'landlordism', he argued,

> should be the system under which land is held by individual owners as private property, and it is thus properly opposed to Communism . . . But this is not the way in which the word is used in Ireland, where it was certainly first used, nor is it the sense with which it is beginning to be employed in England. Mr Parnell, Mr O'Connor Power, and their like use 'landlordism' to convey that peculiar form of quasi-theological hatred which in a Catholic country naturally attaches to every word ending in 'ism'.

As used, it has become 'a term belonging to the ordinary vocabulary of Socialism . . . [and landed property] has been very distinctly pointed out as the first and most hopeful object of attack . . . It is opening the road for those who hold the land of every country to be the common patrimony of all born on it, and whose opinion about property generally was never better expressed than by saying "it is theft"'.[39]

The various plans for Irish land reform were threatening the very essence of private property; once started, the assault on property was unlikely to stop. 'The truth is that landed property, from the very antiquity of its origin, is naturally the most secure of all property . . . When, then, landed property, the oldest of all property, is in danger, all property is in danger, and the entire doctrine of ownership is in a fair way to be soon denied.'[40]

[T]he first attack will necessarily penetrate to the very centre of the institution. Property is nothing if it be not old . . . There is a far vaster mass of human sentiment at present latent which is ready at any moment to array itself against private property if it be seriously threatened. It consists of the innumerable and irresistible emotions which will flow from the appetites, once roused, of those who have nothing and want something, and of those who have something and want more. Beneath private property and the prodigious mass of interests clustered round it there is an abyss which soon after it has begun to heave, will burst forth in lava and fire.[41]

'Let any man try to frame an argument against the Irish land system and see whether it does not resolve itself into an argument against the institution of landed property.' The Irish quack diagnoses and remedies, such as the extension of Ulster Custom, fair rents etc., were wrong – 'giving to one man without compensation that which the law has hitherto given to another'. One consequence was that all capital was threatened. Capital, he believed, instancing the banks, was leaving Ireland.[42] The attack on property was rooted in socialistic ideas:

The agitators are openly Socialistic – partly because they are ignorant, but partly also because they are honest. They have no knowledge of all that depends on such institutions as property and contract, or of the infinity of delicate fibres which spread from them through every part and organ of the body politic . . . They believe, and say it, that they deny the right of one man to have what another has not. They have for the first time in very modern history expressed in the language of common life the epigram of the French Destructive, that Property is Theft.[43]

And, once started, the assault would not stop.

It is assuredly probable that if the Land League succeeds, the tenant farmers' agitation will be followed by a labourers' agitation. There are no doubt 423,000 farmers in Ireland and 440,000 labourers, regarding their employers with the same jealousy with which the employers regard their landlords. It is beyond dispute that the right of property is openly attacked, that Communism is struggling for ascendancy, that terrorism prevails everywhere, that credit is vanishing, that wages must soon fall, and that the small traders must presently be ruined.[44]

THE DANGERS OF DEMOCRACY AND THE THREAT
TO THE BRITISH CONSTITUTION

Maine believed that aristocracy (including an aristocracy of intellect), which for him provided the skill and prudence necessary to control public affairs, was threatened by events in Ireland. The spread of the opposite to aristocracy, democratic ideas, was cause for alarm. Maine argued that virtually all authority had been destroyed in Ireland: the Irish Protestant Church, the Roman Catholic Church, and now the landlords. 'This crop of evil will never be got out of the Irish soil.' A further threat came from the lowering of the county franchise and the substitution of county boards for grand juries. Democracy, he wrote, was a 'cobweb spun by our own minds'. The (secret) ballot, the county boards, the lowering of the franchise; these were new and not inevitable. It was secret voting (the ballot), which enabled Parnell to double his contingent. In a piece on 'The Irish nightmare', Maine ended with the call 'Wake up'.[45] He feared that the expansion of the franchise in Ireland would mean that the new representatives would reflect the electorate's 'average ideas', such as ignorance and hatred of England, superstitious reverence for the Church, and Communistic ideas. Only England kept all this in check.[46] Ireland was still a barbarous country and had never got 'strong systematic government' from England. But an even worse misfortune was 'modern Constitutionalism', which had an uncertain future even where it was best suited, in England. None was less fitted for it than Ireland.[47]

He paid a grudging compliment to Parnell for his leadership qualities, granting that Parnell possessed 'some of the qualities of a great captain in irregular civil war', for 'it has not been given to everybody to deal two such blows in the cause of disorder' as Parnell had succeeded in doing. The first came from the policy of obstructionism in the House of Commons: 'Delivering his stroke at the rules of the House of Commons, he produced confusion, hesitation, and real and perfectly justifiable perplexity on all sides.' Part of his hold on the Irish people, Maine felt, 'arises from their admiration for the one man who openly dishonoured one of the greatest of British institutions'. The second blow derived from Parnell's leadership of the Land League and 'the anarchy which he at once spread through Ireland'. Once more, he 'knew where there was a weak point, and he struck at it'.

Once he detected the weakness, 'he began his campaign against the civil rights of the Irish owner of land; and, as he had fully expected, the Government of the country became on the instant speechless and helpless. They could not move; they could not parry his blow, because the brain of the collective Cabinet was muddled with theories of Land Reform. The result is that something is happening in Ireland far more serious than even the spread among the masses of Communistic opinion. The Government has fallen into contempt . . .'.[48]

Writing in October 1881, Maine claimed that the then state of Ireland was worse than that during the previous winter. While the normal condition should be that people derive safety and so on from support of the government, the reverse was the case in Ireland, where it was normal to be against the government. He instanced shooting and boycotting. There were, in fact, two governments in Ireland: the nominal and the real – the real being the Land League – to which people paid, in effect, tax. Security and other functions of government stemmed from subscribing to the Land League. It was inevitable that the 'Castle' and the League would soon come into conflict and he believed that the League was vulnerable through its treasury.[49]

> Within the last few years there has arisen in Western Europe a community of a new type, answering to none of the definitions of a civilized State which have formed part of political philosophy during the last hundred and fifty years. There is a country within a few miles of our coast in which there is no sanctity of property; there is no regular performance of contract; there is no invariable punishment of detected crime.

Ireland, too, lacked another characteristic of civilised states, a Sovereign, defined as 'an irresistible power, residing somewhere, which forced every man to follow a definite course of action by the commands, which are called laws'. 'There is', he argued,

> no Sovereign in Ireland. There may be discerned there the rudiments or relics of three Sovereigns – the powerless Government, the headless Land League, and a sort of voluntary authority about to exert itself, subsidized by English subscriptions. There is no doubt that every single thinker who has occupied himself with political philosophy would, from the dry scientific point of view, have to describe the social condition of Ireland as a State of anarchy, differing from the anarchy occasionally seen in Europe by its long duration.[50]

Reflecting on calls for Irish Home Rule, he asked what Ireland's future would be if enfranchised? Other than what was forced on Ireland by England or what was simulated, he believed that not one of the elements of political liberty is to be found in Ireland . . . In communities constitutionally liable either to acute or to chronic anarchy – and among these communities we must place all those of Celtic origin – there is an irresistible tendency to the executive despotism of the individual.

If, as the land reforms suggested, Irish tenants were incapable of contracts, then someone else must make decisions for them. Then, referring to his own formulation, he says:

> The sociological rule which affirms that the progress of society is from status to contract only expresses one aspect of the truth that societies in time become civilized and free because the individuals contained in them learn to manage their own affairs, instead of requiring other persons to manage for them.

If the present Bill passes, it is certain that Ireland will become despotic. He instanced France under Napoleon III, Egypt under the Pharaoh, and the Inca. The Irish Land Court was an example of such despotism. India was not a relevant example, he argued, giving a backhanded compliment to the Irish in the process. The Indian ruler was concerned with producing bare maintenance for huge numbers and 'not in the least concerned with the preparation of the Indian millions for liberties quite foreign to their minds', but '[s]ome races find some measure of political freedom as essential to life as food.' What of Ireland? Its capacity for liberty was being slowly destroyed.[51]

THE THREAT OF THE IRISH ABROAD

While Maine was a strong advocate of Irish emigration, he pointed to the dangers that lay in Irish emigration to other parts of the British Empire. These areas were already full, of different religion, and not suited in habits and forms of government to Irishmen. Concerning a proposal by the Cape Government to take an Irish contingent, he spoke of 'the dangerousness of such an addition to the explosive materials already contained in South Africa', asking 'is an Irish colony likely to live in comfort with the Boer or Africander for a neighbour? The races would have nothing in common but their disaffection to British rule'.[52]

Similar dangers attended the prospect of Irish emigration to Britain and North America, as Ireland, a 'half barbarous country', was sending crowds of barbarous emigrants among the civilised, whereas the Greeks and Phoenicians sent out civilised colonists among barbarians. And if the Peleponnesian War started as a colonial quarrel, so a war against contract and property had been started by the Irish in the United Kingdom and in the

United States. Though the ability to go to the UK was, at first sight, a good thing for Ireland, lacking resources as she did and benefiting as a province of a larger entity, the Irish unfortunately remained open to 'any incendiary'. This was even more so in North America, where American money was keeping the Land League alive. Dynamite was bad, but the 'moral catastrophes' being produced were worse.[53]

Focusing on the danger of transferring what he called the 'Irish condition' to England, in particular, he wrote:

> Let it be remembered that there are plenty of outworks belonging to Ireland in England. There are Irish colonies in most of our large manufacturing towns, and much of the affected tenderness of a certain class of politicians among us for the liberties of the Irish subject is merely anxiety of the local Irish vote. Here are the weak points of our economical system into which the poison of Communistic conspiracy is already distilling; and from them, if no timely surgery should save us, it will penetrate into all the inmost recesses of the body politic and social.

One of Maine's fears related to the impact of Irish voters in English cities; he referred to 'political partisans', 'political managers', the 'machine', and the fear among Liberal politicians of losing the Irish vote in 'the great cities'.[54]

Maine concluded by arguing that, while maintenance of order needed much greater force in countries to the east of Great Britain, such force was not needed in Britain because of

> the long-settled habit of obedience to the law, to a frame of mind which hardly admits of an Englishman in his senses resisting legal process, however much he may dislike and disparage the law in virtue of which it issues. But his habit and state of mind depend largely on universality.

This was threatened by the 'Irish colonies'. 'Already one of the chief duties of the British police is to keep the Irish colonies in order. They are now regarded as repulsive examples of a barbarism in which we have no part or interest . . .'[55]

In the light of these worries, what was Maine's alternative? '[T]he Catholic races of Europe', he pointed out, 'have their own special fields of emigration to which they resort in far larger numbers than we here are aware of'. These were the temperate regions of South America.[56]

> Properly speaking, indeed, these regions are not peopled at all . . . There is little or no population in these countries except on the seashore and along the courses of the great rivers. It is a mighty region, capable of holding a dozen Irelands. Much of it is temperate, much of it is rich; it all belongs to the Catholic Church.

A policy of organised emigration would be 'not only possible but easy, and not half as costly as some of the plans which have been advertised for the temporary alleviation of the present troubles'.[57]

CONCLUSIONS

Maine's writings, notably *Ancient Law*, using his comparative and historical method, outlined a process of legal and social evolution where advanced progressive society emerged from an earlier stage of stagnancy. Advanced society was marked by contractual as against status relationships, by individualism as against kinship bonds, by private as against communal property. The contrasting stages were visible in the contrast between east, e.g. India, marked by village communities, and west. The emergence of progressive civilised society was, in Burrow's words, 'a rare and fortunate mutation, but one that was not irreversible – it was a vulnerable stage and could be undermined.'

In the four essays that comprised *Popular Government*, written towards the end of his life, Maine revealed his thinking on the political systems of his day and on how they conformed or deviated from the principles he saw as vital to a progressive society. He was no believer in mass democracy nor in the pursuit of egalitarianism, which he saw as threats to progress; rather he was a passionate defender of the type of mid-Victorian government he was familiar with, which drew on the combined skills of hereditary aristocrats and a middle-class elite of knowledge. On economic issues government involvement should be kept to a minimum and the two foundational principles of contract and private property were to be treated as sacrosanct.

His unsigned *St James's Gazette* articles on Ireland provide the most concrete of historical clothing to the more general arguments presented in *Ancient Law* and *Popular Government;* they starkly reveal the depth and strength of Maine's fear of and opposition to the direction of events in Ireland at the time of the Land War. In Maine's view, the historical English confiscations of land in Ireland were no different from what had occurred elsewhere in Europe; they were part of the wars of religion and were defensible because vital to protect Protestant liberties. Besides, the new landlord system that emerged from these confiscations was less exploitative than the indigenous pre-conquest one and by the nineteenth century the landlord had become a progressive capitalist farmer. Any attempt to interfere with the principles of private property and contract, upon which this system and the British system in general depended, would threaten the very foundations of civilisation. This is what the Gladstonian reform proposals, under pressure from Irish agitators, threatened to do. The Irish (who 'have not quite emerged from barbarism') 'have no knowledge of all that depends on such institutions as property and contract, or of the infinity of delicate fibres which spread from them through every part and organ of the body politic . . . (see p. 83 above). They seem bent not only on reverting to barbarism themselves but of undermining the basis of British material prosperity and civic order. Beset as she is on the one hand by the worst climate in Europe, by poor soil and lack of mineral resources, and on the other hand by over population, the true remedy for Ireland's ills is not the confiscation and re-distribution of land but the encouragement of emigration, not though to Britain itself or to British colonies, where the anarchic Irish can create further dangers, but to the Catholic territories of Latin America.

The ideas of Maine, as formulated in his published works in historical jurisprudence, had considerable influence on the way in which British (Anglo-Indian) officials approached the administration of India, especially landlord and tenant relations. In the earlier part of the nineteenth century, British administrators, driven by utilitarian ideology, saw Indian communal institutions, such as the village community, the caste system, communal tenures and joint cultivation, and so on, as 'so many shackles on the maximizing entrepreneur', which ought to be swept away. By the 1890s, a fundamental ideological reversal had taken place. Indian communal institutions were now looked on much more positively and administrators were fearful of producing a state of *anomie* by undermining such bases of group coherence. Legislation was now designed to prop up such institutions. There is an irony in this, which Clive Dewey draws attention to. Referring to India and to the fact that Maine's ideas were of such a nature as to be usable by people of very different political tendencies than his own, he comments:

> If Maine had lived long enough to read the proceedings of the legislative council when they were sent to the India Office, he would probably have cringed to see the use his admirers were making of his methods. But it was too late. The genie was out of the lamp. (Diamond, 375)

The same could be said of the application of his ideas to Ireland; here his influence on Irish land reform was more indirect than in India, but significant, nonetheless. Those who were influenced by him and who, in turn, influenced Irish land legislation were trained in law and political economy. His ideas had a significant influence on Gladstone's land acts of 1870 and 1881, mediated by such men as T. E. Cliffe Leslie, Sir George Campbell, Alexander Richie and W. Neilson Hancock. They led to policies that caused great alarm to Maine, as seen in his *St James's Gazette* articles.[58]

Maine was elected to membership of the Royal Irish Academy on 16 March 1882, presumably to honour his studies on early Irish law.[59] Again, there is a certain irony in this, coming as it did not long after he had been writing his impassioned articles on Ireland in the *St James's Gazette*. Had the proposers known of these writings and the attitudes he had been expressing in them about Ireland, one wonders if they might not have been more hesitant in forwarding his name.

Notes

1   The *Saturday Review* 'maintained a rigid system of anonymity' from the conviction that 'anonymity was conducive to the public interest; scores of men of affairs who had full-time professions or vocations could publish in its pages their opinions and judgements without fear of disparagement or reprisal'. The *Review* 'appealed to middle to upper class highly educated people . . . [and] was explicitly geared to university-educated men with classical educations, it was often quite rude about people who lacked these "advantages"'. *Waterloo Directory of English Newspapers and Periodicals, 1800–1900*, Series Two (Waterloo, Ontario, Canada: North Waterloo Academic Press, 2003).

2   Cocks (57) adds: '. . . he never claimed that he had fully explained the occurrence of progress; he never arrived at a final, all-inclusive generalisation.' For a lucid summary of Maine's ideas and their context, see Adam Kuper, 'Henry Maine's patriarchal theory', in *The Reinvention of Primitive Society: Transformation of a Myth*, 2nd edn (London: Routledge, 2005), 39–58.

3   Burrow similarly points out that Maine's status to contract formula is not just a historical generalisation, it is also a moral evaluation:

> . . . for Maine expresses not merely an historical truth ('hitherto') but a moral polarity, which no future social development could cancel; a distinction between two moral as well as social worlds: custom set against analysis and intellectual energy, tradition against expediency, dependence against self-reliance, superstitious fear against mutual trust. Maine is strikingly insistent on the moral growth implied by 'the virtues on which Contract depends . . . good faith and trust in our fellows'.

Burrow, 1991, 56–7, quoting *Ancient Law*, 272.

4   It comprised four essays published between 1883 and 1885 in the *Quarterly Review*. I have drawn heavily for this discussion of *Popular Government* on the unpublished thesis of the late W. N. Coxall, *Two Victorian Theorists of Democracy: a Comparative Study of Sir Henry Maine and Matthew Arnold*, PhD thesis, University of London, 1977.

5   According to Coxall (152) he shared his Liberal elitism with Mill and Morley.

6   For Maine the Anglo-Saxon model was the sound form, based on ancient Teutonic freedom, as opposed to pejorative images of democracy, e.g. French anarchy and revolutionary dictatorship (Coxall: 97–8).

7   A number of specific changes to the British constitution Maine feared. He was a strong advocate of bicameralism and he associated 'unicameralism' with revolution, the French

Revolution, for example. He was worried by: the widespread talk of the abolition of the House of Lords, changes in the House of Commons brought in to accelerate the legislative process (partly due to 'obstructions of Irish members'), the flow of power from the Commons to Cabinet (he termed the Cabinet: 'a constitutional Juggernaut'), the emergence of party organisation, electoral reorganisation, the (secret) Ballot, and substantive issues of empire and Ireland.

8   Frederick Greenwood left the *Pall Mall Gazette* to found *St James's Gazette and Evening Review and Record of News*, 1: 1 of which appeared on 31 May 1880. Mitchell's *Newpaper Press Directory and Advertiser's Guide* (London, 1900) described it in the following terms:

> It was a trenchant, if often too indignant and ungenerous, critic of the second Gladstone administration through its five years' life, opposing the Conservatives as zealously as the Liberals when it saw occasion for doing so, and has been a powerful factor in the political settlements and unsettlements that have taken place or have been in process since it was started . . . The St James's Gazette is an independent and progressive newspaper, which, while consistently supporting constitutional principles, the maintenance of the empire, and the supremacy of the law in every portion of the dominions of the Crown, is in favour of moderate and ordered reform. It gives with point, brevity, and accuracy all the most important news of the day, the latest money market reports, sporting news, Parliamentary Intelligence, Foreign Telegrams, etc. Special attention is given to American, Continental, and Indian Intelligence.

Waterloo Directory of English Newspapers and Periodicals, 1800–1900, Series Two (Waterloo, Ontario, Canada: North Waterloo Academic Press, 2003).

9   There is no reference to them, for example, in Diamond's impressive centenary volume, published in 1991. Feaver became aware of these essays from a handwritten list found among Maine's papers.

10   'Irish land and English justice' (29 June, 1880), 403.

> Those who have any knowledge of Ireland are aware that here has been distress, and sometimes terrible distress, among the land-holding class. But Englishmen in the mass have only had before their eyes the great estates which in the maps published by some of the newspapers were made to take up the largest part of the surface of Ireland.

'Landed properties, large and small' (26 Sept., 1881), 1,123.

11   'Irish distress and its remedies' (14 Sept., 1880), 1,459.

12   'Irish facts and English emotions' (1 Dec., 1880), 2,531.

> Is it really forgotten that the poor are always with us? and that the man who bids them mend their poverty by breaking the law will always find a hearing, and a hearing which will end in overt acts of violence unless the law asserts itself instantly, conspicuously, and sternly?

('Why the revolution makes way' (10 Dec., 1880), 2,659.)

13 The following titles are examples: 'Irish distress and its remedies' (14 Sept., 1880), 1,459; 'Irish disease and quack remedies for it' (21 Oct., 1880), 1,979–80; 'Medicine for the Irish malady' (7 Dec., 1880), 2,611; 'The Irish nightmare' (15 Mar., 1881), 1,123; 'The medicines and the quackeries of the land bill' (23 Apr., 1881), 1,531–2; 'Remedies for agricultural distress' (22 Oct., 1881), 1,555.

14 'The dependence of Ireland on Great Britain' (10 Jan., 1881), 115.

15 'Malthusianism and modern politics' (7 July, 1880), 524–5.

[Malthus's] positions have now become the one firm spot from which the most advancing sciences of our day work their leverage; and the argument which rests upon them has thus the same certainty as an argument pointing to the results of combining mechanical or chemical forces.

'The medicines and the quackeries of the land bill' (23 Apr., 1881), 1,531–2.

16 'The survival of the unfittest' (22 Dec., 1880), 2,819.

17 Ibid.

18 'Malthusianism and modern politics' (7 July, 1880), 524–5.

19 'Medicine for the Irish malady' (7 Dec., 1880), 2,611.

20 'Irish disease and quack remedies for it' (21 Oct., 1880), 1,979–80.

21 'The Irish paradox' (5 Dec., 1881), 2,155–6.

22 'French opinion on Irish affairs' (4 Jan., 1881), 35–6.

23 'The new nation' (21 Dec., 1881), 2,371.

24 'The misfortunes of Ireland' (30 Aug., 1880), 1,259–60.

25 Ibid.

26 'Irish agitators and the Church of Rome' (27 Sept., 1880), 1,635. Elsewhere he refers to the memoirs of English statesmen – all of whom had hoped for a conservative Roman Catholic Church in Ireland. It was not so; there was a peasant clergy, trained like peasants, dependent on peasants. 'The Land League and the Catholic bishops' (21 Feb., 1881), 692. In another article Maine defended Froude, who had been attacked by the Radical press because of views he expressed in the preface to a new edition of *The English in Ireland*. Froude had suggested the suspension of the constitutional system in the west of Ireland and ruling it like a Crown colony. In considering granting Irish independence, Radical theorists would, according to Maine, 'annul the one indispensable condition of British greatness . . . the British commonwealth "one and indivisible" as regards the islands which are its heart'. Froude had identified three pre-1870 English-derived institutions, which were meant to imbue Irish with English ideas: i) the Established Church; ii) absolute property in land; iii) a national system of education. Maine held that Gladstone destroyed the first two and weakened the third, though the first two were actually working and the third too new to judge. 'Mr Froude and his critics' (17 Jan., 1881), 211.

27 'Some certain results of the land bill' (14 Apr., 1881), 1,411.

28 'The measure of English responsibility for Ireland' (9 Mar., 1881), 915.

29 'Landlordism' (17 June, 1880), 243–4.

30 'Landed properties, large and small' (26 Sept., 1881), 1,187–8. Maine's defence of the landlord system was consistent with the historical role he saw played by aristocracy. Reacting to a speech by John Bright, which laid all crimes in history at the door of 'monarchs and statesmen', he claimed that the worst historical excesses in Ireland had been when England was most democratic – namely the Commonwealth period – and were based on the knowledge of ills done by Catholics on Protestants abroad; they were perpetrated in defence of English liberties. 'Mr Bright's political and historical philosophy' (19 Nov., 1880), 2,379–80.

31 'The survival of the unfittest', I (22 Dec., 1880), 2,819. William Bence Jones's *The Life's work in Ireland of a landlord who tried to do his duty*, appeared in London in December 1880.

32 'The Irish paradox' (5 Dec., 1881), 2,155–6.

33 'Unnoticed dangers of Irish example' (20 Dec., 1880), 2,795–6.

34 'Budgets and land bills', II (2 Mar., 1881), 819. Moreover, the principles of private property and free contract had 'brilliant success' in the past.

> They were twice applied boldly, unshrinkingly, and conspicuously, in the reform of the poor Laws and in the repeal of the corn Laws. There were objections to the first on the score of its initial severity; there are objections to the second on the ground of public international dangers; but between the two English pauperism has disappeared in the most populous parts of the country, and has become manageable in the rest.

'Radicalism old and new' (25 Jan., 1881), 331–2.

35 Ibid. John O'Connor Power (1846–1919) took part in the Fenian movement, served as an Irish Parliamentary Party MP (pioneering the practice of obstructionism), and was one of the founders of the Land League.

36 'The projected economic revolution in Ireland', II (12 Apr., 1881), 1,379–80.

37 'Modern mysteries' (23 June, 1881), 2,355.

38 'Free contract and free trade' (10 Aug., 1881), 547.

39 Ibid.

40 'Perils of old and new wealth' (4 Nov., 1881), 1,731–2.

41 'The agitation against private property' (24 Nov., 1880), 2,443–4.

42 'Irish disease and quack remedies for it' (21 Oct., 1880), 1,979–80.

43 'French opinion on Irish Affairs', II (4 Jan., 1881), 35–6.

44 'French Opinion on Irish affairs', II (4 Jan., 1881), 35–6.

45 'The Irish nightmare' (15 Mar., 1881), 1,004.

46 'Franchises and opinions in Ireland' (14 June, 1880), 195–6.

47 'The misfortunes of Ireland' (30 Aug., 1880), 1,259–60.

48 'Catalinarian victories and their fruits', I (16 Nov., 1880), 2,332.

49 'The demoralization of a people', III (7 Oct., 1881), 1,347.

50 'The new nation' (21 Dec., 1881), 2,371.

51 'The Irish land court as a school of liberty' (13 May, 1881), 1,795. And see a second comparison with Inca despotism ('now extinct') in 'The projected economic revolution in Ireland' (12 Apr., 1881), 1,379–80. Extreme centralisation, he believed, led to despotism, as did hindering the free exercise of contract making. He cited George Campbell on India, suggesting that the case there was 'manifestly different from that of the Irish Bill'.

52 'The medicines and the quackeries of the land bill' (23 Apr., 1881), 1,531–2.

53 'A message to a wrong address' (4 Aug., 1881), 467–8.

54 'The superstition of ordinary law' (31 Dec., 1880), 2,931.

55 'Unnoticed dangers of Irish example' (20 Dec., 1880), 2,795–6.

56 'The medicines and the quackeries of the land bill' (23 Apr., 1881), 1,531–2.

57 'Medicine for the Irish malady', 1 (7 Dec., 1880), 2,611.

58 For detailed discussion of the impact of Maine's ideas in India and Ireland, see the essays by Dewey.

59 The Royal Irish Academy Committee of Polite Literature and Antiquities included at this time Alexander G. Richey, Robert Atkinson, John Kells Ingram, and the Very Rev. W. Reeves, while the Committee of Science included Alexander Macalister, George Sigerson, and Sir Robert Kane.

Bibliography

Works by Maine

Maine, Henry Sumner, 1908 [1861]. *Ancient law: Its Connection with the Early History of Society and its Relation to Modern Ideas*. London: John Murray.

Maine, Henry Sumner, 1895 [1871]. *Village-Communities in the East and West: Six Lectures delivered at Oxford*. 7th edn. London: John Murray.

Maine, Henry Sumner, 1905 [1875]. *Lectures on the Early History of Institutions*. 7th edn. London: John Murray.

Maine, Henry Sumner, 1901 [1883]. *Dissertations on Early Law and Custom*. New impression. London: John Murray.

Maine, Henry Sumner, 1897 [1885]. *Popular Government: Four Essays*. 5th edn. London: John Murray.

Unsigned articles by Maine with reference to Ireland in the St James's Gazette, 1880 to 1881

'Franchises and opinions in Ireland', 1 (14 June, 1880), 195–6.

'Landlordism', 1 (17 June, 1880), 243–4.

'Irish land and English justice', 1 (29 June, 1880), 403.

'Malthusianism and modern politics', 1 (7 July, 1880), 524–5.

'The lesson to liberals', 1 (14 July, 1880), 611–12.

'Probable effects of past blunders', 1 (9 Aug., 1880), 963.

'The misfortunes of Ireland', 1 (30 Aug., 1880), 1,259–60.

'Irish distress and its remedies', 1 (14 Sept., 1880), 1,459.

'Irish agitators and the Church of Rome', 1 (27 Sept., 1880), 1,635.

'Law and law amendment in Ireland', I (5 Oct., 1880), 1,755–6.

'Now and then', I (11 Oct., 1880), 1,827.

'Some results of nonconformist success', I (14 Oct., 1880), 1,883–4.

'Irish disease and quack remedies for it', I (21 Oct., 1880), 1,979–80.

'Some advantages of the recognition of barbarism', I (10 Nov., 1880), 2,251–2.

'Catalinarian victories and their fruits', I (16 Nov., 1880), 2,332.

'Mr Bright's political and historical philosophy', I (19 Nov., 1880), 2,379–80.

'The agitation against private property', I (24 Nov., 1880), 2,443–4.

'Irish facts and English emotions', I (1 Dec., 1880), 2,531.

'Medicine for the Irish malady', I (7 Dec., 1880), 2,611.

'Why the revolution makes way', I (10 Dec., 1880), 2,659.

'Extraordinary law', I (18 Dec., 1880), 2,771.

'Unnoticed dangers of the Irish example', I (20 Dec., 1880), 2795–6.

'The survival of the unfittest', I (22 Dec., 1880), 2,819.

'The superstition of ordinary law', I (31 Dec., 1880), 2,931.

'French opinion on Irish affairs', II (4 Jan., 1881), 35–6.

'The dependence of Ireland on Great Britain', II (10 Jan., 1881), 115.

'The two voices', II (11 Jan., 1881), 139–40.

'Mr Froude and his critics', II (17 Jan., 1881), 211.

'Radicalism, old and new', II (25 Jan., 1881), 331–2.

'The ordinary law of Ireland and what should be done with it', II (10 Feb., 1881), 517.

'Disillusion', II (17 Feb., 1881), 643.

'The Land League and the Catholic bishops', II (21 Feb., 1881), 692.

'Mr Parnell and foreign opinion', II (22 Feb., 1881), 716.

'Budgets and land bills', II (2 Mar., 1881), 819.

'The measure of English responsibility for Ireland', II (9 Mar., 1881), 915.

'The Irish nightmare', II (15 Mar., 1881), 1,123.

'The projected economic revolution in Ireland', II (12 Apr., 1881) 1,379–80.

'Some certain results of the land bill', II (14 Apr., 1881), 1,441.

'The medicines and the quackeries of the land bill', II (23 Apr., 1881), 1,531–2.

'The Irish land court as a school of liberty', II (13 May, 1881), 1,795.

'The precedent of fifty years since', II (8 June, 1881), 2,147.

'Modern mysteries', II (23 June, 1881), 2,355.

'Veracity in politics', III (4 July, 1881), 35.

'The crime of Guiteau', III (7 July, 1881), 83.

'The Irish land bill as a source of revolution', III (16 July, 1881), 227–8.

'A message to a wrong address', III (4 Aug., 1881), 467–8.

'Free contract and free trade', III (10 Aug., 1881), 547.

'Orating and legislating', III (22 Aug., 1881), 707.

'The farmer and his friends', III (14 Sept., 1881), 1,027.

'The radicals and the farmers', III (21 Sept., 1881), 1,123.

'Landed properties, large and small', III (26 Sept., 1881), 1,123.

'The demoralization of a people', III (7 Oct., 1881), 1,347.
'Remedies for agricultural distress', III (22 Oct., 1881), 1,555.
'Perils of old and new wealth', III (4 Nov., 1881), 1,731–2.
'Free trade and how it is threatened', III (11 Nov., 1881), 1,827.
'Confusion of thought about the land', III (22 Nov., 1881), 1,979–80.
'The Irish paradox', III (5 Dec., 1881), 2,155–6.
'The new nation', III (21 Dec., 1881), 2,371.

Secondary Works

Black, R. D. Collison, 1960 [reprinted, Gregg Revivals, 1993]. *Economic Thought and the Irish Question 1817–1870*. Cambridge: Cambridge University Press.

Bull, Philip, 1996. *Land, Politics and Nationalism: A Study of the Irish Land Question*. Dublin: Gill & Macmillan.

Burrow, J. W., 1966. *Evolution and Society*. Cambridge: Cambridge University Press.

Burrow, J. W., 1991. 'Henry Maine and mid-Victorian ideas of progress', in Alan Diamond (ed.), 55–69.

Cocks, Raymond, 1988. *Sir Henry Maine: a study in Victorian Jurisprudence*. Cambridge: Cambridge University Press.

Collini, Stefan, Donald Winch and John Burrow, 1983. *That Noble Science of Politics: A Study in Nineteenth-Century Intellectual History*. Cambridge: Cambridge University Press.

Coxall, William Norman, 1977. *Two Victorian Theorists of Democracy: A Comparative Study of Sir Henry Maine and Matthew Arnold*, unpublished PhD dissertation, University of London (LSE).

Dewey, Clive, 1972. 'Images of the village community: a study in Anglo-Indian ideology', *Modern Asian Studies*, 6, 291–328.

Dewey, Clive, 1974. 'Celtic agrarian legislation and the Celtic revival: historicist implications of Gladstone's Irish and Scottish land acts 1870–1886', *Past & Present*, 64 (August), 30–70.

Dewey, Clive, 1991. 'The influence of Sir Henry Maine on agrarian policy in India', in Alan Diamond (ed.), 353–75.

Diamond, Alan (ed.), 1991. *The Victorian Achievement of Sir Henry Maine: A Centennial Reappraisal*. Cambridge: Cambridge University Press.

Feaver, George A., 1969. *From Status to Contract: A Biography of Sir Henry Maine 1822–1888*. London: Longmans.

Harris, Marvin, 1968. *The Rise of Anthropological Theory*. N.Y.: Columbia University Press.

Kuper, Adam, 1988. *The Invention of Primitive Society: Transformations of an Illusion*. London: Routledge.

Macfarlane, Alan D. J., 1991. 'Some contributions of Maine to history and anthropology', in Alan Diamond (ed.), 111–42.

CHAPTER 6

The Irish Question in Karl Marx's and Friedrich Engels's Writings on Capitalism and Empire

Chandana Mathur and Dermot Dix

Few nineteenth-century formulations of Ireland's suffering under British rule were as explicit as those of Karl Marx and Friedrich Engels in focusing away from essentialist explanations cast in the language of British villainy, and in concentrating instead on material factors, on the conjoined expansion of capitalism in Britain and underdevelopment in Ireland. This is plainly evident even in the very manner in which Ireland features in the chapter organisation of their explicitly theoretical work. Ellen Hazelkorn points out that, by placing consideration of Irish agriculture in the chapter headed the 'General Law of Capitalist Accumulation', Marx scorned the historicist argument that focused attention on the Act of Union and English anti-Irishness, and turned to evaluate how the transference of capital, foodstuffs, and labour from Ireland to England formed an integral and necessary part of their respective economic growth (Hazelkorn 1981: 26).

The systemic underpinnings of British rule in Ireland have subsequently tended to be under-discussed: it is hard to believe that it is still necessary to go back to the writings of Marx and Engels to be reminded of this key element in the relationship between England and Ireland. Indeed, Eamonn Slater and Terrence McDonough have observed that even the rise of postcolonial theory in Ireland has not helped to mitigate the inattention to political economy that characterises the field of Irish studies (Slater and McDonough 1994: 63-4).

THE TRANSITION FROM FEUDALISM TO CAPITALISM IN IRELAND

It will be a useful first step to consider commentaries on Marx's and Engels's writings on Ireland that do echo their political economy emphasis. In their work on Ireland, Marx and Engels wrote mainly in the second half of the nineteenth century *about* the second half of the nineteenth century. The literature on their Irish writings quickly leads into a transition debate transposed to Ireland, the central issue being what Karl Kautsky called 'the agrarian question' and defined as follows:

> Is capital, and in what ways is capital, taking hold of agriculture, revolutionizing it, smashing the old forms of production and of poverty and establishing the new forms which must succeed? (Kautsky 1988: 46)

Ellen Hazelkorn's starting point is a little-noticed passage about Ireland in *Capital* Volume One where Marx argues that capitalist relations were beginning to take hold in Irish agriculture after the famine. Agricultural production was increasingly being moulded to British requirements (for example, by the substitution of pasture for tillage), there was greater consolidation and concentration of land ownership, and rapid proletarianisation in the Irish countryside was giving rise to emigration and the swelling of the industrial reserve army of labour in Britain. This transition had been hastened after the famine, in Marx's view, by the repeal of the Corn Laws and the Encumbered Estates Acts.

Using historical research by David Fitzpatrick and Cormac Ó Gráda, Hazelkorn shows that Marx was mistaken about the emergence of capitalist agriculture in Ireland, and that small farmers had successfully been able to resist proletarianisation for a good while longer. The tendency towards centralisation and consolidation that Marx saw in the immediate post-famine years was stalled, even reversed in later decades. The political consequence of this misreading, she says, is that Marx and Engels were unprepared for the way that the Land League movement evolved. Much later, in 1888, Engels ruefully admitted to the true property-desiring character of the movement:

> A purely socialist movement cannot be expected in Ireland for a considerable time. People there want first of all to become peasants owning a plot of land, and after they have achieved that mortgages will appear on the scene and they will be ruined once more. But this should not prevent us from seeking to help them to get rid of their landlords, that is, to pass from semi-feudal conditions to capitalist conditions (Marx and Engels 1971: 343).

Hazelkorn faults the inadequacy of their analysis of class in the Irish countryside – a dismal contrast to their sophisticated analysis of the French agrarian classes – for their misrecognition of land politics and economics in the second half of the nineteenth century.

Slater and McDonough cast the transition debate in entirely different terms. They note that, in *Capital* Volume Three, Marx states correctly that the feudal mode of production was still intact in Ireland in the nineteenth century, as evidenced in the fact that the Irish rental form was not yet a capitalist ground rent (Slater and McDonough 1994: 73–4). So their argument is that it is not Marx, but the conventional readings of Marx, that are mistaken. For example, they fault Mokyr and Ó Gráda for not discussing the feudal nature of the rent relationship (Slater and McDonough 1994: 111n). For Slater and McDonough, this amounts to an implicit acceptance of the notion of a capitalist rent relationship. Somewhat surprisingly, they do not challenge Hazelkorn's reading of Marx, which is very much at odds with theirs, but they do explicitly take issue with Ó Gráda, even though his findings about the postponement of proletarianisation basically buttress their thesis of the continued existence of feudalism.

In any case, even if we go along with Hazelkorn's reading that Marx and Engels mistakenly saw capitalist relations developing in Irish agriculture, they were off by only a few decades. Hazelkorn herself admits that capitalist relations came to prevail in Irish agriculture quite soon after. Also, if they were wrong about the Land League, they were certainly not alone; Michael Davitt was famously disappointed in the failure of his land nationalisation project to take hold among small farmers (Davitt 1991: 280).

ASIATIC MODES AND OTHER ANALYTICAL HAZARDS

A comparison with that other colonial context which Marx discussed extensively – India under British rule – helps place in perspective the flaws in their analysis of Irish agriculture. A relatively minor error of periodisation in Ireland is emphatically not a clunker of the magnitude of the 'Asiatic' mode of production, a conception that resulted in Marx arguing – over a fairly sustained period – that colonialism had beneficial tonic effects for its Asian subjects. By contrast, he never presented the colonial relationship as an even potentially positive one for Ireland; notwithstanding changes in emphasis and at times even a change of mind on key processes, his analysis of Irish history and society under British rule was always more critical.

Despite the risk of being sidetracked into the issues and debates raised by the unfortunate formulation, it may be worthwhile to remember that the two key characteristics of the Asiatic mode were seen by Marx to be the unchanging village community and the despotic nature of the Oriental state, where rent and tax were coterminous because the sovereign owned all land. According to Irfan Habib (30–4), it is evident that Marx began to entertain serious doubts about the whole 'Asiatic' concept after 1867, going by marginal notes he took on later readings – on Elphinstone's *History of India*, Maine's *Lectures on the Early History of Institutions* and most notably Kovalevsky's

Communal Landholding. He came seriously to doubt the idea of the stagnant, unchanging village community. He also came to realise that land ownership in pre-British India was a far more complex issue than he had at first grasped.

Later doubts about the Asiatic mode notwithstanding, Marx was decidedly positive about colonialism's transformative possibilities in his Indian commentary, a mood that one does not encounter in the Irish material. In an 1853 *New York Tribune* article, he describes the railways as being 'truly the forerunner of modern industry' in India (Marx and Engels 2001: 73). He referred to England's 'double mission in India: one destructive, the other regenerating – the annihilation of old Asiatic society, and the laying of the material foundations of Western society in Asia'. Asiatic village life, he thought, 'restrained the human mind within the smallest possible compass, enslaving it beneath traditional rules, depriving it of all grandeur and historical energies' (Marx and Engels 2001: 65). It is this passage, and the numerous others like it scattered through his articles on India, that prompted Edward Said to label Marx an 'orientalist'.

However, even in this early (1853), apparently positive mindset in regards to colonialism in India, Marx was clear that the misery inflicted by the British was 'infinitely more intensive' (Marx and Engels 2001: 62) than anything experienced to date on the subcontinent; British rule was nothing short of 'swinish' (Marx and Engels 2001: 18).

Marx particularly, and Engels to a lesser degree, followed the insurgency of 1857 in India closely. In September of that year, Marx wrote that 'the outrages committed by the revolted sepoys in India are indeed appalling' – and then proceeded to offer a luminous, excoriating critique of British hypocrisy and brutality in the following words: the outrages, he wrote, were of a type that 'respectable England' used to admire when committed against the old enemy, France. More tellingly, however, he offers the following explanation for the violence:

> However infamous the conduct of the sepoys, it is only the reflex, in a concentrated form, of England's own conduct in India . . . even during the last ten years of a long-settled rule. To characterize that rule, it suffices to say that torture formed an organic institution of its financial policy. There is something in human history like retribution; and it is a rule of historical retribution that its instrument be forged not by the offended, but by the offender himself. (Marx and Engels 2001: 82)

This insight about the violence of the anti-colonial movement would reappear almost exactly one hundred years later in the work of writers such as Frantz Fanon and Albert Memmi.

Marx describes reading letters of British officers that were 'redolent of malignity' (Marx and Engels 2001: 83). Indeed, some of the offending passages he selected, together with the summary justice meted out to many an innocent, are starkly reminiscent of the aftermath of the 1798 Rebellion in Ireland.

Marx preferred the term 'First War of Indian Independence' to the more demeaning 'mutiny' as a label for the events of 1857; but he saw quickly that there would be no sustained movement in the immediate future. Still, four years before 1857, he was abundantly clear about the desirability of Indian independence. Both Habib and Aijaz Ahmad make a great deal of the following 1853 quote from Marx:

> The Indians will not reap the fruits of the new elements of society scattered among them by the British bourgeoisie, till in Great Britain itself the new ruling classes shall have been supplanted by the industrial proletariat, or till the Hindus [read, Indians] themselves shall have grown strong enough to throw off the English yoke altogether. (Marx and Engels 2001: 73)

Ahmad points out that 'no influential Indian reformer of the nineteenth century . . . was to take so clear-cut a position on the issue of Indian independence' (Marx and Engels 2001: 20), and that Gandhi would spend the years of the First World War recruiting soldiers for the war effort (in much the same way as did Redmond in Ireland, and for near-identical reasons).

Nearly thirty years after that breathless 1853 ode to the railways, Marx was to become more cautious about colonialism's offerings. In 1881 he wrote, in a letter to N. F. Danielson, about the 'bleeding process' that empire forced on India, and even referred to the previously much-vaunted railways as 'useless to the Hindoos' (Marx and Engels 2001: 104). There are, thus, ambiguities and significant changes of position in Marx's and Engels's corpus of writings on India. However, although we too disagree with Edward Said's dismissal of Marx as a 'romantic orientalist', it nevertheless seems to us that scholarship such as Ahmad's and Habib's doth protest too much on this point.

Consider Habib's response to the following line from the same 1853 article by Marx: 'Modern industry, resulting from the railway system, will dissolve the hereditary divisions of labour, upon which rest the Indian castes, those decisive impediments to Indian progress and Indian power' (Marx and Engels 2001: 73). Determined to rehabilitate even such an extravagant claim as this, Habib writes: 'This was confident prophecy; and the Indian working class has largely fulfilled it though not to the extent, perhaps, that Marx might have expected' (Habib 1995: 56). It takes a staggering amount of wishful thinking to imagine that caste has been 'largely' broken down in contemporary India. Similarly, while Ahmad concedes that 'the writings of Marx and Engels are indeed contaminated in several places with the usual banalities of nineteenth-century Eurocentrism, and [that] the general prognosis they offered about the social stagnation of our societies was often based on unexamined staples of conventional European histories' (Ahmad 1992: 229), he does seem to go to an inordinate amount of trouble to demonstrate the relatively unchanging character of the Indian village community.

It seems to us that honest criticism needs to play a crucial role in any serious engagement with the colonial writings of Marx and Engels. It is precisely the unsatisfactory nature of some of their analysis of colonialism which helps account for twentieth-century Marxism's preoccupation with the subject, from Lenin's pioneering *Imperialism* to Ernest Mandel's finely drawn picture of combined and uneven development in his *Late Capitalism*.

While it is important to be critical, we remain acutely aware of the danger of the false paradox. For example, in the context of the very comparison that we have been making between Marx's writings on Ireland and India, Ivan Vujacic detects, in our view unjustly, an analytic slant in favour of Ireland. Juxtaposing one of those passages where Marx congratulates British colonialism for breaking up India's stagnant social structure with his analysis of Ireland in *Capital*, Vujacic writes:

> His analysis of the situation in Ireland, which was also a colony of Great Britain, is quite different. In the chapter on the general law of capitalist accumulation in *Capital*, Marx draws an empirical sketch of the systematic impoverishment of Ireland and the subjugation of its economic structure to the needs of English capital, with all the social consequences that spring from such a process. (Vujacic 1988: 476)

According to Vujacic, Marx is discriminating in favour of Ireland here in the sense that Ireland enters centrally into his analysis of capitalism whereas India does not. In fact, it is not Marx but British imperial policy on migration that happens to be discriminating in favour of Ireland. The Irish people fleeing rural poverty could find employment in the mills of industrial Britain, whereas Indians fleeing rural poverty were not allowed to exercise such an option. Chapter twenty-five of *Capital* Volume One deals with the industrial reserve army of labour, and Ireland enters here precisely because it had been enabled by colonial policy to make a sizeable labour contribution to the industrial revolution in Britain. Even granted the lack of peasant proletarian-isation in Ireland in the second half of the nineteenth century, as noted by Hazelkorn, and also by Slater and McDonough, it is nonetheless true that there were significant numbers of Irish workers to be found in every British industrial town. Given that Indians were dragged to various parts of the British Empire as indentured workers, but were prevented from freely emigrating in search of work to any part of the Empire or to Britain, it is hardly surprising that an analysis of the British working class should exclude a consideration of the Indian colonial context. These issues of labour mobility and restrictions thereon were crucial then and still have resonance today.

IN DEFENCE OF NATIONALIST MOVEMENTS

Perhaps the most important emphasis we have derived from Ahmad and Habib is their stress on Marx's and Engels's unambiguous support for anti-colonial movements. The latter did, certainly, have a great deal to say on the subject, both in the Irish and Indian contexts. Indeed, the anarchist Bakunin famously attacked Marx and the Communist International for being overly interested in Irish nationalism, at the expense of the international working-class movement.

Marx and Engels took an active interest in the Fenian movement; they were closely involved in the attempt to force the British government to put an end to the cruel treatment of Fenian prisoners in British and Irish jails in the aftermath of the Fenian rising of 1867. Marx between 1869 and 1870 wrote stinging critiques of this treatment, in which he argued that 'there is no country in Europe where political prisoners are treated like in England and Russia' (Marx and Engels 1971: 153). His comments also demonstrate an intimate knowledge of the situation of particular prisoners (such as O'Donovan Rossa, kept for 35 days in a darkened cell, hands tied behind his back; Martin Carey, locked up in a lunatic asylum; Denis Mulcahy, harnessed to a cart and bound with a metal band around his neck) – a knowledge that may surprise those who think of Marx as being interested solely in the broad sweep of history (Marx and Engels 1971: 164–5).

Engels, on a personal level, was closer than Marx to the Irish situation through his long association and marriage ties with the Lancashire-Irish and Fenian-connected Burns family. Around 1870 he prepared a large amount of material for a history of Ireland, and completed two chapters – one on 'Natural conditions' and the other on 'Ancient Ireland'. He visited Ireland three times, in 1856, in 1869, and again in 1891. Just after the second visit (two years after the Fenian Rising) he described the country in a letter to Marx as being in a

state of war. . . There are squads of Royal Irish all over the place, with sheath-knives, and occasionally a revolver at their side and a police baton in their hand; in Dublin a horse-drawn battery drove right through the centre of town, a thing I have never seen in England, and there are soldiers literally everywhere. (Marx and Engels 1971: 273–4)

However, it was Engels rather than Marx who tended to be much more immoderate in the remarks he indulged in on the nature of 'the Irish'. Often in the context of a positive line (e.g. 'Give me 200,000 Irishmen and I could overthrow the entire British monarchy'), he could apparently happily conjure up the image of 'wild, headstrong, fanatical Gaels', or dismiss 'the Irishman' as a 'light-hearted, cheerful, potato-eating child of nature' who, 'straight from the moorland, where he grew up under a leaky roof fed on weak tea and short commons . . . is suddenly flung into our civilisation'. Another vivid psycho-social picture is that of the Irishman who gets his political education in England (in the 'mechanistic, frigid and egoistic bustle of the English industrial town') and who returns home with a point to his rage, 'capable of anything', and ready to lash out furiously whenever he sees an opportunity (Marx and Engels 1971: 33–4). There is no shortage of this kind of cartoon-like characterisation and, of the two, Engels tends to be the more guilty of it; but Marx too could slip into a mode of analysis whereby he contrasted the firebrand Irish with the stolid Anglo-Saxon.

This curious use of stereotype, paradoxically, goes hand in hand with Marx's perceptive refutation, in the *Capital* chapter already discussed, of the Malthusian view that Ireland's poverty was caused by its over-population. Just as it is today, Malthusian language was an important idiom in which racism was expressed in the nineteenth century, and Marx used the Irish example to articulate a powerful critique.

Although stereotype occasionally appeared in their writing, their political arguments did not hinge on it. Marx and Engels admired the Fenian movement for being 'socialist', 'lower-class', 'republican' and non-sectarian (Marx and Engels 1971: 124). Marx, in a November 1867 letter to Engels, reports that he had been planning to make a speech on Ireland at a meeting of the International's General Council, only to yield the floor because 'our subject, Fenianism, was liable to inflame the passions to such heat that I . . . would have been forced to hurl revolutionary thunderbolts instead of soberly analysing the state of affairs and the movement as I had intended' (Marx and Engels 1971: 147). This was clearly a subject close to Marx's engagé heart. Notwithstanding their broad support for the Fenian movement and instinctive humanitarian outrage about the treatment of Fenian prisoners, it must be said that Marx and Engels did come to entertain serious doubts about Fenianism. In a November 1867 letter to Marx, Engels writes as follows:

> As regards the Fenians you are quite right. The beastliness of the English must not make us forget that the leaders of this sect are mostly asses and partly exploiters and we cannot in any way make ourselves responsible for the stupidities which occur in every conspiracy. And they are certain to happen.
> (Marx and Engels 1971: 145–6)

Marx and Engels criticised the tendency of the Fenian leadership and their sympathisers to stick to a narrowly national line. In a letter to Engels of December 1869, Marx complains about the tendency to insist that the 'Irish question' be treated as 'something quite separate, apart from the rest of the world', and to conceal the extent of support for the Irish among certain sections of the English working class (Marx and Engels 1971: 282).

They also had problems with Fenian methods. In a June 1882 letter to Eduard Bernstein, Engels complained that the Fenians 'are . . . increasingly being pushed into a sort of Bakuninism' (Marx and Engels 1971: 336), as evidenced by the Phoenix Park murders which Engels regarded as ill-advised and counter-productive (we know now that he was mistaken in blaming these murders on the Fenians, when they were in fact carried out by a group known as 'The Invincibles'). By this stage, Engels regarded Parnell as Ireland's best medium-term possibility, and he thought that actions like the Phoenix Park murders would only serve to impede Parnell's work.

Marx, who had previously held the view that Ireland would be freed by the revolution of the working class in England, now came to have serious doubts on this score. He says as much in a December 1869 letter to Engels:

> For a long time I believed that it would be possible to overthrow the Irish regime by English working-class ascendancy. I always expressed this point of view in the *New-York Tribune*. Deeper study has now convinced me of the opposite. The English working class will never accomplish anything before it has got rid of Ireland. The lever must be applied in Ireland. (Marx and Engels 1971: 284)

This lever, successfully 'applied', would short-circuit what Marx one year later described as the profound antagonism between the Irish proletariat and the English proletariat (Marx and Engels 1971: 293). His hope was that some kind of resolution of the national question in Ireland, together with revolutionary success in Ireland – identified as the fall of landlordism – would lead to something similar in England. This notion of Ireland exporting revolution to England might seem curious (in the same piece, Marx writes that of all countries in Europe 'England alone can serve as the lever for a serious economic revolution'); it is worth bearing in mind that he makes this claim for Ireland partly by way of answering Bakunin's critique. But this was no mere defensiveness on Marx's part. His response to Bakunin was forceful and persuasive (as judged by votes in the General Council of the International and within the Geneva branch). Indeed, in this interchange it is Bakunin who sticks to what some might see as a 'rigid Marxian position' that keeps nationalist struggles strictly at arm's length, and Marx who shows himself to be the more flexible thinker.

James Connolly would later say something similar about the social and national questions: with the national question resolved, Irish working-class voters in English cities would end their counter-intuitive connection with the Liberal Party and start to vote for the Labour Party, the party they should naturally support (Connolly 1991 [1914]: 726). Connolly also, of course, saw resolution of Ireland's national question as a precursor to any transformation of Irish society (Connolly 1991 [1897]: 718–9).

So, we can be clear on the later Marx's hopes for the Irish question's impact on English labour. But how did he and Engels see the development of an independent (or semi-independent) Ireland? They do not offer a great deal of analysis on that score, though they did support Home Rule as the optimum medium-term solution for Ireland. Firstly, however, in that same December 1869 letter, Marx says that, quite aside from any benefit that might accrue to English labour, resolution of the Irish question was a matter of '"international" and "human" justice for Ireland' (Marx and Engels 1971: 284). In other words, it is far from the case that he concerned himself with Ireland solely owing to the role he foresaw it playing in the more significant English context.

CONCLUSION

We see a readiness in the writings of Marx and Engels to change their perspectives in the light of new evidence on the socio-economic transformation in Ireland and the Irish political situation – for example, on the development of capitalist relations in agriculture, or about the nature of the Land League, or on the revolutionary potential of the Fenians. What remains constant, however, is their solid grasp of the material underpinnings of the colonial relationship, as shown for example, in chapter twenty-five of *Capital* Volume One: they saw agrarian change and political movements in Ireland as being inextricably tied in with the shifts in industrial capitalism in Britain. This is a key issue about the Irish–English relationship which they grasped while it was still in motion, and which gets passed over all too often in more recent historical treatments.

Bibliography

Ahmad, Aijaz, 1992. *In Theory: Classes, Nations, Literatures.* London: Verso.

Connolly, James, 1991. 'Socialism and nationalism' [1897], in Seamus Deane (ed.), *The Field Day Anthology of Irish Writing*, III. Derry: Field Day Publications, 718–19.

Connolly, James, 1991. 'Socialism and nationalism' [1914], in Seamus Deane (ed.), *The Field Day Anthology of Irish Writing*, III. Derry: Field Day Publications, 725–29.

Davitt, Michael, 1991. *Some Suggestions for a Final Settlement of the Land Question* [1902], in Seamus Deane (ed.), *The Field Day Anthology of Irish Writing*, II. Derry: Field Day Publications, 280.

Habib, Irfan, 1995. *Essays in Indian History: Towards a Marxist Perspective.* New Delhi: Tulika Press.

Hazelkorn, Ellen, 1981. 'Some problems with Marx's theory of capitalist penetration into agriculture: the case of Ireland', *Economy and Society*, 10, 284–315.

Kautsky, Karl, 1988 [1899]. *The Agrarian Question.* London: Zwan Books.

Lenin, V. I., 1996 [1917]. *Imperialism: the Highest Stage of Capitalism*, Norman Lewis and James Malone (eds). London: Pluto Press.

Mandel, Ernest, 1978. *Late Capitalism.* London: Verso.

Marx, Karl and Frederick Engels, 1971. *Ireland and the Irish Question*, R. Dixon (ed.), Moscow: Progress Publishers.

Marx, Karl and Frederick Engels, 2001. *On the National and Colonial Questions: Selected Writings*, Aijaz Ahmad (ed.), New Delhi: Left Word Books.

Slater, Eamonn and Terrence McDonough, 1994. 'Bulwark of landlordism and capitalism: the dynamics of feudalism in nineteenth century Ireland', *Research in Political Economy*, 14, 63–119.

Vujacic, Ivan, 1988. 'Marx and Engels on development and underdevelopment: the restoration of a certain coherence', *History of Political Economy* 20: 3, 471–98.

CHAPTER 7

Destinies Intertwined

The Metaphysical Unionism of James Anthony Froude

Ciaran Brady

In the early 1870s the distinguished historian and man of letters James Anthony Froude embarked upon a mission to bring the Irish question to the centre of British political and moral argument which over the following two decades was to establish his reputation in England as a formidable, if controversial, authority on Ireland, and render him notorious in Ireland as a malignant and slanderous provocateur.[1] In the remaining years of the century English intellectuals, scholars and journalists were, with few exceptions, to show themselves to be, like Froude, unconditionally hostile to Irish nationalism.[2] But Froude's attack upon even the mildest aspirations to Home Rule for Ireland was in several ways distinctive. It was among the earliest, launched even before Isaac Butt's modest movement was properly under way. It was likewise among the most uncompromising and vituperative, founded on assumptions uncritically asserted and couched in a rhetoric of breathtaking condescension that seemed calculated to provoke outrage and offence. Yet it was also among the least consistent and most contradictory of unionist polemics, combining a dogmatic assertion of the Irish people's incapacity for self-government with a damning indictment of the persistent failure of England itself to provide the Irish with a worthy and just alternative. And finally, Froude's offence to both Irish nationalist and Anglo-Irish unionist opinion was compounded by the fact that, of all English-born commentators, he alone could claim to have long had a deep personal experience of Ireland, having repeatedly spent long periods in the country living among its people from the early 1840s to the early 1870s. The distinctive features of Froude's unionism are sufficient, perhaps, to warrant separate enquiry. But it will also be suggested below that they are symptoms of an ambition and an anxiety of far greater significance than a desire to hold Ireland for England's strategic and economic interests.

I

Though it was soon to acquire its fiercely polemical character, Froude's crusade against Irish independence began gently enough with a pair of ostensibly light but politically pointed travel essays entitled 'A fortnight in Kerry' which appeared in *Fraser's Magazine* (the journal of which he was himself editor) in April 1870 and January 1871.[3] Adopting, disingenuously, the guise of an innocent but well-meaning visitor to Ireland, Froude announced breezily that the character of the Irish had changed in the years since the famine. Those who had survived the great trauma and those who had succeeded them were determined that the wretchedness into which their forefathers had sunk would never again be repeated. From henceforth their approach towards making and increasing their livings would be frugal, responsible and shrewd. This, then, said the much-encouraged visitor, was the time for England to respond to the needs of the new generation. The moderate tenurial reforms introduced by Gladstone in the recent Land Act (1870) were to be welcomed, and in time developed. There should be more state investment in education of a practical or vocational kind; more younger sons of the peasantry should be given places in the public service; and those who could not make an honest living from their meagre tenancies or other employments should be granted state subsidies to emigrate to the growing British colonies in Canada, Australia and New Zealand where they could start anew. But amidst all this England must be careful not to listen to the demands once again being raised by some self-appointed leaders in Ireland that the Union should be dissolved and Ireland should have self-rule.

This negative political stance, adopted only fleetingly in the articles on Kerry, was made explicit in two further articles which were published shortly after in *Fraser's Magazine* of which one had been commissioned by Froude from 'An Irish Liberal', and the other was most probably authored by Froude himself.[4] In these frankly political pieces the case against a re-emerging campaign for Home Rule, now being championed by Isaac Butt, was frankly stated. Repeal of the Union at this juncture, it was claimed, was an historical anachronism. For all its horrors, the calamity of the Great Famine had removed most of the principal causes of the poverty, misery and vulnerability of Irish rural society in the early nineteenth century. Unfortunate but feckless elements within the peasantry had starved or been forced to flee; tyrannous, irresponsible and absentee landlords had paid the price for their neglect; middlemen, the great exploiters of both groups' weaknesses, had been ruined. And Britain itself, whose indifference and neglect had been every bit as responsible for the catastrophe, was at last finally beginning to acknowledge its fault. Yet it was precisely because Britain's responsibility had only tentatively been admitted that it was essential now that she should be required to make good the damage done, not by allowing injured Ireland to go its own way where all its wounds would continue to fester, but by granting her a full and equal place within the expanding British Empire.

Despite the uncompromising nature of their case, the tone in these articles remained moderate and apologetic. Yet within a year Froude's rhetoric had become suddenly and sharply offensive. Between October and December 1872, in a series of lectures on the course of Irish history from the twelfth-century Norman Conquest to the present, which he delivered on a tour of New York, Boston and Philadelphia, Froude unfolded an interpretation that seemed purposely designed to antagonise and infuriate all interested parties, English and Irish, Catholic and Protestant alike.[5] Conceived ostensibly as a response to popular nationalist histories recently published in the United States by John Mitchel and Jeremiah O'Donovan Rossa, Froude's lectures propounded a resolutely unionist case. Throughout their history, he asserted, the native Irish had repeatedly proven themselves quite incapable of self-government. It was the barbaric state of the whole island in the twelfth century, its political and moral decline from the golden age of saints and scholars to the degeneracy of the warring petty-kingdoms and the virtual disappearance of the Christian Church that had induced Pope Adrian IV to undertake the conquest of Ireland for the salvation of its own people. Left to their own devices once more, however, through the neglect of the English kings in the later middle ages, the Irish and the descendants of their one-time conquerors once again descended into an anarchy which was to be suppressed only by the force of the Tudor conquest. Yet this opportunity was soon squandered by further neglect and corruption, which was to suffer its nemesis in the bloody rebellion of 1641. Only with the coming of Cromwell, the smashing up of the old elites, and the initiation of a radical political, religious and tenurial restructuring of the whole island did the promise of making Ireland at last capable of peaceful government seem possible. This brief experiment, however, was also quickly abandoned. By the end of the century the Irish were therefore again in rebellion against England and bloody repression was again required. But the pattern of English rule repeated itself in the following century until at its close the bloodiest repression of all was required.

Even in the present century the Irish capacity for rebellion had been shown at least twice in 1848 and 1867. But the short-lived and feeble character of both of these efforts gave grounds, Froude affected to believe, for hope. The changes that had been brought about in the aftermath of the calamity of the famine were, Froude argued, the primary causes for this change in temperature. The large-scale emigration of the underemployed peasantry, the ruin of idle and absentee landlords, the gradual development of a more economically sound approach to estate management, and the emergence on the part of the British government of a more responsible policy towards land-tenure as evidenced in Gladstone's Land Act ('the most healing measure that has been devised for Ireland during two centuries at least') had all contributed to a fundamental change in Irish society and Irish attitudes towards England. Ireland, Froude concluded, had been given 'a fair start now'.

> She has better laws than England has. Let her point to any other measure of practical advantage to her and no matter what interests are affected, she will not ask for it in vain.[6]

But there was one exception: Ireland must never be conceded Home Rule. It had always been impossible, and now, when so much was promised under a newly reconstructed Union, it was totally insupportable. For left to itself Ireland would return rapidly to the cycles of corruption, poverty, division and violence which had characterised all her previous history.

Though Froude's lectures were generally well received by the conservative press in Britain and by Republican Party organs in America, they could hardly have been more offensive to nationalist opinion on both sides of the Atlantic.[7] Infuriated by his bias, his arrogance and his dogmatism, nationalist spokesmen responded immediately. In America Froude was directly challenged by the formidable public speaker Fr. Thomas N. Burke, who embarked on his own lecture tour – 'The sophistries of Froude refuted' – which purported to provide a point-by-point rebuttal of Froude's arguments.[8] John Mitchel contributed his own well-publicised rebuttal, and large sections of the American popular press expressed such dissatisfaction that the tour's financial promoters felt obliged to cut it short.[9] In Ireland nationalist responses to the lectures and to the first volume of *The English in Ireland* were equally heated. The historian J. P. Prendergast who had been Froude's guide to the Irish Record Office composed a lengthy and highly vituperative response which appeared for days in the *Freeman's Journal*, while *The Nation* and the *Cork Examiner* were strongly critical.[10]

The vigour and passion of the nationalist response to Froude served, however, to obscure a second and quite contrary theme, the importance of which in Froude's thought was to be more fully appreciated only as the interpretation underpinning his extensive three-decker monograph on *The English in Ireland in the Eighteenth Century* began to be more fully digested. Published in instalments, with volume one appearing at the end of 1872 and volumes two and three following in April 1874, the impact of the complex polemic embedded within the book was somewhat delayed. The first volume opened with a rehearsal of the argument concerning the fundamental themes of Irish history which would have been familiar to readers of his American lectures but stated now in an even more terse and uncompromising manner.[11] In encapsulating his thesis that history had shown Ireland and the Irish to be altogether unsuited for self-government, Froude began with geographical determinism. When two countries are so close to each other it is inevitable that the stronger one will determine the character of the weaker. Next, moral determinism was pressed into service: as with individuals so with communities, the state of liberty is not simply a given condition, to be passively accepted, it was a fragile possession maintained only when people were prepared to fight for or defend it. The strength of each country was thus determined by its ability to assert and defend its liberty against all comers. And it was on this basis that Froude finally invoked history: this hard-fought-for liberty was one which England had manifestly achieved, and one from which, with equal historical certainty, Ireland had been pre-cluded. Incapable either of maintaining their autonomy or yet, like the Welsh and Scottish, of accepting a peaceful union and integration with their English neighbour, the Irish had remained in a chronically inchoate state and had never matured as a freeborn people:

> Unstable as water the Irish temperament wanted cohesiveness to bear the shapes which were imprinted upon it . . . Passionate in everything – passionate in their patriotism, passionate in their religion, passionately courageous, passionately loyal and affectionate [the Irish] are without the manliness which will give strength and solidity to the sentimental part of their disposition . . . The incompleteness of character is conspicuous in all that they do and have done; in their history, in their practical habits, in their arts and in their literature.[12]

This being so clearly the case, the right of England to claim responsibility for the Irish, to govern them with firmness and justice, was incontestable; and the feeble resistance of the Irish, so painfully illustrated throughout their history, just another telling sign of their continuing cultural immaturity. The absorption of Ireland within the United Kingdom of England, Scotland and Wales was, therefore, neither a great political injustice nor an unfortunate accident; it was the necessary outcome of an inevitable historical process.[13]

With all of this nationalists were, of course, exasperated; and unionists contented. But in what followed a gradual reversal of responses was put in train. For now, having laid down all of the *a priori* reasons demonstrating the superiority of the English over the native Irish and justifying on historical grounds their right to govern Ireland, Froude set about devoting the remainder of his text to the development of the proposition that the English themselves were, through their neglect, corruption and injustice, culpably responsible for all of Ireland's grievances. Slowly emerging in the later pages of his first volume but gathering pace as the other two appeared, Froude's indictment of the English rather than his excoriation of the native Irish was at last seen to be the central theme of his major historical study.

Alternating between total neglect, susceptibility to vested interest and simple greed, the English administration in Whitehall, Froude argued, had inflicted innumerable injustices on Ireland since the beginnings of its involvement there. Its authority once established, the English parliament had proved itself even more selfish and greedy. In Dublin the executives of the Crown had, with few honourable exceptions, shown themselves either stupid, corrupt or vainglorious in their management of the charges. And most of all, the English settlers themselves, from the Normans down to the representatives of the so-called Protestant nation had shown an irresponsibility, a viciousness and a reckless divisiveness that repeatedly stifled any chance of bringing about just government in Ireland.[14] And so Froude's unrelenting censure of the English in eighteenth-century Ireland reached its climax in the opening pages of his narrative of the bloody rebellion in which the century closed:

> The long era of misgovernment had ripened at last for the harvest. Rarely since the inhabitants of the earth have formed themselves into civilized communities had any country suffered from such a complication of neglect and ill-usage. The Irish people clamoured against Government, and their real wrong from first to last had been that there was no government; that under changing forms the universal rule . . . had been the tyranny of the strong over the weak . . . justice had been blotted out . . . They had appealed to England and England had for bread given them a stone, for a fish, a serpent.[15]

'For a hundred years', Froude concluded, 'the English and Irish Protestants had been affecting to govern Ireland. They had not governed Ireland. They had left it to ignorance and misery'.[16] On these grounds it is hardly surprising that Froude should have come round to a denial of his supposed premises with the admission that it would have been far better if England had never arrogated to itself the right of ruling Ireland. 'It would have been better and happier by far had England never encompassed the rule of the Irish and never attempted to force upon them a landed gentry of alien blood.'[17]

II

What kind of thinking could have underpinned this deliberately perverse narrative? For Froude's Anglo-Irish critics, now infuriated as much as the nationalists had been by his unrelieved sententiousness, Froude's was an exercise in vanity and folly, a reckless exposure of his own intellectual confusion. The great Anglo-Irish historian W. E. H. Lecky, who would soon be sufficiently provoked to mount a full-scale rebuttal of *The English in Ireland*, by devoting almost half of his *History of England in the Eighteenth Century* (eight volumes, 1878–90) to his own account of Ireland in the period covered by Froude, began the counterattack with two lengthy reviews of Froude's book which aimed not only to expose Froude's factual and inter- pretative errors, but also his pathological obsession with 'moral paradox', which Lecky concluded had driven Froude to the edge of unreason.[18] In a cooler but no less hostile review, the Anglo-Irish political economist, John Elliot Cairnes, conducted a systematic demonstration of what he claimed were Froude's many contradictions and incoherencies in regard, for example, to the penal laws whose inadequate enforcement Froude castigated at the outset of his book but whose continuing application he saw as a principal source of discontent in the island later on; or to the Celtic race whose anarchic traits Froude regarded as incorrigible but who, Froude conceded, could 'rise to his natural level whenever he was removed from his own unfortunate country'.[19]

Exposures of the surface inconsistencies of his text by Froude's Anglo- Irish critics helped, no doubt, to assuage the resentment of offended readers. But they obscured other, deeper features of *The English in Ireland* concerning its structure, its distribution of emphasis, its language, and its very subject matter which suggest that Froude had more complex motives in composing his work than an irrational desire to offend. Among these the most curious is his very choice of subject matter.

Though Froude had repeatedly claimed both in his public utterances and in his private correspondence that the single most important event in modern Irish history was the rebellion of 1641, it is odd that he should have decided to devote such relatively little attention to it in his own historical work. We know, for instance, that he visited the library of Trinity College, Dublin, and inspected there the large body of depositions pertaining to this supposedly epoch-making event. But for all his insistence upon their impor- tance, he himself declined to investigate the atrocities of 1641, arranging instead that the work be delegated to an unknown scholar, the talented but impecunious Mary Hickson whom he persuaded his friend Lord Carnarvon to fund.[20] No less intriguing than this shying away from the obvious is the fact that in the preliminary section of *The English in Ireland* he devoted less than twenty of 240 pages to the outbreak of the rebellion itself, making no reference there to the great scholarly project he had initiated at Trinity. Likewise, though Froude proudly asserted that the Cromwellian period represented the noblest epoch of English rule in Ireland, he gave little more than twenty pages to the 1650s, basing his account largely on Carlyle's *Cromwell*, and on the far from congenial authority of J. P. Prendergast.[21] A similarly surprising distribution of emphasis is evident in Froude's treatment of the eighteenth century itself, for though his narrative seems to build towards the grand climacteric of the rebellion of 1798 which is foreshadowed at several times in the text, it is curious how relatively little space is actually provided for it in the end: a mere 100 pages in a history of some 1,600.

If Froude had been primarily concerned to demonstrate the instability, treachery and violence of the Irish and the need to reassert firm English rule over them, it is surely towards these rebellions that he might have been expected to drift, in a narrative reaching from 1641 to 1798. That he elected to diminish their importance both in his research and writing, and to allot priority instead to the ceaseless bickerings of the Irish parliament, the restless changes of policy and personnel of the Dublin administration, and the recurrent surfacing of terror, crime and vice in the country at large in the century between 1690 and 1790 (over half of which he claimed had no real history) is an indication that something more deliberate lay at the root of Froude's ambiguous polemic.

Froude's tone supplied a further unsettling element in his supposedly misguided tirade. The authorial voice he adopted in *The English* was extraordinary: so dogmatic and rebarbative in its moral judgements, whether it was denouncing the viciousness of the Celt or the corruption of the Saxon, that it was bound to alienate any readers who were not already sympathetic to his case. It not only differed significantly from that which he had adopted in his American lectures and in the essays on contemporary Ireland, it is also quite unlike the one he had assumed in his earlier *History of England from the Death of Wolsey to the Defeat of the Armada* (1856–70). There, while Froude's polemical purposes were equally explicit – he was determined to defend the Protestant Reformation against all modern ecumenical tendencies – no *a priori* principles were stated in advance and the argument was developed in open debate with previous opinion.[22]

The tone with which Ireland was treated in the earlier history is, moreover, significantly different. There the great opponents of Tudor rule in Ireland – Kildare, Desmond and Shane O'Neill – are depicted not as representatives of a dark primeval world, but as agents of a more immediate and pressing danger: the Counter Reformation and the possibility of imminent invasion. The threat posed to English rule by Catholic reaction is one of the central themes in the Irish sections of Froude's sixteenth-century history. But increasingly as the narrative proceeds, a second acquires greater prominence. This is the record of English atrocity. Beginning with the massacres of Sir Peter Carew in the 1560s, sequentially recounting those of Humphrey Gilbert, the earl of Essex, and ending in the horrors of the Desmond rebellion, Froude records the slaughter of non-combatants, and especially of women and children, with undisguised disgust. Lest the point be lost, moreover, Froude expanded upon the Elizabethans' misconduct in

Ireland in a separate article published under the deeply ironical title 'The government of Ireland in the sixteenth century', which ended with a disturbing judgement already stated in the *History* and soon to be echoed in the *English*: 'It cannot be said that England deserved to keep a country which it mismanaged so disastrously'.[23]

The contrasting tones but similar conclusions in regard to England's role in Ireland reached in Froude's two histories and his article suggest that they were in some fashion crucially interlinked in Froude's mind. And the fact that in 1870 Froude abandoned his English *History*, ending its narrative abruptly in the year 1588 rather than with the death of Elizabeth in 1603 as had been originally planned, in order to commence work on his Irish study lends additional strength to the notion that in doing so Froude was engaged upon a further stage in his general campaign to underline the urgency of history's moral and spiritual lessons to his readers.[24]

Yet why Ireland in 1870 should have presented itself to him as the focus for this redirected mission is not easy to determine. For many of the most obvious candidates for such a development seem hardly of themselves to have been sufficient to bear the portentous burden being placed on them. Of itself the re-emergence of Home Rule was hardly a sign of imminent crisis. The aims of the Home Government Association formed by Isaac Butt in 1870 were remarkably modest and the movement in any case had hardly taken shape at the time Froude first began his researches in the Irish State Paper Office and was still in its infancy at the time of the appearance of the first volume of the *English in Ireland*.[25] When Home Rule eventually began to establish itself as a significant movement, a formidably solid coalition among English intellectuals including Mill, Freeman, Morley and Goldwin Smith against repeal of the Union did indeed materialise. But Froude was unique in reacting so early to the re-emergence of anti-unionist sentiment in Ireland; and his early reaction suggests that it was a symptom of a process already under way in Froude's mind rather than a motivating factor.

Other specifically Irish factors which might be adduced as possible provocations of Froude's early anxieties are equally inconclusive. Froude did not, for example, share in the disquiet provoked among some Tories both in Ireland and Britain by Gladstone's mildly reformist Landlord and Tenant Act of 1870. Instead, as we have seen, he positively approved of the reforms and hoped for more to come.[26] Similarly, though fear of Fenian terror had been a nagging anxiety throughout the late 1860s and early 1870s in England, Froude was unimpressed. 'A few attacks on handfuls of police or the blowing in of the walls of an English prison with the wanton destruction of innocent life may suffice', he wrote contemptuously, 'for a scene or two in a melodrama, but they will not overturn an Empire . . . Fanians, *Faineants*, Do-Nothings!'[27] An evil portent for the future, perhaps; but in the short term Fenianism hardly seemed sufficient justification for the launch of his urgent polemic. Finally, among the remaining issues of distinctly Irish relevance, only the disestablishment of the Church of Ireland enacted in 1869 and put into effect in 1871 is of any significance. But here Froude's attitude was also clear. He strongly approved: just as he hoped and argued for disestablishment in England; and his sustained condemnation of the weakness and corruption of the eighteenth-century Irish episcopacy in *The English in Ireland* was designed to offer little succour for their successors.[28]

So the difficulty persists. Developments in Ireland itself in the late 1860s and 1870s supplied of themselves insufficient reason to even the most alarmist of souls to conclude that England was on the point of losing Ireland. Yet when the frame of analysis is moved beyond Ireland, other influences more pertinent to Froude's particular preoccupations come into view. Shortly before he had begun his research in the Irish archives and published his first sympathetic essays on Ireland, Froude had been intensely engaged with a rather different problem then confronting the English government: that of managing England's overseas colonies. In his private correspondence in the mid 1860s and increasingly in the columns of *Fraser's* Froude was professing his deepening dissatisfaction with the colonial policies of successive governments.[29] His objections were several. But two salient points always featured. First, he resented the careless laissez-faire attitude adopted by the government towards movements of independence which were arising in Canada, Australia and South Africa. The colonies, Froude insisted, were not to be permitted to go their own way, and all necessary inducements to bind them close to the mother country were to be applied. Secondly, he objected to the equally careless way in which government had tolerated the free flow of emigration from England, Scotland and above all from post-famine Ireland to territories other than the British colonies, and in particular to the United States. He pleaded for an active emigration policy to subsidise, organise, direct and reward settlement in the British colonies themselves.

It would be easy at this distance to credit Froude with an early version of the new imperialism of the later 1880s and 1890s. But, though he sometimes sought to justify his case on commercial, industrial and demographic grounds, Froude's concerns were not, at bottom, economic. They were, rather, historical and above all moral. Thus, while he sometimes engaged in disputation in political economy, challenging the prevailing Liberal view that it was impossible to encourage investment against the flow of existing market forces, he preferred to argue that the development of the colonies was a priority in itself, a higher good than mere profit making. Froude was no simple jingoist, however, insisting that trade should follow the flag. His attitude towards Britain's territorial expansion was, in fact, especially modest. Thus in the 1850s and the 1870s he strongly criticised British imperialist *démarches* in the

Balkans and Asia (he was part of the lonely band that vigorously opposed the Crimean War); and he took the then enlightened view that the Boers should be given equal constitutional status in the Cape colony.[30] At the time he raised these anxieties in the late 1860s and early 1870s, Froude, however, was, as he had been in the 1850s, something of a lone voice. The Great Depression was almost a decade away. And these were years of unprecedented prosperity, remarkable market stability and substantial improvement in living conditions. Though criticism of successive governments' colonial policy was more common than has sometimes been assumed, confidence in the wisdom and effectiveness of laissez-faire remained strong.[31]

What separated Froude from conventional opinion on British policy in the 1850s and 1860s, was the fact that he, unlike so many of his contemporaries, remained committed to the powerful convictions he had held in the crisis years of the 1840s. This was the belief, which in his own distinctive way he shared with both Newman and Carlyle, that England was on the edge of an immense and catastrophic historical epoch: a spiritual and moral crisis signalled and epitomised by the degeneration and ossification of English Protestantism in general and of the Church of England in particular.[32]

Froude's preoccupation with the problem of Protestantism's decline was rather more subtle than the crudely anti-Papist and boldly Evangelical impulse that has sometimes been depicted.[33] Far from supporting the great Evangelical revival, he despised it, regarding it as a mere conjuring trick blinding the people to the historical and metaphysical reality of Protestantism's exhaustion. In his private correspondence and more circumspectly in a series of essays on Calvinism, Catholicism, biblical criticism and speculative theology published in the 1850s and 1860s he was prepared to grant that the religion of the sixteenth century had run its course, that it was now as out of tune with the state of our knowledge of the world as the scholasticisms and superstitions of Catholicism had been in 1517.[34] The point now was not how it might be salvaged but how its people might be prepared for the next great spiritual and moral challenge that was soon to face them. And from his earliest days as a writer, Froude's fiction, his extended philosophical essays and his Tudor *History* had all been conceived as contributions to this missionary cause.

It is in this light that Froude's apparent anti-Catholicism is best understood. It was not, as has frequently been assumed, the reaction of one who had once been tempted and had fallen. Froude, in fact, had never contemplated going over to Rome with Newman.[35] Rather, the breach within the Church of England opened by Newman's defection had convinced him of the imminence of Protestantism's fall – the consequences of which formed the central theme of his novel *The Nemesis of Faith*. But Protestantism's decline had never persuaded him of the likelihood of

Catholicism's revival; because, for Froude, Carlyle, Fichte and the German historicists, its fate too had been determined by the processes of unfolding Creation as revealed in human history.[36] Even in the mid-1860s, amidst some signs of a Catholic revival in England under the energetic leadership of the recently established Catholic archbishop of Westminster, Edward Manning, Froude remained unperturbed. In a thoughtful essay on Newman's *Grammar of Assent* published in 1870, which incidentally differs markedly both in its intellectual sophistication and in the moderation of its tone from the voice adopted in the near-contemporary *English in Ireland*, he could confidently conclude that Newman's enticing sophistries amounted to no more than a galvanic stimulation of a long dead corpse.[37] With Catholicism dead or moribund as a spiritual force there remained only a few places in the world where it still demonstrated a vitality of sorts. But these, he came increasingly to believe, were crucial.

The first was Ireland. That Catholicism had survived long after its historical deadline there was due not to its intrinsic strength, but entirely to the sins of commission and omission perpetrated by the English whose historic destiny it had been to see it off. It is within this world-historical perspective that a key to the seeming contradictions of Froude's attitude towards Ireland which exasperated so many of his critics is ultimately to be found. As a visitor to Ireland on the eve of the famine, Froude's deeply Romantic sensibility had been struck by the parallel worlds which appeared to exist side by side in Ireland. All around him he witnessed poverty and misery, indifference and corruption: defining characteristics of contemporary Ireland and dire warnings of the catastrophe to come. But at the same time, as he travelled along the western seaboard, he encountered in the surviving antiquities of the Celtic past the remnants of a once great and profoundly spiritual civilisation that had once been pervasive throughout Ireland.[38] Their very endurance, and their continuing power to evoke an occasional spiritual awakening among the now degenerate Irish – as evidenced in the survival of pattern days, pilgrimages and practices of annual retreat – was an indication at once of how much potential remained latent in Ireland and of how much had been lost: lost in the centuries of English misrule.[39] It was in this insight that the seeming paradox that underlay Froude's fierce assertion of England's metahistorical obligations to Ireland and his equally outraged condemnation of England's historical failures was rooted. Having been charged by destiny, or more precisely by the unfolding spirit of Creation, with responsibility for the cure of Ireland, England had failed disastrously, at every turn, from the time of the Conquest down to the famine.

The historical and moral burden imposed on England by its failures in Ireland was always, for Froude, a heavy one.[40] But what gave it renewed urgency, driving his moral polemic to the edges of contradiction, was a second and wholly unexpected occurrence of the revival of Catholicism in one of its least likely breeding grounds: the United States of America. In the years in which he undertook the writing of the *English In Ireland*, the remarkable advance of Catholicism, and of Irish Catholicism in particular, in the United States could be registered in a number of alarming milestones: in the extraordinary support given to the Fenians throughout the north-eastern states, in the establishment of the Irish Catholic Benevolent Union in Ohio and of Clann na Gael as an openly revolutionary organisation in New York, in the establishment of a potent propagandist weapon, *The Irish World*. Even more alarming were the revelations of the power and corruption of Irish machine politics in the big urban centres of the north-east made through the investigation of the Tweed circle of Tammany Hall.[41]

Though not in themselves remarkably threatening, these developments were symptoms of more profound forces now converging in the United States. The first and most recent of these was the triumph of the North in the Civil War, a result which signalled the victory for populist democracy, party politics, special interest groups, patronage, kick-backs and ballyhoo: in fact all of the mechanisms which had allowed the politics of Irish American Catholicism to survive and flourish. The second was the even more devastating impact of the Irish famine. Though it had not been deliberately caused by England, it was English greed and neglect which had been largely responsible for its scale, and through her continuing inaction England was now sowing dragon's teeth in the form of the massive numbers of profoundly hostile Irish who were now establishing themselves in America determined to take revenge on England.[42]

Froude had no fears of a Fenian invasion. Rather what made the threat from Irish-America profoundly alarming were the broader global implications of America's transformation. Its own internal contradictions having been resolved in civil war, the United States was now embarking on a course of development that had already enabled it to rival and would soon enable it to overtake Great Britain as the pre-eminent world power. Though relations between the two countries remained amicable, the rivalry and the coming challenge, Froude knew, was inevitable.[43] And in this confrontation the match between the rivals was profoundly uneven. While Britain with her laissez-faire economy was disastrously alienating countless numbers of her English, Scottish and above all Irish subjects, and was likewise with her laissez-faire politics happily considering the abandonment of all her colonies and the fatal release of Ireland under Home Rule, America was expanding both politically and economically, welcoming all the discontented of the world to aid her in the construction of an industrial and commercial empire which would soon surpass any in history.

It was in such circumstances that in Froude's eyes Ireland acquired renewed world-historical significance. Having for centuries served as an aching reminder of England's failure to discharge the primary historical obligation placed upon it by the unfolding process of Creation, Ireland, by means of the extraordinary influence now exercised by its angry emigrant Catholics, was threatening to overturn the very purpose for which England had been chosen in the first place, that is the advance of Christianity beyond its medieval phase, and to be preparing the world for the greatest retrogression in history, the reassertion of Romanism, as a fully integrated element in the newly emerging American empire, even as the Reformation had run its course.[44]

It was this terrifying vision that inspired and shaped the character of Froude's unionist crusade. In embarking upon his American lecture tour, even as the first volume of *The English in Ireland* was in the press, Froude was taking his war to the frontiers of history, deliberately cultivating Protestant America's support in an attempt to forestall the integration of the Catholic Irish into the transformed American polity, before moving on to present the heart of his message to those who alone could take effective action in curing Ireland: the English. For with its fiercely dogmatic assertions of power, responsibility and historical necessity and its condemnation of Irish anarchy, English misrule and Anglo-Irish corruption, *The English in Ireland* was consciously addressed to the opponents of liberal laissez-faire from all sides of the political spectrum in England itself.[45]

In the early 1870s there was as yet no cause for Froude to conclude that England's destiny was already sealed. Though the clouds now gathering in the West represented a final sign that England's long moral indebtedness was at length being called to account, America's as yet unrealised potential sustained hope that it was not yet too late. In the years immediately following the appearance of *The English in Ireland* the prospects for Froude's mission appeared relatively fair. The book enjoyed something of a *success de scandale*, it prompted a heated correspondence in *The Times*, and as the campaign for Home Rule developed in the late 1870s and early 1880s it was cited as an authority by both sides in the case. As the Irish claim for Home Rule moved, under the shrewd and hard-nosed management of Charles Stewart Parnell, towards the top of Westminster's political agenda, Froude, like many other pro-unionist men of letters, adopted a public stance, giving lectures, publishing letters and articles in newspapers, and on one occasion standing on an election platform to speak in favour of a unionist candidate.[46] A second edition of *The English in Ireland* which appeared in 1884 contained an additional chapter and extra footnotes which confirmed the overtly political polemic of Froude's history.[47] But as the challenge of Home Rule rose, and its pressures on the character and structures of British parliamentary politics increased, so the arguments about the implications of allowing Ireland some form of self-determination became more complex and more diffuse, and so Froude's early and distinctive contribution, with its apparent contradictions, its susceptibility to exploitation by both sides of the argument, and the dogmatism of its rhetoric rhetorical dogmatism became submerged and marginalised within the general clamour. Thus Froude's own attitudes towards the debate on Home Rule became more ambivalent; and his relative disengagement from the struggle as it reached its crisis in the mid-1880s in contrast to his deep engagement with the issue at it very inception in the early 1870s is in part a reflection of his own apprehension that its character had changed substantially in the intervening period. But the deeper impulses underlying his original address survived the public debates of the 1880s and surfaced once again at the end of the decade in far darker but quite explicit terms when Froude eventually succeeded in bringing to fruition the Irish fiction which he had for long envisaged as an accompaniment to his Irish history and which he entitled *The Two Chiefs of Dunboy or an Irish Romance of the Last Century*.

III

Though *The Two Chiefs* appeared only at the end of the 1880s, Froude had first conceived the idea of writing a fiction to accompany his formal history while *The English in Ireland* was still being written, and he published a shorter version of the main plot as early as 1872.[48] In the interim, however, major distractions, including his involvement in government policy in the Cape Colony and the immense labours involved in the composition of his *Life of Carlyle*, had intervened. In the meantime also the understanding of the Irish question had undergone decisive changes in English public opinion; and the fears first harboured by Froude in the early 1870s about a gradual acceptance among the English political elite of Ireland's eventual release from the Union grew stronger. It is not surprising, therefore, that both in its mood and in its address the novel is in several ways markedly different from the history. It was likewise natural that, amidst increasing pessimism about the future of the Union, the powerful motivating forces left largely hidden under Froude's fiery historical polemic should become urgent and more explicit But on the surface at least it is the correspondences between Froude's history and his novel that are most obvious.

The Two Chiefs is set in the mid-eighteenth century – the centre of gravity of *The English in Ireland*. Many of its main characters are representations of actual historical figures who are introduced in the history and bear the same name; several others, such as Lord B– or Dr S–, are indicated in such a way as to be easily identified by readers of the earlier book. Several of the principal events in the novel are based upon verifiable historical evidence first supplied in the history, while one of the central themes in Froude's history – the pervasive and nefarious practice of duelling in Ireland – is converted into the central trope of the novel. Froude was cavalier in his treatment of the historical record as it suited him; and departures from truth were mercilessly exposed by the novel's first reviewers.[49] But such criticisms were largely beside the point. For Froude was not seeking merely to rewrite his history. Rather than straining after a false verisimilitude, Froude was instead seeking to exploit the generic possibilities of the historical romance in a manner which enabled him at once to address his readers in a more intimate register than that he had employed in *The English*, to make more explicit his deepest feelings about the historical role of Ireland in relation to England which had either been ignored or misapprehended by readers and critics of the history, and most importantly of all to elicit a more sensitive and self-reflective response from his audience. It cannot be said that he succeeded in this last ambition to any great extent and the most perceptive of his critics pointed to his failure fully to escape from the framework of the earlier polemic.[50]

The plot of *The Two Chiefs* is as thin as the conventions of the genre allowed. Two men – one a brave, honourable and determined Englishman, Colonel John Goring, the other a brave, honourable but impulsive Irishman, Morty Sullivan – are pitted against each other through the intertwining of their lives in a variety of circumstances. They had fought each other at Culloden; the Irishman had been captured by the Englishman but had subsequently escaped. The Englishman now occupied the patrimony of the exiled Jacobite. He was introducing English Protestant colonies there, suppressing the smuggling trade by which the natives had earned their crust, and to rub salt in the wound he had evicted the Irishman's sister from her tenancy for aiding the smugglers. A duel was therefore inevitable, but it proves frustratingly difficult for Morty to organise. On his first return to Dunboy his challenge to the interloper goes sour as his own weapon misfired and Goring, refusing to engage, fires over Morty's head. The duel is then suspended. On the second, Morty, against his better judgement and his sense of honour, is goaded into having Goring brought to face him by a ruse. But again the brave colonel refuses to honour the Irish outlaw by conniving in an act of lawlessness. He struggles to break free from the trap, wounds the Irishmen who are attending upon Morty and is immediately shot dead by Morty. Morty is distraught by the outcome. This was not the honourable challenge he had sought, but a sordid intrigue in which his antagonist had been unfairly trapped and brutally done away with. Disgusted with himself for his part in the shameful conspiracy, and even more contemptuous for those companions who had persuaded him to take part, he leaves, swearing never to return. But a short time later, and again under pressure from his followers, he returns to take his sister and her son, the heir to the O'Sullivan lordship, out of Ireland for good. On arrival he is betrayed by a kinsman moved to hatred by the scorn which Morty had poured on him after the killing of Goring, and is himself killed while trying to escape.

The novel's characters are hardly more compelling than its plot. They are largely representative types, uncomplicated and predictable. The English are almost invariably good: like Goring, they are noble, brave and industrious. The Irish are almost invariably defective: cowards and traitors such as Sylvester O'Sullivan, or figures filled with rancour and bitterness, such as Morty's sister, Ellen. Even Morty is fiery, erratic, too sensitive to his standing in other men's eyes.

Amidst all this there are, however, exceptions whose subtleties may easily be overlooked. Not all of the English are good. An interlude in Dublin which disrupts the main lines of plot development allows Froude the opportunity of etching an acid sketch of the Anglo-Irish establishment whose leading figures (chief among whom are Archbishop Stone, Speaker Ponsonby, Henry Flood and Lord Chancellor Bowes) are presented as the very epitomes of cynicism, corruption and irresponsibility. The degeneracy of this ruling class is symbolised by an evening which Goring spends with them at the baths run by Dr Achmet Borumborad, an enigmatic Turk who is a highly fashionable figure in Dublin society. In the middle of their drunken cavortings which involve throwing each other into the baths, Achmet is exposed as an imposter, a pretend foreigner, who proudly declares himself to be:

'No Turk at all, at all. Sure it is Pat Joyce from Kilkenny I am – no less – and as good a Christian as the Pope of Rome'[51]

The lesson is clear: amidst this fun and frivolity, the papists are all around, deceptive and disguised, but proud and confident of their future. And all the while the irresponsible leaders of the Protestant Ireland can do nothing but laugh at their own condition. Thus the heritage which Cromwell's virtuous republicans had bequeathed was being drowned (literally) in a luxury that was as corrosive as it was illusory.

The symbolism here is obvious. But other specimens of human nature in Froude's Dublin project more ambivalent images. One is a Mr Fitzherbert, a Fellow of Trinity College. Fitzherbert's ancestry is as ambiguous as his name: it suggests but does not confirm an Anglo-Norman origin, and we are given no first name to offer a further clue. Fitzherbert speaks of himself as Irish but in a disturbing way:

What we are today [he tells Goring] we have been for a thousand years neither worse nor better. If the English wanted order in Ireland, they should have left none of us alive. We were but half a million when the Tudor princes began interfering. At that time they might have made a clean sweep, and the world would have been better for the want of us. We are a beggarly race wherever we go, and what you can't mend you had better end.[52]

Here is the very model of the self-hating Irishman (and a Trinity don into the bargain). But it should not be inferred that Froude presents Fitzherbert for unqualified approval. Goring strongly dissents from such opinions, and Froude offers his own reservations: 'A critic and man of the world . . . he had not sought admittance to either of the learned professions . . . had never invited the suffrages of a constituency, and had amused himself with watching the action from outside of the most corrupt assembly in the world.'[53] Such amused detachment was an attitude which Froude abhorred among his own contemporaries since his own deeply troubled days as an Oxford don. The defeatism of Fitzherbert's view of the Irish is, moreover, directly contradicted at the outset of the novel where the wealthy, commanding figure of Patrick Blake is held up as 'an instance – one among many to be observed in that epoch – of what an Irishman could do when transplanted from the land of his birth'.[54] Fitzherbert's world-weary passivity is further contrasted with his cousin's endeavours, establishing a colony, mining for copper, reforming the agricultural practices on his estate. He himself dimly perceives the contrast during his stay at Dunboy, but to the end he cannot fully abandon his lassitude.

Fitzherbert's character is also set against that of another Englishman, the senior artillery officer General Vavasour. In addition to his military profession, the general is also an enthusiastic student of Irish antiquities, and his discovery of a set of engraved stones at an ancient site on Dursey Island provides Froude with the opportunity of revealing the strengths and limitations of the central characters. Fitzherbert is quite uninterested in the discovery, his curiosity piqued only by his amusement at the general's innocent engagement. Goring is more respectful, but sees in the site only the remains of an old cattle pen which in medieval times the Gaelic chieftains had used to protect their cattle from rustlers or to house cattle they had rustled themselves. The general is prepared to allow this as a later function in degenerate times; but continues to maintain with the support of some technical mathematical and astronomical calculations (of which Fitzherbert, significantly, is ignorant) that the site provided evidence of the residence there at some time in the past of a sophisticated, learned and spiritually minded people. The debate ends inconclusively: the general goes silent, but does not withdraw from his views: the others remain sceptical. But echoes of the young Froude's intense experience of Ireland in the 1840s are audible here; and his readers may be expected to retain respect for the general's opinion by the way in which he then sets about the practical defence of the island in the face of an imminent pirate attack.[55]

More interesting is the fact that the general's metaphysical speculations are echoed in an adjacent chapter by those of the Morty Sullivan himself. Strolling disconsolately along a nearby strand, his confidence in the possibility of raising a rebellion from the unpromising conspirators with whom he has come in contact declining rapidly, Morty muses on the ceaseless motion of historical change:

> For how many ages had the bay and the rocks and the mountains looked exactly the same as they were looking then? How many generations had played their part on the same stage, eager and impassioned as if it had been created only for them! the half naked fisherman of forgotten centuries who had earned a scanty living there; the monks from the Skelligs who had come in on highdays in their coracles to say mass for them, baptize their children or bury their dead; the Celtic chief with saffron shirt and battle axe, driven from his richer lands by Norman or Saxon invaders . . . the Scandinavian pirates . . . these had all played their brief parts there and were gone, and as many more would follow in the cycles of the years that were to come, yet the scene itself was unchanged and would not change. The same soil had fed the departed . . . The same landscape had affected their imaginations with its beauty or awed them with its splendours; and each alike had yielded to the same delusion that the valley was theirs and was inseparably connected with themselves and their fortunes.[56]

Unlike Vavasour, Morty relates his own career to this ceaseless process of change. As a child he had played on the same beach, had 'kindled with enthusiasm at the tales which were told him of his forefathers'; had fought 'in the holy cause', and now was it all for nothing?

> What was he? What was anyone? To what purpose the ineffectual strivings of short-lived humanity? Man's life was but the shadow of a dream, and his work was but the heaping of sand which the next tide would level flat again.[57]

Here is a profoundly Romantic apprehension (one which echoes the young Froude's experience on his recovery from a bout of fever during a stay in the west in 1844) which shows that, even in his reduced condition, Morty retains the vestiges of the spiritual nature of the people from whom he is descended.[58] Unlike Fitzherbert, moreover, Morty is not paralysed by this desolating revelation. Rather like Goring, he is a man of action who will go on to do his duty as he sees it in an adopted course that will end in both of their deaths.

This insight that is granted to Morty should dispel any notion that he is being portrayed by Froude as a wild and passionate primitive. Instead, from his first appearance, Morty is presented as a gentleman, a brave and noble soldier whose acute sense of honour makes the service he must do for the cause as a pirate on the high seas painfully disagreeable to him. Morty's position as a pirate in Froude's novel is curious. For this adventurer on the high seas whose daring raids on British merchantmen and naval frigates made his name a terror in the Caribbean and elsewhere could easily be seen as simply re-enacting in the eighteenth century the achievements of Drake, Hawkins and the other sea dogs of the sixteenth century which Froude had celebrated in earlier historical writings. There is no likelihood that the eulogist of 'England's forgotten worthies' was unaware of the parallel. But the point was that the English privateers of the sixteenth century had contributed to a profound historical change which had made their own activities thereafter redundant and illegitimate. They had, in other words, saved the Protestant Reformation and helped establish Britain as the leader and guardian of that world historical movement. In the wake of this epoch-making revolution Morty's attempts to mount a counter-revolution were therefore not only too late by two centuries and doomed to failure, by extension they were also, as he himself is privately aware, as unjustified as the contemporary actions of the English pirates Morgan and Kidd.[59]

This was, of course, a distinctly self-serving theory of historical justification. But Froude was now willing to apply the implications of this form of argument beyond the plight of the historically retarded Irish. He applied them also to his English hero, John Goring, who was almost equally out of date in eighteenth-century Ireland. From the first Goring is presented in historical terms. He had served at Culloden against the Jacobites; he had come to the aid of Colonel Eyre in Galway where Patrick Blake is told by one of his sea captains:

> he was like one of Cromwell's troopers, the Lord confound them! With a sword in one hand and a pistol in the other, and the Bible on the lips of him.[60]

Always a religious man:

> Under Cromwell he would have been the most devoted of the Ironsides . . . an Englishman of the old Puritan school . . .[61]

Inheriting Dunboy through the death of his brother, he regarded this run-down estate 'as a direction of Providence to him' to revive the spirit of the Protestant settlers of Cromwell's day. But his mission had not gone well for him. Even as he is being introduced readers are made aware of the troubles surrounding him. Though just 32, the same age as Morty, his hair has already begun to grey, 'as if life had brought anxieties, which were leaving their marks upon him'.[62] Though married, his wife Elizabeth is a shadowy, passive figure, troubled by their settlement there. He is under threat of death. They have no children. His situation deteriorates steadily throughout the novel. Surrounded by hostile natives and unsupported by the other local gentry, his colonists grow anxious by the day and seek permission to leave. Goring's attempts to encourage them are everywhere frustrated. He built a chapel for them and appointed a nonconformist clergyman to minister to them. But these actions and the fact that he had occasionally preached to them himself had been a scandal to the local Established clergy, and he had been rebuked. Innocently he travels to Dublin to seek a licence from the primate and is curtly refused. Meanwhile, agrarian terror accelerates the decline of the colony which is already on the point of failure before Goring is killed. On his death, we are told, his estate will descend to the sterile Fitzherbert. Like Morty, Goring is also an historical anachronism, of only a slightly later vintage; and his enterprise is as doomed to failure in the eighteenth century as his enemy's. In this sense they have equal status as chiefs of Dunboy, that is, as principal representatives of integral, distinct, and mutually incompatible cultures whose time had passed.

For all its clumsiness, Froude's romance casts important light on the fundamental concerns which had engaged him in all his previous writings on English and Irish history. Several of the themes first developed in the two histories are rehearsed again but in a subtly modulated way. The inability of the native Irish adequately to govern themselves in the island is again asserted, but qualified now by the recognition that this had not always been the case, and that in other places it was not so now. Such historically based reservations, however, served to intensify rather than alleviate England's moral responsibility. As a politically more stable and militarily more powerful culture, geographical propinquity had made the English conquest of Ireland inevitable. But this legitimate event had been rapidly succeeded by a series of historical developments of disastrous moral import. Not only had the conquest not resulted in the moral development of the weaker people through their integration with the stronger (as had supposedly been the case in England), their defects had become grossly accentuated in a process for which the conquerors themselves must assume responsibility. Set against the contrasting evidence of their advancement once they had emigrated, this was a devastating revelation of weaknesses and vices inherent in the conquerors themselves which required immediate and urgent address if the process of decay was not to work its natural effects on them also. Geographically and culturally determined, the destinies of Ireland and England had been inexorably intertwined in their histories. And in the process history had reshaped them as moral co-dependants in which the fate of the one was ineluctably bound to that of the other. As the moral vitality of English Protestantism had been sapped by its own internal exhaustion, and by the complacent culture of laissez-faire which replaced it, so the assertion of responsibility for the government of Ireland now presented a final trial for England's spiritual redemption. Once again Ireland would supply the test: the occasion either of England's atonement, or of her damnation.

Notes

1   On Froude in general see W. H. Dunn, *James Anthony Froude: A Biography, 1: 1818–56; 2: 1856–1894*, 2 vols (Oxford, 1961–3); see also the insightful sketch by A. F. Pollard in the *Dictionary of National Biography*.

2   Tom Dunne, 'La trahison des clercs: British intellectuals and the first home-rule crisis', *Irish Historical Studies*, 23: 90 (1982), 134–73.

3   *Fraser's Magazine*, 81 (Apr. 1870), 513–30; 83 (Jan. 1871), 28–45, reprinted in J. A. Froude, *Short Studies on Great Subjects* (London, 1894) vol II, 217–58; 259–307.

4   'Home government for Ireland', *Fraser's Magazine*, 84 (July 1871), 1–12; the author may possibly have been Richard Mahony, Kerry landlord and friend of Froude's, who was the author of two near-contemporary pamphlets which expressed similar arguments in similar formulations; 'Irish experiences of Home Rule', *Fraser's Magazine*, 85 (Feb 1872), 206–17.

5   Widely reported on in the American, British and Irish press, texts of Froude's lectures were printed in the *New York Times* on 29 Oct. and 2, 21, 22 Nov. 1872; in the *New York Freeman's Journal and Catholic Register*, 2, 9, 16, 23, 30 Nov. 1872; and in *The Times*, 29 Oct., and 6, 7, 8, 18, 22 Nov. 1872.

6   'Ireland since the Union', final lecture in the series reprinted in Froude, *Short Studies*, II, 514–62 – the quotation is from p. 561.

7   In addition to the *New York Times*, the *New York Herald* and the *New York Tribune* reported favourably on Froude's tour; in Britain *The Standard* gave a brief approving notice; for a useful anthology of editorial responses see, James W. O'Brien, *Froude's Crusade: Both Sides* (New York, 1873).

8   Published as T. N. Burke, *Ireland's Vindication*. Glasgow, n.d. [1873?].

9   Mitchel, 'Froude from the standpoint of a protestant Irishman', *New York Times*, 21 Dec. 1872; see also commentaries in the *New York Daily Journal*, 2, 4, 14 Nov. and the *New York World*, 14, 15, 22, 30 Nov. 1872.

10   *Freeman's Journal*, 30–31 Oct., 11, 19, 20, 21, 29, 30 Nov.; *The Nation*, 2, 16, 13 Nov.; *The Cork Examiner*, 7 Nov. 1872.

11   *The English in Ireland in the Eighteenth Century* (London: Longmans Green and Co., vol. I, Nov. 1872; vols II and III, Apr. 1874), Book One.

12   Ibid., I, 22–3.

13   Ibid., I, Book One, sections ii–iv.

14 For central passages developing this indictment see *The English in Ireland* I, 215–39, 371–95; II, 84–122, 453–75; III, 469–505.

15 *The English in Ireland*, III, 355. The allusion at the end of this quotation is to Luke 11: 11: 'if a son shall ask bread of any of you that is a father, will he give him a stone, or if he ask for a fish will he for a fish give him a serpent?' (King James version): the paternalistic assumptions underlying Froude's position are obvious.

16 *The English in Ireland*, III, 442.

17 *The English in Ireland*, III, 462.

18 *Macmillan's Magazine*, XXVII (Jan. 1873), 246–64; XXX (June 1874), 166–84.

19 *The Fortnightly Review*, XVI (Aug. 1874), 171–91; Cairnes was citing from *The English in Ireland*, II, p. 127, where Froude also conceded: 'The modern Irishman is of no race, so blended now is the blood of Celt and Dane, Saxon and Norman, Scot and Frenchman.'

20 M. A. Hickson, *Ireland in the Seventeenth Century; or the Irish Massacres of 1641–2 with a preface by J. A. Froude* (London, 1884); the book was published by Froude's publishers, Longmans; Froude offered to write the preface, but agreed to make several changes to it at Hickson's request – Hickson's 'Note' in *The English Historical Review*, 2 (1887), p. 527; on Froude's support for Hickson see Froude to Lady Carnarvon, 18 Aug. and 5 Sept. 1885, British Library, Carnarvon MSS, Add MS 60799B, ff 96–100.

21 *The English in Ireland*, I, Book one, ch. ii.

22 For discussions of this text see J. W. Burrow, *A Liberal Descent: Victorian Historians and the English Past* (Cambridge, 1981), chs 9–10; Rosemary Jann, *The Art and Science of Victorian History* (Ohio, 1985), ch. 4.

23 Ciaran Brady, 'Offering offence: James Anthony Froude, moral obligation and the uses of Irish history', in Vincent Carey and Ute Lotz-Heuman (eds), *Taking Sides: Colonial and Confessional Mentalités in Early Modern Ireland* (Dublin, 2004), 266–90; J. A. Froude, 'The government of Ireland in the sixteenth century', *Fraser's Magazine*, 71 (Mar. 1865), 312–15.

24 Brady, 'Offering offence', 281–89.

25 David Thornley, *Isaac Butt and Home Rule* (London, 1965).

26 Froude described Gladstone's act as 'the most healing measure that has been devised for Ireland during two centuries at least'. 'Ireland since the Union', 553.

27 'Ireland since the Union', 550–1.

28 Under Froude's editorship in the 1860s *Fraser's* had published several articles in support of the disestablishment of the Church of Ireland; his views on the disestablishment of the church of England are trenchantly expressed in the closing chapter of his *History of England: Elizabeth I* (1912, Everyman edn), V, 466–73.

29 'England and her colonies', *Fraser's Magazine*, 81 (Jan. 1870), 1–16; 'The merchant and his wife: an apologue for the Colonial Office', *Fraser's Magazine*, 81 (Feb. 1870), 246–7; 'The colonies once more', *Fraser's Magazine*, 82 (Sept. 1870), 269–87; 'England's war', *Fraser's Magazine*, 83 (Feb. 1871), 135–50.

30 'The four empires', *Westminster Review*, 68 (Oct. 1857), 415–40; Froude's highly individual stance on the Cape Colony is a topic in need of further investigation; the best available discussion at present is to be found in Dunn, *James Anthony Froude*, II, chs 26–7; but a succinct personal statement is to be found in his *Two Lectures on South Africa* (Edinburgh, 1880).

31 C. A. Bodelsen, *Studies in Mid-Victorian imperialism* (London, 1960); C. C. Eldridge, *England's Mission: The Imperial Idea in the Age of Gladstone and Disraeli, 1868–1880* (London, 1973) and *Victorian Imperialism* (London, 1978).

32 Among many studies of the crisis of faith see B. M. G. Reardon, *Religious Thought in the Victorian Age: A Survey from Coleridge to Gore* (London, 1995, 2nd edn); also Howard R. Murphy, 'The ethical revolt against Christian orthodoxy in early Victorian England', *American Historical Review*, 60 (1955), 800–17; Froude's personal and highly illuminating account is supplied in 'The Oxford Counter-Reformation', in *Short Studies on Great Subjects*, IV, 231–360.

33 See, for example, P. R. Frothingham, 'Froude: or the historian as preacher', *Harvard Theological Review*, 2 (1909), 481–99; Andrew Fish, 'The reputation of Froude', *Pacific Historical Review*, 1 (1932), 179–92.

34 'The philosophy of Christianity', *The Leader* (n.d. 1851) reprinted as 'The philosophy of Catholicism', in *Short Studies*, I, 188–201; 'A plea for the free discussion of theological difficulties', *Fraser's Magazine*, 68 (Sept. 1863), 277–91, reprinted in *Short Studies*, I, 202–40; 'Criticism and the Gospel history', *Fraser's Magazine*, 69 (Jan. 1864), 49–63, reprinted in *Short Studies*, I, 241–80; 'Conditions and prospects of Protestantism', *Fraser's Magazine*, 77 (Jan. 1868), 56–70; 'Calvinism: an address to the students at St Andrews', in *Short Studies*, II, 1–59; see Micheal Madden, 'Curious paradoxes: James Anthony Froude's view of the Bible', *Journal of Religious History*, 30 (2006), 199–206.

35 For such a suggestion see Hilaire Belloc's 'Introduction' to Froude's *Essays in Literature and History*, London (1904), xii–xiv, xxi; see also Kingsley Badger, 'The ordeal of Anthony Froude: Protestant historian', *Modern Language Quarterly*, 13 (1952), 41–55.

36 For discussions of Froude's *Nemesis of Faith* (1849) see Rosemary Ashton's 'Introduction' to the 1988 edition; and Robert Wolff, *Gains and Losses: Novels of Faith and Doubt in Victorian England* (London, 1977), 389–404.

37 'Father Newman's "The grammar of assent"', *Frasers' Magazine*, 81 (May 1870), 561–80, reprinted in *Short Studies*, 101–45.

38 Froude's 'Autobiography' printed in Dunn, *Froude*, 68–71, 88–90, 122–6.

39 'Autobiography'; see also Froude to Clough, 15 June, 12 Aug 1848, Clough MSS, Bodleian Library, Eng.lett, C190, ff. 302–7; and for the continuance of such sentiments in Froude's thinking, Froude to Lord Derby, 26 Oct. 1880, Liverpool Record Office, Derby MSS.

40 See the closing comments on Ireland in his *History of England: Elizabeth I*, IV, ch. xxiv; and 'The government of Ireland in the sixteenth century', 314–15.

41 See in general, Thomas N. Brown, *Irish-American Nationalism, 1870–1890*, (Philadelphia, 1966); Steven P. Erie, *Rainbows End: Irish Americans and the Dilemmas of Urban Machine Politics, 1840–1985* (Berkeley, CA, 1988).

42 Froude, 'Romanism and the Irish race in the United States', *North American Review*, 129 (Dec. 1879), 519–37; 130 (Jan 1880), 31–51; Brown, *Irish-American Nationalism*, chs 5–6; also Edward T. O'Donnell, '"The scattered debris of the Irish nation": the Famine Irish and New York City, 1845–1855', in Margaret Crawford (ed.), *The Hungry Stream: Emigration from Ireland during the Great Famine* (Belfast, 1997), 49–60.

43 This is a frequent theme in Froude's correspondence with Charles Butler, his American stockbroker – Edinburgh University Library, Butler MSS, E.87. 105; see *inter alia* Froude to Butler, 22 Dec. 1877; 6 July 1878, 1 Jan. 1892; see also Froude to Carnarvon, 7 July 1885, 'If we let them have independence we shall have to interfere in a year or two and perhaps get into a scrape with the United States in turn'. British Library, Carnarvon MSS. Add MS 60799B, f. 90.

44 Froude, 'Romanism and the Irish race in the United States', part II.

45 The pseudo-theoretical assertions with which Froude begins the book are strikingly reminiscent of the arguments advanced by his close friend James Fitzjames Stephen whose polemic against liberal laissez-faire, *Liberty, Equality and Fraternity*, appeared in 1872 while Froude was publishing the first volume of *The English*.

46 See, for example, *The Times*, 25 Nov. 1876, 8 col. B; 4 Oct. 1880, 10 col. A; 12 Oct. 1880, 6 col. B; 10 Jan 1881, 4 col. A; 11 Feb 1886, 10 col. B; for Froude's address to a Conservative meeting at Salcombe, 3 July 1886 6 col. D; 22 July 1886, 7 col. B; 11 Mar. 1889 7 col. A.

47 *The English in Ireland* (London, 1884, 2nd enlarged edn); see also Froude's comments on the overtly anti-Gladstonian stance of his revisions – Froude to Carnarvon, 20 Jan. 1886, Carnarvon MSS, British Library, Add MS 60799B, ff. 1–2.

48 *The Two Chiefs of Dunboy or an Irish Romance of the Last Century* (London, Longman, Green, 1889); an early version of the plot appeared in Froude, 'Stories of the Irish smugglers', *Scribner's Monthly*, 5 (Dec. 1872), 221–33; for Froude's long struggles with composition see Froude to Lord Derby 13 Apr. [1889], Liverpool Record Office, Derby MSS, no. 7.

49 See *inter alia*, *The Athenaeum*, 13 Apr. 1889, 469–70; *The Nation*, 16 May 1889, 403–4; *The Saturday Review*, 20 Apr. 1889, 474; the exchanges in *Notes and* Queries, 18 May and 8 June 1889; *The Times* 12 Apr. 1889, 12 col. A; A. J. Fetherstonhaugh published a lengthy factual refutation in 'The true story of the two chiefs of Dunboy' in *Journal of the Royal Society of Antiquaries of Ireland*, 24 (1894), 35–43, 139–49.

50 This was the burden of Oscar Wilde's witty demolition, 'Mr Froude's blue book', *Pall Mall Gazette*, 13 Apr. 1889 (repr. in *The Artist as Critic: Critical Writings of Oscar Wilde*, ed. Richard Ellmann (Chicago, 1968)), which in contrast to those preoccupied with questions of historical accuracy suggested that there was far too much history in the book for it to succeed on any grounds as a novel.

51 *Two Chiefs*, 304. This incident in the novel is based directly on an anecdote related in Jonah Barrington's *Personal Sketches* of which Froude had made considerable use in *The English in Ireland*. But while in Barrington's text Joyce is reported to have said that he was 'as good a Christian as the archbishop' of Dublin, Froude in his novel silently but significantly alters Joyce's allegiance to the Pope of Rome; see Hugh B. Staples (ed.), *Sir Jonah Barrington's Ireland: selections from his Personal Sketches* (Seattle and London, 1967), 166–7.

52 *Two Chiefs*, 260.

53 Ibid., 237.

54 Ibid., 2; also 3–8.

55 Ibid., chs xxiii–iv.

56 Ibid., 366–7.

57 Ibid., 368.

58 On this see the relevant passage in Froude's fragmentary autobiography printed in Dunn, *Froude*, I, 88–90.

59 Froude, 'England's forgotten worthies', *Westminster Review*, 58 (July 1852), 32–67; for a revelation of Froude's highly relativist attitude towards the Elizabethan privateers see Froude to [?], 6 Oct. 1862, Beinecke Library, Yale University, Hilles MSS Box 9, file F.

60 *Two Chiefs*, 46.

61 Ibid., 59.

62 Ibid., ch. v.

Bibliography

Badger, Kingsley, 1952. 'The ordeal of Anthony Froude: protestant historian', *Modern Language Quarterly*, 13, 41–55.

Bodelsen, C.A., 1960. *Studies in Mid-Victorian Imperialism*. London.

Brady, Ciaran, 2004. 'Offering offence: James Anthony Froude, moral obligation and the uses of Irish history', in Vincent Carey and Ute Lotz-Heuman (eds), *Taking Sides: Colonial and Confessional Mentalités in Early Modern Ireland*. Dublin, 266–90.

Brown Thomas N., 1966. *Irish-American Nationalism, 1870 –1890*. Philadelphia.

Burke, T. N., n.d. [1873?]. *Ireland's Vindication*. Glasgow.

Burrow, J.W., 1981. *A Liberal Descent: Victorian Historians and the English Past*. Cambridge.

Dunn, W. H., 1961–3. *James Anthony Froude, A Biography, 1: 1818–56; 2: 1856–1894*. 2 vols. Oxford.

Dunne, Tom, 1982. 'La trahison des clercs: British intellectuals and the first home-rule crisis', *Irish Historical Studies*, 23: 90, 134–73.

Eldridge, C. C., 1973. *England's Mission: The Imperial Idea in the Age of Gladstone and Disraeli, 1868–1880*. London.

Eldridge, C. C., 1978. *Victorian Imperialism*. London.

Erie, Steven P., 1988. *Rainbows End: Irish Americans and the Dilemmas of Urban Machine Politics, 1840–1985*. Berkeley, CA.

Fish, Andrew, 1932. 'The reputation of Froude', *Pacific Historical Review*, 1, 179–92.

Frothingham, P. R., 1909. 'Froude: or the historian as preacher', *Harvard Theological Review*, 2, 481–99.

Froude, J. A., 'Ireland since the Union', reprinted in Froude, *Short Studies*, II, 514–62.

Froude, J. A., 1872–4. *The English in Ireland in the Eighteenth Century*. vol. I, Nov. 1872; vols II and III, Apr. 1874. London: Longmans Green.

Froude, J. A., 1889. *The Two Chiefs of Dunboy or an Irish Romance of the Last Century*. London, Longman, Green.

Froude, J. A., 1894. *Short Studies on Great Subjects*. London.

Hickson, M. A., 1884. *Ireland in the Seventeenth Century; or the Irish Massacres of 1641–2 with a Preface by J. A. Froude*. London: Longmans.

Jann, Rosemary, 1985. *The Art and Science of Victorian History*. Ohio.

Madden, Micheal, 2006. 'Curious paradoxes: James Anthony Froude's view of the Bible', *Journal of Religious History*, 30, 199–206.

Murphy, Howard R., 1955. 'The ethical revolt against Christian orthodoxy in early Victorian England', *American Historical Review*, 60, 800–17.

O'Brien, James W., 1873. *Froude's Crusade: Both Sides*. New York.

O'Donnell, Edward T., 1997. '"The scattered debris of the Irish nation": The Famine Irish and New York City, 1845–1855', in Margaret Crawford (ed.), *The Hungry Stream: Emigration from Ireland During the Great Famine*. Belfast, 49–60.

Reardon, B.M.G., 1995. *Religious Thought in the Victorian Age: A Survey from Coleridge to Gore*. London, 2nd edn.

Wolff, Robert, 1977. *Gains and Losses: Novels of Faith and Doubt in Victorian England*. London, 389–404.

CHAPTER 8

Race Theory and the Irish

Peter J. Bowler

Historians such as Perry Curtis have focused on the way in which popular literature in nineteenth-century Britain depicted the Irish as having a simianised or ape-like character (Curtis 1968, 1997; Foster 1993: ch. 9; Urry 1993). The beetling eyebrows, receding forehead and non-existent chin were all invoked to create a derogatory caricature that helped to shore up the Anglo-Saxons' sense that here in Ireland they were dealing with a mentally and indeed biologically inferior people who could never hope to be lifted out of their barbarous cultural state. From Charles Kingsley's claim that he had seen creatures resembling chimpanzees in Sligo through numerous *Punch* cartoons to Madison Grant's claim that Neanderthals could still be found roaming in the west of Ireland, this imagery helped to sustain several generations of anti-Irish prejudice. Not all depictions of the Irish were like this, of course, and one can debate the relative strength of the pro- and anti-Irish sentiment, and how it fluctuated, in the course of the nineteenth century. But the use of biological and evolutionary imagery was certainly a factor, and leads to the natural conclusion that the sciences of physical anthropology and evolutionary biology must have played a role in either creating or sustaining it.

In this essay I wish to examine that claim and argue that the role of science in creating this imagery has probably been exaggerated. I shall certainly not be denying that the scientists were deeply involved in supporting the notion of a hierarchy of races by using anatomical characteristics to depict other races as having smaller brains and more ape-like features than the Anglo-Saxons. The image of the ape-like, almost sub-human 'lower' races certainly predates the theory of evolution, but the idea that some races had been left behind in the advance of mankind from the ancestral ape resonated well with the flourishing of Darwinian imagery and metaphor in the mid and late nineteenth century. If evolutionary anthropology did not create this imagery, it certainly helped to sustain it. But most of that imagery was targeted on demeaning the status of the black and coloured races. I want to argue that, although it was applied to the people of Ireland, the proportion of effort devoted to this target was much more limited than we might expect from the prevalence of the demeaning images in popular culture. Far from seeing science as the origin of this picture of the Irish, I would suggest that we see the scientists responding – but only in a limited way – to the popular culture in which they operated. In the end, I suspect, they were reluctant to get too deeply involved because they realised that to attack the character of another white race too blatantly would undermine the credibility of the far more important project that underpinned the Europeans' exploitation of non-white races in so many parts of the world.

There is, of course, some anti-Irish activity in the literature of physical anthropology and evolutionary racism, but it is of relatively limited extent, at least when compared with that directed against the non-white races. And some of the most blatant examples turn out to have little scientific input: what we find are scientists promoting the same anti-Irish rhetoric as one finds elsewhere in Victorian culture, but being remarkably shy about actually substantiating their invective with the kind of anatomical measurements that were so extensively used to depict blacks as small-brained and ape-like in appearance. Science reflected the anti-Irish racism of the nineteenth century, but it does not seem to have been the driving force in establishing the imagery of the simian Paddy.

Before outlining my evidence for these claims, I want to say something about the conceptual structure of nineteenth-century race theories, and about contemporary ideas on the prehistory of Europe (for more details see Bowler 1986). Traditional interpretations of the history of race science recognise a distinction between monogenism and polygenism, a distinction which becomes partially blurred after the introduction of evolutionism. Polygenists argued that there were a number of distinctly created human species corresponding to the major racial types. There were many who saw the white and black races as separate species, but this approach began to seem somewhat artificial if it were applied to the separate divisions within the white race, such as that between the Anglo-Saxon or Teuton and the Celt. After all, how many distinct human species could one plausibly believe God to have created? Some extremists did argue for this position, of course, but they were widely recognised as such. Polygenists had little interest in the origin of the species they postulated, except to insist that they could not have evolved one from another. Evolutionism seemed to imply monogenism for the human race: all races could interbreed and thus had to be counted as varieties or at best subspecies evolved from a common ancestor. But it was certainly possible to argue that the separation had taken place deep in the past, perhaps even before the final steps in the ascent of humankind from the ancestral ape. In principle, Darwin's was a theory of branching evolution in which no living species could preserve the exact form of the common ancestor from which it and its closest relatives had diverged. But in practice it was relatively easy to suppose that some branches of the human species had advanced less rapidly than others, and thus preserved some of the original ape-like character. Evolutionists could thus certainly be racists (in modern terminology), although they could not realistically invoke the absolute differences between racial types that were central to polygenism. Another point which it is important to stress is that the polygenists were just as willing to depict the lower races as ape-like, even though they did not believe we had evolved from the apes. The notion of a linear chain of being was still influential, and all the polygenist had to do was imagine the various human species to be individual links in a chain stretching from the ape to the highest human type.

Polygenists and evolutionists were thus both in a position to supply an apparently scientific basis for depicting other races as biologically inferior to Europeans. In both Britain and America, supporters of both positions certainly did participate in the attempt to show that the coloured races were inferior to the whites, although in general the polygenists took a far more extreme position on this. There was also a general agreement that the population of Europe, although broadly 'white', was composed of a number of racial types. It was widely assumed that in comparatively recent times a race of round-headed Teutons or Anglo-Saxons had gradually displaced a long-headed Celtic race, the latter still surviving on the margins of the continent. But it was gradually realised that there were remnants of even older races. The fair Celts had actually displaced an older Iberian or Mediterranean type, which was much darker in appearance. It was this Iberian race which survived in Wales and especially in western Ireland. The notion that the anti-Irish component of race science was directed primarily against the Celts is thus a misconception. It is based largely on the example of Robert Knox, whose invective against the Irish in his *Races of Men* of 1850 did focus on the Celts. But by the 1860s no one familiar with the latest developments in philology, archaeology or anthropology thought that the Celts were a truly primitive people. The revival of interest in Celtic art and culture in the 1860s did not necessarily affect the issue, because by then the Celts were not the real target.

There was general agreement on the 'primitive' cultural state of the Iberian remnants in western Ireland. But was it possible to apply the sciences of physical anthropology and biology to show that – like the blacks – the Iberians were biologically and hence mentally inferior to the Teutons (and the Celts)? There were certainly attempts to develop such a case, but my argument is that they are of relatively limited scope when compared with the amount of effort that went into simianising the non-white races. When we rule out comments that limit themselves to attacking Irish culture and Irish habits, we find that there are few extended arguments intended to depict the Iberian as noticeably closer to the ancestral ape than the Teuton. There are short passages in some of the 'usual suspects' of nineteenth-century race science, but they seldom represent a really well-developed attempt to provide scientific evidence for the simian Paddy of popular caricature. The Irish were inferior, perhaps, but by no means so inferior that one might try to pretend that they were some sort of link back to humankind's ape ancestry.

Note first that anti-Irish prejudice does not loom large in the standard modern histories of race-science and racism. Stephen Jay Gould's controversial *Mismeasure of Man* (1981) focuses almost exclusively on anti-black prejudice. I have not seen any reference to the Irish in the book, and neither Ireland nor the Irish appear in the index. Frank Spencer's monumental *History of Physical Anthropology* (1997) similarly contains no article or index entry on Ireland or the Irish, and none of the references to the Celts relates to Ireland. Nancy Stepan's *The Idea of Race in Science* (1982) makes only brief references to the popularity of the distinction between Anglo-Saxon and Celt. George Stocking's *Victorian Anthropology* refers to the Anglo-Saxon hostility to the Celt (1987, ch. 2), but notes that it was only loosely biological in nature. If authors interested primarily in Ireland have chosen to stress the role of physical anthropology, historians dealing with the history of that science and its links to racist thought do not seem to find the Irish dimension looming very large in their work.

Let me now start to put some flesh on the bones of my argument by bringing in the primary sources. Let's start with the most obvious one, Robert Knox's *Races of Man* of 1850 (2nd edn. Knox 1862). Knox's invective against both the mental character of both the blacks and the Irish is so well known as to scarcely need repeating. He did not recognise a non-Celtic component in the Irish population, and hence focused all his invective on the Celt. For him the Celts were natural Catholics who could be ruled only by force from above, characterised by 'furious fanaticism, a love of war and disorder; a hatred for order and patient industry; no accumulative habits, restless, treacherous, uncertain: look at Ireland'. (Knox 1862: 25). Knox was an eminent anatomist, although discredited because he bought cadavers from the bodysnatchers and murderers Burke and Hare. He was a follower of Continental transcendental anatomy, which sought to understand the relationships between species in terms of idealised morphological patterns. If anyone was in a position to back up his anti-Irish rhetoric with anatomical evidence, it was he. Yet his book is curiously devoid of anatomical evidence and argument. He makes no effort to depict the Irish as having smaller brains or more ape-like features than Anglo-Saxons. Indeed, even his anti-black tirades are pretty thinly supported by anatomy – there is a diagram of the facial angle towards the back of the book (1862: 404) which presents a negro as having more ape-like characters than a classic white profile, but there is nothing on brain size or structure anywhere. Knox is a very good source to illustrate anti-Irish prejudice in a scientist, but not to illustrate the actual application of science to provide evidence supporting the denigration of the Irish character.

What then of the classic supporters of polygenism who tried to support their position with anatomical evidence based on brain size and so on? Here we find the some evidence, but put in the context of the sheer volume of this literature, it is fairly limited – we are almost invariably dealing with a few paragraphs on the Irish in books that spend hundred of pages on the overall topic. The polygenists were, in any case, on shaky ground when dealing with differences within the peoples of Europe – after all, everyone accepted that the Celts were part of the Aryan family either linguistically or racially, so was it really plausible that they could be made to represent an intermediate form between true humans and apes? The Iberians were supposed to be a more ancient and probably non-Aryan race, and they were sometimes described with the skull characters that imply an ape-like appearance (low forehead, massive brow-ridges, prognathous jaw). But to carry this effect too far would put them on a par with the most despised black races, such as the Hottentots and the Australian aborigines, and this was hardly plausible or appropriate.

Irish skulls do not appear in Samuel George Morton's *Crania Americana*, although according to his followers he had a few Irish skulls in his collection. Morton mentions the primitive nature of Irish culture in his introduction, but says nothing to imply that the people are biologically inferior (Morton 1839: 15–18). Josiah C. Nott and George R. Gliddon do not refer to Ireland in their *Types of Mankind* (1854), but an essay by J. A. Meigs in their *Indigenous Races of the Earth* has a brief description of the Irish skull as typically having a low forehead and large brow ridges (Meigs 1857: 302). These are certainly features which would support the portrayal of the Irish as ape-like in appearance. This characterisation also finds its way briefly into D. Mackintosh's article on the 'Comparative anthropology of England and Wales' published in the *Anthropological Review* (1866). This was the journal of James Hunt's highly racist Anthropological Society of London, and it is here if anywhere that one would have expected to find anti-Irish material – it reprinted a summary of Knox's views (anon 1868). Yet the journal presents very little of this, and seems surprisingly even-handed on the topic, publishing several articles taking a very positive attitude towards the character of the Celtic race in the late 1860s (e.g. Jackson 1869). In his *Races of Britain* John Beddoe endorses the view that the low forehead and prognathous jaw are typically found in the west of Ireland, but focuses far more on his index of nigrescence (1885: 293; see also Beddoe 1870–1). The claim that the Iberians were of a darker skin and hair colour than the Anglo-Saxons (or the true Celts) might have been used as a sign of inferiority, but it would not have carried the same weight as the presumed anatomical differences. Everyone, in any case, agreed that the intermingling of the races in Ireland, as elsewhere, made clear-cut judgements impossible. This was a point displayed in Alfred Cort Haddon's studies of Irish skulls (1892, 1893, 1897), where again there is no sign of an effort to depict those studied as being of ape-like appearance (see Ashley 2001). Indeed, Haddon comments on the fine features of some of the skulls.

What of the actual size of the brain? Given the almost universal assumption in the late nineteenth century that brain size was correlated with intelligence, the attempt to prove that there were significant differences between the average brain sizes of different races was a central feature of physical anthropology. The black races were almost invariably presented as having average cranial capacities significantly lower than whites. The same technique was certainly applied to the various races of Europe, and here we find the Irish frequently depicted as having brains slightly smaller than the Anglo-Saxons – but the differential is very small and would hardly support the claim that the Iberian represents a relic of the distant evolutionary past. There seems to be a fairly general agreement among authorities that the average capacity of the Irish skull is around 87 or 88 cubic inches (Meigs 1857: 305; Nott 1856: 466: Quatrefages 1879: 383, the latter quoting figures from Morton). The same authors have the Anglo-Saxons or Teutons with skulls averaging between 90 and 96 cubic inches. There is a difference, but it is much less than that presented for the black races – the Hottentots and Australian aborigines were generally portrayed as having an average of 75 cubic inches. Nott and Gliddon also note that there is a good deal of variation in the Irish skulls, suggesting once again that the Irish people are actually a compound of two racial types, the average being brought down by the inclusion of the smaller brained Cymbric (Iberian) type. This is hardly a heavy-handed attempt to depict the whole Irish people as intellectually inferior. If the purpose of craniometry was to show that certain races would never be capable of contributing to modern culture and civilisation, the big guns were aimed at the blacks, not the Irish.

At the same time, of course, the negative view of the Celtic character expressed by Knox and others was being undermined. There was a growing feeling among scholars that the Celtic race had much to contribute to modern culture. As noted above, this view even found its way into the pages of the *Anthropological Review*, for instance in an article by J. W. Jackson (1869). Some scientists certainly shared this view, including Thomas Henry Huxley. Although not noted for his willingness to concede the equality of the black and white races, Huxley poured scorn on the idea of an inferior Celtic character in his 1871 article 'On some fixed points in British ethnology' (reprinted Huxley 1894). Observing that there was no physical difference between the peoples of the west of England and the east of Ireland, he suggested that the differences in their typical behaviour could be explained by something more than an appeal to 'the idle pretext of "Celtic blood"'. Like most authorities, Huxley recognised that it was the Iberians, rather than the Celts, who were the more ancient race in Ireland. But he made no effort to portray them as relics of the truly distant past who might have retained ape-like characters. For Huxley and his disciples, the real problem in Ireland was the Catholic Church, not the Celtic race. They hoped that a scientific education would break the Church's hold on the Irish people – but for this programme to be successful they must have felt that Irish children could benefit from such an education. This is hardly evidence of a sense that the Irish were racially inferior, and indeed it was widely realised that Irish people were playing a vital role in the running of Britain's overseas empire.

Many of the early Darwinians had a negative view of the Irish character, but were similarly reluctant to engage in a serious effort to apply the evolutionary model in a way which would depict the Irish as relics of the distant past. One exception is Charles Kingsley, who wrote of a journey in Co. Sligo in 1860: 'I am haunted by the human chimpanzees I saw along that hundred miles of horrible country' (in F. E. Kingsley 1877: II, 107). He was particularly shocked by the fact that these were white chimpanzees – it would not have been so bad if they had been black. But although he supported Darwin, Kingsley was a clergyman and historian, not a scientist, and his remarks were contained in a private letter. I know of no equivalent comment on the appearance of the Irish in his published works. Kingsley's *Water Babies* explores the themes of evolutionary progress and degeneration, and it does refer to the Irish. But where one representation of the 'poor Paddy' presents him as amiable but feckless, there is also an Irishwoman from Galway who is 'very tall and handsome, with bright gray eyes . . .' (Kingsley, 1889: 116 and 9).

In his *Descent of Man*, originally published in 1871 (1879 edn: 138), Darwin himself repeated some rude comments about the improvidence of the Irish character from W. R. Greg. But this was in the context of the differential rates of reproduction among different groups, and he made no effort to link his view of Irish improvidence to physical characteristics. When it came to listing average cranial capacities he cited figures from J. Barnard Davis which treated Europeans as a single unit in order to bring out their collective superiority over the black races (1879: 54). John Lubbock's anthropological and archaeological writings were based on the assumption that the non-white races lagged behind the Europeans both mentally as well as culturally, but I have found no references to Irish mental inferiority in his work (Lubbock 1865, 1870). Herbert Spencer had no very positive view of the Irish character, but when he looked for an example of a white race whose culture had encouraged the development of an improvident character, he cited the English! (Spencer 1887: 367–8)

The point that needs to be stressed here is that the prevailing view of how the British Isles had been peopled did not encourage an attempt to link the Irish back to an early stage in human evolution. Whatever one's feelings about the Irish character, the most ancient inhabitants of the island were probably the Iberians, and they were a Neolithic people. To find remnants of older, Palaeolithic races in the world one normally had to look much further afield. William Boyd Dawkins (1880) popularised the view that the Eskimos were relics of the Magdalenian reindeer hunters, driven northwards by later invaders. This view was taken up in William Johnson Sollas's *Ancient Hunters* of 1911. Sollas also tried to claim the Australians as genuine relics of the Neanderthal race or species, although he was forced to abandon this claim in his later editions and treat them as only cultural rather than bio-logical relics of the Mousterian period (Sollas 1924; see Bowler 1986: 85–7). The Neanderthals had come to be regarded as possible ancestors of modern humanity by some authorities in the late nineteenth century, but by the time Sollas published most thought that they had been completely wiped out when modern humans invaded Europe.

Was there a possibility that traces of Palaeolithic races had survived in Ireland? Haddon claimed that Beddoe had thought that there might be traces of the ape-like Neanderthals left in the British Isles, but he does not specify Ireland and gives no source for the claim (Haddon 1898: 80). Beddoe (following Hector Maclean) does identify the late Palaeolithic Cro Magnon and Eskimo-like races as surviving in remote parts of Ireland (Beddoe 1885: 9–10). But these were early types of modern humans – in fact it was the Cro Magnons who were soon being presented as the race which wiped out the Neanderthals. They were not the most attractive of people, according to Beddoe, having large heads, but of low intelligence – the character of Sancho Panza in Don Quixote typifies the type. But they were fully human and there was no suggestion of an ape-like appearance. It was the Neanderthals, and sometimes the non-white races of the modern world, that were depicted as being so far down the evolutionary ladder that they still preserved an ape-like appearance. No race living in modern Europe could be pushed that far down the scale without undermining the credibility of the attempt to depict the negroes and the Australians as relics of earlier states in cultural and mental development.

When the American exponent of white supremacy, Madison Grant, wrote of 'ferocious gorilla-like living specimens of Palaeolithic man' on the West coast of Ireland (1921: 108), he was endorsing an image of the Neanderthal Paddy that had gone out of fashion decades before. No serious writer on physical anthropology or human origins had ever suggested that the

Iberians were a Palaeolithic type – this label had always been reserved for the 'lowest' black races, and had been discredited in the early twentieth century as the view began to prevail that the Neanderthals were not, in any case, on the direct line of ancestry leading to any modern humans. If more ancient types survived in Ireland, they were nevertheless fully human. Interestingly, Carlton Coon's much later *Races of Europe* notes the heavy brow-ridges found in some parts of Ireland, but argues that this character is found more commonly in Ulster than in the southwest. (Coon 1939: 376–84)

My last example of anti-Irish racism in science is the embryologist Ernest William MacBride. He was one of the last major supporters within science of the Lamarckian theory of the inheritance of acquired characteristics, which he defended against the growing influence of genetics in the early twentieth century. The writer Arthur Koestler once described MacBride as the Irishman with a heart of gold, because he defended Paul Kammerer, the Austrian biologist discredited in what Koestler called *The Case of the Midwife Toad* (Koestler 1971). What Koestler did not spot was that MacBride – an Ulster Protestant by birth – was a prominent supporter of eugenics who held that the Irish component of the British population should be sterilised (see Bowler 1984). He believed that the swarthy Iberian or Mediterranean race had evolved in a softer and less demanding climate than that of the more northern regions which had produced the hardy and more self-reliant Nordics. In his *Introduction to the Study of Heredity*, published in the popular Home University Library series in 1924, MacBride wrote as follows:

> The Mediterranean race forms the aboriginal stratum of the population. They are characterized by a mercurial temperament, prone to quarrel and quick to take revenge, with musical and poetic gifts, but without the courage and organizing power of the Nordic race or the plodding industry of the Alpine. Their natural organization, as Irish legends show, is a division into warring and treacherous clans. When they drift into the towns they tend to form the 'submerged tenth,' i.e. the inhabitants of the slum. (MacBride 1924: 244–5)

It was essential for the preservation of the Empire, he argued, that the breeding of this submerged tenth should be restricted.

As a scientist, MacBride was an anachronism by the 1920s, and his extremism on the race question was widely recognised – he was even ousted from the Eugenics Society. The real point that I want to make, though, is that – despite his commitment to a progressionist evolutionism – MacBride made no effort to depict the Iberians of Ireland as small-brained throwbacks to an era when humans were closer to the apes. He had an explanation of their inferior character based on adaptation to a less-demanding environment, but would never have endorsed the idea that they were living

Neanderthals. Indeed, he went on to argue that the worst features displayed by this race were found in those members now living in the slums of the great cities, and was the result of recent degeneration. This was caused by damage to their reproductive systems inflicted by the harsh conditions in which they now lived (MacBride 1924: 247–8).

MacBride allows me to bring my argument to a conclusion by providing an example of anti-Irish prejudice which in many respects parallels that offered by Knox nearly a century earlier. Both had very negative views of the Irish character (though MacBride recognised that it was the Iberians, not the Celts, who had to be targeted). Both were morphologists who would have been well situated to bring the resources of comparative anatomy to bear in order to sustain an image of the Irish as ape-like relics of the past. Yet neither did so: their antagonism was based on colloquial impressions of the Irish character rather than on anatomical features such as brain size and brow ridges. In between these very early and very late examples of extreme anti-Irish prejudice, we find a generation of physical anthropologists and evolutionists who certainly shared the prevailing anti-Irish prejudice, and made limited efforts to justify their preconceptions on biological grounds, but who seem to have been remarkably reluctant to allow this particular case to figure very largely in their writings.

The argument I have presented is that this reluctance can be understood in terms of the wider agenda shared by the advocates of European racial superiority. The real purpose of race science in the late nineteenth century was to justify the enslavement or domination of the non-white races in the parts of the world that the Europeans had conquered or colonised. It was vitally important to this agenda that the blacks and Australian aborigines were depicted as little better than survivals of the ape-human links missing from the fossil record. To try to shoehorn a white race, and one which archaeology declared to be of Neolithic, not Palaeolithic origin, into the slot reserved for the blacks would have made nonsense out of the whole enterprise. There was thus a very good reason why both physical anthropologists and evolutionists would have been reluctant to engage in a serious effort to substantiate the popular caricature of the Neanderthal Paddy. That caricature may have flourished in the popular imagination, but it was not something the scientific community was prepared to endorse. Furthermore, the limited hostility displayed by scientists toward the Irish had little to do with the alleged antagonism between Teuton and Celt, because almost everyone after Knox realised that the main aboriginal stratum of the Irish population was of Iberian rather than Celtic origin. If we wish to identify the source of the popular caricature, we need to look not to science but to deeper prejudices which projected an ape-like appearance on to despised races long before evolutionism became widely accepted.

Bibliography

Anonymous, 1868. 'Knox on the Celtic Race', *Anthropological Review*, 6, 175–91.

Ashley, Scott, 2001. 'The poetics of race in 1890s Ireland: an Ethnography of the Aran Islands', *Patterns of Prejudice*, 35, 5–18.

Beddoe, John, 1870–1. 'The Kelts of Ireland', *Journal of Anthropology*, 1, 117–31.

Beddoe, John, 1885. *The Races of Britain: A Contribution to the Anthropology of Western Europe.* Repr. London: Hutchinson, 1971.

Bowler, Peter J., 1984. 'E. W. MacBride's Lamarckian eugenics', *Annals of Science*, 41, 245–60.

Bowler, Peter J., 1986. *Theories of Human Evolution: A Century of Debate, 1844–1944.* Baltimore: Johns Hopkins University Press.

Coon, Carlton S., 1939. *The Races of Europe.* New York: Macmillan.

Curtis, L. Perry, 1968. *Anglo-Saxons and Celts: A Study of Anti-Irish Prejudice in Victorian England.* Bridgeport, Conn.: Conference on British Studies.

Curtis, L. Perry, 1997. *Apes and Angels: The Irishman in Victorian Caricature.* Revised edn. Washington: Smithsonian Institution Press.

Darwin, Charles, 1879. *The Descent of Man.* London: John Murray.

Dawkins, W. Boyd, 1880. *Early Man in Britain and his Place in the Tertiary Period.* London: Macmillan.

Foster, R. F., 1993. *Paddy and Mr Punch: Connections in Irish and English History.* London: Allen Lane.

Gould, Stephen Jay, 1981. *The Mismeasure of Man.* New York: Norton.

Grant, Madison, 1921. *The Passing of the Great Race.* London: George Bell, 4th edn.

Haddon, Alfred Cort, 1892. 'Studies in Irish craniometry', *Proceedings of the Royal Irish Academy*, I, 759–67.

Haddon, Alfred Cort, 1893. 'Studies in Irish craniometry', *Proceedings of the Royal Irish Academy*, II, 311–16.

Haddon, Alfred Cort, 1897. 'Studies in Irish craniometry', *Proceedings of the Royal Irish Academy*, IV, 570–85.

Haddon, Alfred Cort, 1898. *The Study of Man.* London: John Murray.

Huxley, Thomas Henry, 1894. 'Some fixed points in British ethnology', in Huxley, *Man's Place in Nature.* London: Macmillan. 252–70.

Jackson, J. W., 1869. 'The race question in Ireland', *Anthropological Review*, 7, 54–76.

Kingsley, Charles, 1889. *The Water Babies: A Fairy Tale for a Land Baby.* London: Macmillan.

Kingsley, F. E. (ed.), 1877. *Charles Kingsley: His Letters and Memories of his Life.* London: Henry S. King, 2 vols.

Knox, Robert, 1862. *The Races of Men: A Philosophical Enquiry into the Influence of Race on the Destiny of Nations.* London: Henry Renshaw, 2nd edn.

Koestler, Arthur, 1971. *The Case of the Midwife Toad.* London: Hutchinson.

Lubbock, John, 1865. *Prehistoric Times.* London: Williams and Norgate.

Lubbock, John, 1870. *The Origin of Civilization and the Primitive Condition of Man.* London: Longmans, Green.

MacBride, E. W., 1924. *An Introduction to the Study of Heredity*. London: Williams and Norgate.

Mackintosh, D., 1866. 'Comparative anthropology of England and Wales', *Anthropological Review*, 4, 1–21.

Meigs, J. Aitlan, 1857. 'The cranial characteristics of the races of men', in J. C. Nott and George R. Gliddon, *Indigenous Races of the Earth: or New Chapters of Ethnological Inquiry*. Philadelphia: Lippincot, reprinted Bristol: Thoemmes, 2002, 203–352.

Morton, Samuel George, 1839. *Crania Americana, or a Comparative View of the Skulls of Various Aboriginal Nations of North and South America: to which is prefixed an Essay on the Varieties of the Human Species*. Philadelphia: J. Dobson, reprinted Bristol: Thoemmes, 2002.

Nott, J. C., 1856. 'Appendix', in A. de Gobineau, *The Moral and Intellectual Diversity of Races*. Philadelphia: Lippincott, 466.

Nott, J. C. and George R. Gliddon, 1857. *Indigenous Races of the Earth: or New Chapters of Ethnological Inquiry*. Philadelphia: Lippincot, reprinted Bristol: Thoemmes, 2002.

Quatrefages, A. de, 1879. *The Human Species*. London: Kegan Paul.

Sollas, W. J., 1911. *Ancient Hunters and their Modern Representatives*. London: Macmillan.

Sollas, W. J., 1924. *Ancient Hunters and their Modern Representatives*. 3rd edn. London: Macmillan.

Spencer, Frank (ed.), 1997. *History of Physical Anthropology*, 2 vols. New York: Garland,

Spencer, Herbert, 1887. *The Study of Sociology*. London: Macmillan.

Stepan, Nancy, 1982. *The Idea of Race in Science: Great Britain, 1800–1960*. London: Macmillan.

Stocking, George W., Jr, 1987. *Victorian Anthropology*. New York: Free Press.

Urry, James, 1993. 'Englishmen, Celts, and Iberians: the ethnographic survey of the United Kingdom', in Urry, *Before Social Anthropology: Essays on the History of British Anthropology*. Chur, Switzerland: Harwood Academic Publishers. 83–101.

CHAPTER 9

Celticism

Macpherson, Matthew Arnold and Ireland

George J. Watson

In James Joyce's *Dubliners* story, 'A little cloud', written in the early 1900s, the protagonist Chandler's pathetic aspiration to fame as an artist is mercilessly exposed in all its unreality:

> He tried to weigh his soul to see if it was a poet's soul. Melancholy was the dominant note of his temperament, he thought, but melancholy tempered by recurrences of faith and resignation and simple joy. If he could give expression to it in a book of poems perhaps men would listen . . . The English critics, perhaps, would recognise him as one of the Celtic school by reason of the melancholy tone of his poems; besides that, he would put in allusions. He began to invent sentences and phrases from the notices which his book would get. *Mr Chandler has the gift of easy and graceful verse . . . A wistful sadness pervades these poems . . . The Celtic note*. It was a pity that his name was not more Irish-looking. Perhaps it would be better to insert his mother's name before his surname: Thomas Malone Chandler, or better still: T. Malone Chandler. (Joyce 1968: 73–4)

Joyce's feline denigration of 'the Celtic note' is more subtle than the brutal assault of the formidable controversialist and journalist D. P. Moran, whose philosophy of 'Irish Ireland' was expounded vigorously in the columns of the *New Ireland Review* between 1898 and 1900. W. B. Yeats was a special target for Moran's vituperation, and Yeats's chief crime was to claim that his writing was Irish. Moran fulminated against 'a mongrel thing . . . called Irish literature in the English language' (Moran 1905: 43). Worse, Yeats was spoken of as the leader of 'the Celtic Revival'. Moran reserved his fiercest words for the 'Celtic note':

> an intelligent people are asked to believe that the manufacture of the before-mentioned 'Celtic note' is a grand symbol of an Irish national intellectual

awakening. This, it appears to me, is one of the most glaring frauds that the credulous Irish people have ever swallowed. (Moran 1905: 21–2)

Moran and Joyce, then, in their very different ways identify what they see as the hollowness, the falseness of 'the Celtic', its pandering to a sentimental and anaemic version of nationality. This essay will examine the origins of the cult of Celticism, and concentrate on the significance of Matthew Arnold's classic – and classically ambiguous – arguments in his *On the Study of Celtic Literature*, showing how, despite the scepticism of Joyce and Moran, 'the Celtic note' played its part in the growth of cultural nationalism in Ireland, especially in the formation of the work of Yeats, who gave powerful impetus to that growth.

★   ★   ★

In 1974, the historian J. G. A. Pocock wrote an article called 'British history: a plea for a new subject'. Contesting the Anglocentric bias of traditional 'British' history, Pocock called for a *genuinely* British history, which would be alive, not only to the distinctive histories of the four nations of the 'British Isles', but also to the patterns of interaction between and among the nations and cultures of the islands:

> The premises must be that the various peoples and nations, ethnic cultures, social structures and locally defined communities, which have from time to time existed in the area known as 'Great Britain and Ireland', have not only acted so as to create the conditions of their several existences, but have also interacted so as to modify the conditions of one another's existence. (Pocock 1974: 3)

Celticism plays a part in those 'patterns of interaction' to which Pocock wishes to point us, but as a phenomenon does not belong in diplomatic or constitutional or economic or political history, as historians would define those areas. Rather, it belongs in the more nebulous area of cultural history, of people's imaginings and inventions, in short, of ideology. This word is to be understood in its 'soft' definition as 'a body of ideas reflecting the social needs and aspirations of a group, or culture'. Even that might be going too far, if the word 'ideas' suggests anything very systematic. Celticism, as I am going to use the term, is an ideological construction, originating in the eighteenth century, an attempt to create, re-create or assert, a cultural identity for the peoples of Ireland, Scotland and Wales which will distinguish them from the majority inhabitants of the British Isles, the English. It may be generated internally, or imposed from the centre externally, as may be seen to this day in the common and contentious appellation of these three nations as 'the Celtic Fringe'.

The question I wish to examine is the ambiguous nature of Celticism: did it help or hinder the mutual accommodations that were made between the peoples of the British Isles? In what ways did it 'modify the conditions' (Pocock's phrase) of the differing peoples' existences? Is it merely a kind of safety valve devised by a hegemonic England, by which the pressure of ethnic nationalisms might be harmlessly dissipated in druidic rites, in tartanry, or in fairy brides and changelings? For an example of an extremely hostile view, this time from the Scottish perspective, Tom Nairn speaks of the 'stunted, caricatural . . . cultural sub-nationalism' of tartanry, which, 'uncultivated by "national" experience in the usual sense, [became] curiously fixed or fossilized . . . to the point of forming a huge, virtually self-contained universe of kitsch' (Nairn 1977: 163). Such a view prompts an even more fundamental question: is the subject worthy of scholarly attention in any sense?

Celticism is certainly viewed with scholarly suspicion. Many, especially those versed in the antiquities, the archaeology, and the philology of the Celtic peoples who spread out across Europe from the second millennium BC to the second century AD are irritated by the use of the word 'Celtic' in reference to the peoples of modern Ireland, Wales and Scotland. They feel that, though the term is commonly used as an ethnic signifier, this is misleading, since properly it is primarily a philological term, a group name for a cluster of languages, Indo-European in origin, which include Irish Gaelic, Scottish Gaelic, Welsh, and the now extinct Manx and Cornish languages of the British Isles, as well as the Breton language of France. In this purist view, people should no more say 'I am a Celt' than say 'I am an Indo-European'.

Further, there are those who think that Celticism is just bogus, and thus beneath attention. This hostile dismissal of Celticism as *completely* nugatory rests on its not infrequent associations with the ludicrous and the ersatz. There is a certain amount of damning evidence: one thinks, for example, of the portly George IV, great-nephew of the Duke of Cumberland (the Butcher of Culloden), on the royal state visit to Scotland in 1822, bulgingly encased (by his couturier Walter Scott) in the Stuart tartan, the same tartan proscribed by Hanoverian edict for many years after the Jacobite rebellion of 1745; or of the extended debates at the Pan-Celtic congress in Dublin in 1901 on the choice of proper evening wear for the true Celt (the eleventh century got the *haute couture* vote); or of the popularity of 'Celtic religion' as a kind of spiritual aromatherapy; or of the relentless and occasionally comic commercial hype, as in the 'Past Times' advertisement for 'our Celtic loose leaf tea . . . created in Scotland, it is a fine blend of high-grown teas from India and Kenya'. However, I think (despite this rather worrying evidence) that there is more to Celticism than a cup of tea, even if it manages to blend India and Kenya with Glencoe.

If Celticism had a patron saint, it would have to be the Roman god Janus, who faces both ways at once, as I think will become clearer from a discussion of its two key texts, and of their impact. I will begin with James Macpherson's *Ossian* of 1760, which may be considered the foundational text of Celticism, and which – among other things – embodies two conflicting ways of perceiving Scottish identity. Then I will go on to Matthew Arnold's very influential *On the Study of Celtic Literature* (1866), which seeks to incorporate Ireland more securely into the Union, even as it asserts its fundamental otherness. I will finish with some thoughts on the high tide of Celticism in the later nineteenth century, and its role in the development of cultural nationalism.

MACPHERSON'S OSSIAN

James Macpherson published his *Fragments of Ancient Poetry* in 1760.[1] These short fragments purported to be translations from the Gaelic manuscripts of the bard Ossian, son of Fingal or Finn, who lived in the third century. (In Ireland, where he properly belongs, Ossian is known as Oisín.)[2] They were enthusiastically received, especially in Edinburgh, and Macpherson was encouraged to do more hunting in the Highlands, and duly came up with two more works by Ossian, this time not just fragments but epics, *Fingal* and *Temora*. Doubts about authenticity quickly surfaced, not least those raised by the formidable Dr Johnson and, though the controversy went on for the rest of the century, the issue was settled – for scholarship at least – by the 1805 *Report of the Committee of the Highland Society of Scotland, appointed to Inquire into the Nature and Authenticity of the Poems of Ossian*, edited by Henry Mackenzie: this concluded that Macpherson had based his work on the popular ballads of the Highlands, incorporating some traditional plots and passages of accurate translation in long poems spun from his own imagination. No third century manuscripts, penned or scratched by Ossian, were ever found.

Thus, from the very start, with what I have called its foundational text, Celticism is associated with fraudulence. Nevertheless, the hesitations of scholars had little weight compared to the verdict of the people, and not just the people in Scotland. The fraudulence issue is an irrelevance in terms of the cultural history of the poems, as Fiona Stafford argues, and it blocks 'more constructive approaches' (Stafford 1988: 3). During the century following the appearance of *Fragments of Ancient Poetry*, Macpherson's works were translated into 26 different languages, and into all the major European languages within the first 15 years. They had a tremendous vogue in the new United States, where Thomas Jefferson was an avid enthusiast (and sent to

Edinburgh for a Gaelic grammar and dictionary, so that he could read the bard in the original). Napoleon carried a copy of Ossian on all his campaigns; Goethe and Blake were both keen devotees of Ossian; and the radical William Hazlitt wrote in 1818 – well after the apparent proof of unauthenticity was available – 'I shall conclude this general account with some remarks on four of the principal works of poetry in the world, at different periods of history – Homer, the Bible, Dante, and let me add, Ossian' (Hazlitt 1818: 5,15). How do we interpret this immediate and immense impact?

Ossian may be seen as a fountainhead of European Romanticism and, moreover, as a phenomenon which gave a strong push to the establishment of Romantic Scotland. Macpherson had been born in the Highlands, and it is relevant that as a boy he had witnessed the breaking of the Gaelic world in Scotland with the defeat of the clans at Culloden, and had seen, close-up, the bloody aftermath. Certainly, the Ossianic material focuses exclusively – indeed obsessively – on defeat, doom, death and heroic failure. Yet Macpherson was writing at the very apogee of the Scottish Enlightenment, a time of huge Scottish achievement measured in the names of a glittering group of philosophers, sociologists, historians, economists and rhetoricians, which included David Hume, Adam Smith, Adam Ferguson, William Robertson, Hugh Blair – the brightest gems of that 'hotbed of genius', as the novelist Smollett called the Edinburgh of the Enlightenment. One argument about the significance of Ossian would therefore relate it to its time in an *oppositional* way. Thus Andrew Hook writes:

> The new Scotland, the North Britain of enlightened Progress and Improvement, had nothing in common with the [spectacle of doomed and defeated heroism] that Macpherson was concerned to evoke and make familiar to so many readers everywhere. In the end, *Ossian* represented a challenge to the new material civilisation of Lowland Scotland and to the intellectual and cultural hegemony it had so brilliantly established; Ossian was a kind of Highland counter-attack, an attempt to impose on Scotland, as her truer and more traditional self, a romantic, Celtic image created out of the wild grandeur of her Highland scenery, and the heroic simplicity of a poetic Highland past (Hook 1984: 39).

Robert Crawford, reviewing the new Gaskill 1996 edition of Macpherson, also takes up the Culloden background, and seeks to link content to form, by arguing that Macpherson's poetic use of the fragment reflects a relationship with the realities of the post-Culloden devastation of the Gaelic and Highland world and, perhaps, anticipates the ways in which later poets, notably T. S. Eliot and Ezra Pound, used fragments to write in the wake of a war which shattered the civilisation *they* knew. This may be going too far; more convincing is Crawford's suggestion that when Macpherson wrote typical passages such as this:

Autumn is dark on the mountains; grey mist rests on the hills. The whirlwind is
heard on the heath. Dark rolls the river thro' the narrow plain

he created the tone at the root of Romanticism, the voice we hear in
Wordsworth, Byron and Emily Brontë. Crawford claims that Walt Whitman
grew his long lines out of Macpherson's cadenced prose, that Fenimore
Cooper found indirect sustenance in Macpherson for his translatorese repre-
sentation of Native American languages, and that it was Ossian by way of
Matthew Arnold who structured the Celtic Twilight in Ireland and Scotland
(Crawford 1996: 18). And if Crawford goes too far, it is clear that in his time
Macpherson at very least opened a world of stormy mountain scenery full of
the grandeur and terror demanded by the new taste for the Sublime.

This is the Romantic Ossian; but the case for an Ossian who is of
Enlightenment Edinburgh can be persuasively made, first by noting that all
those luminaries mentioned earlier, the *literati*, were or became friends of
Macpherson, and some of them, notably Hugh Blair, Regius Professor of
Rhetoric and Belles Lettres at the University of Edinburgh, had actively
persuaded Macpherson to his task of collecting the raw materials out of
which he would fashion his dubious epics. These are heavily marked by the
circumstances of their production, as can be seen very clearly from the terms
in which Blair speaks in his 1763 *Critical Dissertation on the Poems of Ossian*
(Gaskill 1996). The context in which Blair's remarks should be understood
is the delicate state of cultural relations between Scotland and England only
some fifty years after the Union of 1707 and the even closer proximity of the
'45. One should not underestimate 'that anxious strain of Scottish patriotic
sentiment which sought to remove the impurities of their own native culture
in order to present a more acceptable face to English polite society' (Gibbons
1996: 282). Despite their intellectual achievements, even the Scots of the
Enlightenment feared the stigma of provincialism. To take just one striking
example, David Hume published a six-page pamphlet in 1752 on Scotticisms,
combed his own prose to extirpate them, wrote again in the *Scots Magazine*
of 1760 on their inadvisability, and is reputed to have died lamenting not his
sins but his Scotticisms (McCrum et al. 1986: 151; Kay 1993: 85, 88, 91;
Jones 1995: 48; Beal 2004: 96). In part, the aim of the *literati* was a general
programme of cultural 'improvement' (a keyword of the whole period) in
Elocution and Rhetoric and Belles Lettres – which included the production
of decorous epics. 'If the Scottish Enlightenment was building its Athens in
the North, then it was fitting it should have its equivalent of Homer, shrouded
in the mists of Celtic antiquity' (Gibbons 1996: 285). This equivalent of
Homer, however, would be thoroughly steeped in the values of the Scottish
Enlightenment. Hugh Blair's is the definitive voice of what I will call 'epical
improvement': he commends Ossian on precisely the grounds that

A variety of personages of different ages, sexes and conditions are introduced into his poems, and they speak and act with a propriety of sentiment and behaviour which it is surprising to find in so rude an age. (Gaskill 1996: 363)

In Blair's description of Ossian, he ascribes the virtues of primitive feeling to the bard, but the terms of the description clearly align this poetic ideal to avowedly contemporary poets of sensibility.

When we open the works of Ossian . . . we find the fire and enthusiasm of the most early times, combined with an amazing degree of regularity and art. We find tenderness, and even delicacy of sentiment, greatly predominant over fierceness and barbarity. (Gaskill 1996: 349)

The 'rudeness' of the primitive is tempered by the 'sensibilities' everywhere on display in the Ossianic world just as they in turn are valorised by its access to fundamental, vigorous experience. In the end, for Blair, sensibility wins out: Ossian stands revealed as one of the earliest exemplars of the Man of Feeling:

Ossian . . . appears to have been endowed by nature with an exquisite sensibility of heart, prone to that tender melancholy which is so often attendant on great genius, and susceptible equally of strong and soft emotions. (Gaskill 1996: 371)

Blair's Ossian does not sound in the least like one engaged in a Highland counter-attack against the new Enlightened Edinburgh.

The argument is that far from writing as a mutinous Celt, Macpherson fabricated the apparently Celtic Ossian, consciously or unconsciously, in the mode of gentility and sensibility which would help to ensure that the Scots had, as it were, the cultural entry-ticket guaranteeing equal status or parity of esteem in the polite drawing rooms of the Union. If so, Ossian – despite initial appearances – is in fact complicit with Unionist tendencies. Buttressing this reading, we could add the overwhelming sense of the Ossianic works as a picturesque mortuary for the Gaelic world. The emphasis is unrelentingly on that world's irrevocable pastness. In Ossian, action and martial conflict take a back seat to a repetitive insistence on fatalistic mourning for inevitable defeat, for the last of the race. The ghosts who return from Culloden, as it were, can only wring their hands and lament. 'The transformation of Gaelic tradition into a Romanticised image of a heroic past, to which Macpherson contributed so significantly, was not [in Scotland] so much a liberation from antiquity as an absorption by modernity. Macpherson's efforts can thus be seen as part of the process of turning a living culture into a safe museum of bits and pieces retrieved from the wreckage of a community' (Stafford and Gaskill 1998: xiii).

However, it may be wrong to polarise Ossian as either mutinous Celt or as the Man of Feeling. In a brilliant recent essay, 'National literature and cultural capital in Scotland and Ireland', Cairns Craig offers another way of looking at Macpherson's work. He charts how, in the 1750s, there began to grow a realisation that a country's capital was as much in its culture as in its counting houses, and argues that 'Gaelic Scotland, in economic ruin in the aftermath of the Jacobite defeat in 1746, was transformed by Macpherson's poetry into one of Scotland's most valuable cultural assets' (Craig 2005: 40). He is pointing to much more than a matter of revenues from cultural tourism, and he is worth quoting at some length:

> Recent theories of the nation – whether from the modernist perspective of Gellner, Hobsbawm and Anderson or from the ethno-symbolist perspective of Smith and Hutchinson – have laid an ever-increasing stress on the role of memory in national identity. Without a core of shared symbolism resting on an accepted body of cultural memory, the modern nation could not exist, which is why in 'new' nations such material must be invented if it cannot be retrieved or discovered. Since, for the 'modernist' theorists, all nations are 'new' in the aftermath of the French Revolution, all nations are mythic inventions of constructed memories; for the ethno-symbolists, on the other hand, the unity of the nation depends on tapping into the symbolic structures of a pre-existent communal memory. In both cases, however, the fundamental asset of the nation is the stored capital it can draw down for future investment in the memorial solidarity upon which its continued existence depends. The impact of Macpherson's Ossian throughout Europe was testimony to the developing awareness of the significance of cultural memory to the prospects of the nation and to the awareness of a new kind of cultural capital which, rather than being merely civic . . . derived from the tissues of memories inhering in the national landscape and in national legend. (Craig 2005: 41)

Craig's is a reading which offers more productive ways of thinking about this most ambiguous of Celtic texts and its embodiment of 'cultural capital'. His work also offers an endorsement of the significance of Celticism in general.

★   ★   ★

MATTHEW ARNOLD: ON THE STUDY OF CELTIC LITERATURE

Matthew Arnold's reputation as the pre-eminent nineteenth-century theorist of Celticism in the Anglophone world rests on the lectures which he gave as Professor of Poetry in Oxford in 1865, and which were published in 1866 as *On the Study of Celtic Literature.*[3] This is another crucial Celticist text which, like Ossian, invites a number of very different responses (and which has had them). Arnold, incidentally, was a great admirer of Ossian – indeed, the epigraph to the printed version of his lectures, 'They went forth to the wars, but they always fell' is from Macpherson, and in them he pays the work a famous compliment on its European impact. Why might contemporary Irish, or Scots, or Welsh readers have been less than enthusiastic in their reactions to this famous work?

In many ways, it is a very bad or at least slipshod book. It exhibits no real knowledge of its ostensible subject, except through secondary sources – Arnold had none of the Celtic languages – and he draws attention to his cheerful dilettantism by including in the published version the series of footnotes from his expert adviser, Lord Strangford, intended to correct the linguistic howlers in his own text, which Arnold, however, blithely left unchanged. Owen Dudley Edwards rightly speaks of Arnold's 'twin epaulettes of confidence and ignorance' (Edwards 1986: 152).

Arnold shows little sense that Celtic cultures might have any living reality. Rather, in a more explicit way than Macpherson, he asserts the pastness of Celtic civilisation, and wishes to embalm it as something fit only for antiquarian study. He writes of 'the Celtic genius of Wales or Ireland':

What it *has* been, what it *has* done, let it ask us to attend to that, as a matter of science and history; not to what it will be, or will do, as a matter of modern politics. It cannot count appreciably now as a material power; but . . . if it can get itself thoroughly known as an object of science, it may count for a good deal. (Super 3: 298)

Perhaps my metaphor of 'embalming' may be too emollient. Arnold speaks forcefully of the need to extirpate Welsh as a spoken language:

The sooner the Welsh language disappears as an instrument of the practical, political, social life of Wales, the better; the better for England, the better for Wales itself. Traders and tourists do excellent service by pushing the English wedge farther and farther into the heart of the principality; Ministers of Education, by hammering it harder and harder into the elementary schools. (Super 3: 297)

On the Study of Celtic Literature might well be seen as a plea for the making the Union of Great Britain and Ireland a living reality and not just a political fiction. Arnold's vision is, however, expressed like this:

The fusion of all the inhabitants of these islands into one homogeneous, English-speaking whole, the breaking down of barriers between us, the swallowing up of separate provincial nationalities, is a consummation to which the natural course of things irresistibly tends . . . and its accomplishment is a mere affair of time. (Super 3: 296)

David Lloyd makes the obvious point about that 'swallowing up': 'the digestive metaphor implicit in the word embodies the relationship of power and consumption involved. It suggests equally the kind of transformation of the colonial subject, his breaking down or disintegration, that is the necessary prelude to his total identification with or absorption into the imperial state' (Lloyd 1987: 7).

In a few pages the Celt is hammered, wedged and swallowed. One might well say, if Arnold is the Celt's friend, who would be his enemy? Yet Arnold was in fact sympathetic to the 'Celtic genius', and paints an attractive picture of the Celt, as spiritual, melancholy, natural and poetic. The contrast is with the materialist, philistine, utilitarian, excessively rational, artificial, industrial-ised and urbanised Saxon. This philistine, according to Arnold, even has a longer length of intestine than the Celt, the better to accommodate all his hearty Teutonic sausages and beer. The Arnoldian balance-sheet works out mostly in favour of the Celt, even in terms of the delicacy and modesty of his intestines; but on the other hand, Arnold points out that the Saxon has qualities that the Celt does not have – he can make locks that work, doors that open, and razors that shave – in other words, he has a practical turn that makes the world work. Not only is the Celt impractical, he has, famously, a fatal 'readiness to revolt against the despotism of fact' (a phrase Arnold borrows from Henri Martin's chapter on the Celts in his *Histoire de France*). This lames him in the world of business and politics, and he is not really capable of governing himself. So, Arnold's repressive tolerance suggests that the Celt is lucky to have the dull and muddy-mettled Saxon to run his affairs for him; in return, the Celt will serve to leaven the Saxon lump, bringing with him to the heavy imperial dining table his passion, his aspiration after life and light and emotion, his capacity for penetrating melancholy – in short his visionary and spiritual qualities, which would not know or care about either end of a German sausage. But still, he is not really capable of looking after himself.

Arnold, in short, created a potent, yet it might be felt, simultaneously disempowering, stereotype of the Celt. *Celtic Literature* is, of course, 'neither the first nor the last text that subordinates a colonised people's culture and literature to the major canon by stereotyping the essential identity of the race concerned' (Lloyd 1987: 6). What is of immediate relevance here is a particular emphasis derived from Macpherson. The single most emphatic element in this stereotype is melancholy. Arnold asks whence English literature gets 'its chord of penetrating passion and melancholy', and answers:

The Celts, with their vehement reaction against the despotism of fact, with their sensuous nature, their manifold striving, their adverse destiny, their immense calamities, the Celts are the prime authors of this vein of piercing regret and passion, of this Titanism in poetry. A famous book, Macpherson's *Ossian*, carried in the last century this vein like a flood of lava through Europe . . . All Europe felt the power of that melancholy (Super 3: 370–1).

From this stress on melancholy and lament comes the Celtic Twilight, with its negative connotations of anaemic and crepuscular emotions, in a setting predictably involving lone tree, heath, mist, reeds, cataracts, the tops of crags, total solitude, and evening. It is most readily found in the writings of the Scot, and friend of Yeats, William Sharp, who knew each other in the 1890s. Sharp had discovered psychic gifts in himself, and had become acquainted with the most spiritual and melancholy Celt of them all – Fiona Macleod. He had done better than merely meet her – he had become her, and kept up an elaborate pretence of the reality of her existence as a kind of Highland poetic seer until after his own death in 1905 (Alaya 1970). 'Her' writing – poetry, short stories, novels and essays – followed the chief Arnoldian formulas almost slavishly, particularly in the steady elegiac emphasis on the Celt as one whose day is over, but whose compensation is the spiritual wisdom hidden from the successful Saxon:

> But we front a possible because a spiritual destiny greater than the height of imperial fortunes, and have that which may send our voices further than the trumpets of east and west. Through ages of slow westering, till now we face the sundown seas, we have learned in continual vicissitude that there are secret ways whereon armies cannot march. And this has been given to us, a more ardent longing, and a more rapt passion in the things of outward beauty and in the things of spiritual beauty. Nor it seems to me is there any sadness, or only the serene sadness of a great day's end, that, to others, we reveal in our best the genius of a race whose farewell is in a tragic lighting of torches of beauty around its grave (Macleod 1910: 178–9).

Slow westering, the sundown seas, serene sadness: 'Fiona's' entire *oeuvre* rings the (very limited) changes on this twilight congeries, which goes back through Arnold to the Ossianic stress on the Celtic endgame, the 'last of the race' syndrome. Arnold wants to embalm Celtic culture; Fiona Macleod wants to make sure that the funeral goes aesthetically to plan. Arnold might not himself have perpetrated Fiona's filmy nonsense, but it could be held against him that his Celticising had made it possible.

From one point of view, not only is Arnold open to the charge of aiding and abetting this kind of kitsch sentimentalising, but, more seriously, as we have seen, as endorsing cultural imperialism. And yet, as so often with Celticism, there is another competing perspective on the impact of Arnold. That most austere and sternly ideological of Irish critics, Seamus Deane, makes the case for the dynamic – if perhaps not fully intended – impact of Arnold's work on Ireland: 'Even now it is difficult to overestimate the importance of Arnold's Oxford Lectures, *The Study of Celtic Literature*' (Deane 1985: 25). Again we are brought back to the inherent ambiguity in Celticism.

Seeking ways in which to justify the idea that *The Study of Celtic Literature* might have had such an impact on Ireland (and the other 'Celtic' countries), we might begin by remembering that Matthew Arnold was one of the great names in the public intellectual life of Victorian Britain. That Arnold should choose, at one of those high tides of anti-Irish prejudice in that Britain, fanned into fury by Fenian outrages, a fury stoked by the vigorous simianisation of Paddy in the Darwinian cartoons of *Punch*, that Arnold should choose at that particular juncture, in his lectures as Professor of Poetry in Oxford, to speak on Celtic Literature, and to express in his peroration his desire to establish a Chair of Celtic Literature in Oxford, and thus 'to send, through the gentle ministration of science, a message of peace to Ireland' (Super 3: 386) – this made unquestionably its own political impact. There was courage as well as the famous Arnoldian liberal humanism in this. In a broader academic sense, it was one manifestation, but a very public one, of the growing significance or appreciation of the Celtic world. The recognition of and fascination with the Celtic world manifested in events like Arnold's lectures, admittedly accompanied by the less public but massive application of scholarship, especially German scholarship to it, offered to the Celtic 'home countries', as it were, a purchase on a wider international world. This boosted cultural and intellectual self-confidence in those countries. One of many small examples: a member of the Ossianic Society of Inverness remarked in 1871 with pleasure, mingled I think with slight bemusement, on how 'the language and the very pastimes of the humblest of our Highland people [are now] mixed up with the great and interesting subjects of philology, ethnology, history and anthropology generally'.

Further, there is the obvious point that must not be overlooked, precisely because of its obviousness, about Arnold's Celt, however stereotypical, and one that was of great importance to the Irish in general and the young Yeats in particular: the melancholy Celt, the idealistic dreamer of Arnold's construction, was a much more agreeable image than Paddy with his pig and potato and his shillelagh and his never-ending store of malapropisms and Irish bulls.[4] Some stereotypes are less damaging than others.

At a less obvious level, and with hindsight, we can see that *On the Study of Celtic Literature* is really a dry run for Arnold's most famous work, *Culture and Anarchy*, published just a few years later in 1869, in which Arnold set himself – consciously and in the wake of such world-historical developments as the French and industrial revolutions – to confront the immense questions of how to reconcile progress or change with order and continuity. So, one of the reasons, perhaps, why *On the Study of Celtic Literature* is weak on its supposed subject matter, about which Arnold was only informed via secondary sources, is that its real subject is this one, in which Celticism is deployed as a cultural force against the narrowing and hardening arteries of Victorian Britain. *On the Study of Celtic Literature* and *Culture and Anarchy* are most compelling and persuasive when attacking what Arnold, who borrowed the word from Heine and gave it wide currency as a term of cultural abuse, called Philistinism. His chief hope in the Celtic lectures is that Celtic values, embodied in their culture, especially in the literature, will prove a powerful inoculation against the toxin of crass Philistinism. *Celtic Literature* is a deeply felt critique of what even the milk-and-water Fiona Macleod was to call later the 'bastard utilitarianism' of the century (Brown 1996: 3). Arnold, and after him Yeats, are profoundly at one in believing that culture must stand and fight against fetishism, literally and originally 'the worship of material substances' (Young 1995: 49).

A positive significance of Arnold's constructed Celt, then, is that he represents the antithesis of Mammonism, materialism, narrow horizons, and the indifference to the deposits of the cultural past which was rampant in Victorian society, as all of the great Victorian novelists attest. Dickens's Gradgrind (in *Hard Times*) was a reality, the 'despotism of fact' a horrible feature of Victorian England. We may even entertain the possibility that Arnold in some perhaps unconscious way *approved* of the Celt's 'readiness to revolt' against that despotism: 'Celtic style has for Arnold a moral content – the refusal to accept the despotism of fact and of the merely practical world' (Trilling 1949: 239). Thus, Yeats, ten years after Arnold's death, points out to him retrospectively what he really meant by using his famous phrase. In an 1898 review of the poems of Lionel Johnson, Yeats writes of his desire to carry out 'that revolt of Celtic Ireland which is, according to one's point of view, the Celt's futile revolt against the despotism of fact or his necessary revolt against a political and moral materialism' (Frayne 2: 90). Getting and spending, the valuation of getting on, the utilitarianism which he saw as the true enemy of vision and dream, and the enemy of what Arnold called 'disinterestedness' – these were Yeats's foes too.

★   ★   ★

The racial colouration in Arnold's writing was his most important if unintended legacy, certainly as far as Ireland and Irish culture were concerned. It is a commonplace that ethnological and racial theories saw their great flourishing in the Victorian period. As Robert Knox put it in his *Races of Man: A Fragment,* 1850: 'Race is everything: literature, science, art – in a word, civilisation depends on it' (Bolt 1971: 1). And indeed, no word appears more often in Arnold's writings than 'race' (Faverty: 1951). While Arnold was intensely interested in them, he was not particularly informed about the 'scientific' racist theories of the period: he could not be called a scientific racist. At times in *Celtic Literature* he speaks as if a people's culture is the product of a biologically rooted aptitude; at other times as if it is the product of a cultivated disposition, something learned, something nurtured by environmental factors. Thus he may talk of a people's 'complexion of nature' suggesting the biological construction of culture, but he also utilises a whole battery of other metaphors which are more ambiguous – 'impulse, bent, force, tendency'. Yet, despite the problems that this equivocation might cause the reader irritably reaching after despotic facts, it is fairly clear that Arnold embraces the whole of the racial assumption; he therefore earnestly distinguishes between the different geniuses of the Teuton and the Saxon and the Norman and the Celt. As Lionel Trilling puts it in his classic study of Arnold: 'Science, the anthropology of his day, told him that the spirit of a nation – what we might call its national *style* – is determined by "blood" or "race" and that these are constants, asserting themselves against all other determinants such as class, existing social forms, and geographical and economic environment' (Trilling 1949: 232–3).

But if, on the whole, he *believes* in the primacy of 'blood' or 'race', he *concentrates* his attention and arguments on cultural matters. The 'genius' of the Saxon or the Celt of which Arnold speaks is mainly carried in cultural terms. Arnold did not go in for craniometrics, or the index of nigrescence.[5] The major carrier of any culture is its literature, its legends and stories and poems, and what Arnold tries to argue in his lectures is that English literature is based on a huge Celtic substratum, that it is a hybrid. Arnold's ostensible purpose was to promote disinterested research into Celtic culture, but his underlying objective was to differentiate the various racial elements that make up English literature and English character. Thus one could say that the aim of *Celtic Literature* was a good one: 'Arnold's's untenable theory of race . . . differs in one important respect from many others – in that it was not intended to separate peoples but to draw them together' (Trilling 1949: 236). The argument of *Celtic Literature* was intended to suggest the merits of their own hybridity to the English; however, what it suggested to the *Irish* was their own fundamental otherness, that what was at stake was a 'collision between two racial types' (Deane 1985: 26).

What Yeats (and other Scottish and Irish cultural nationalists) found so useful about this was that the best known and perhaps most prestigious literary critic of his day acknowledged a racial type called Celtic, and the distinctiveness of its literature, and, further, unlike most other imperial Englishmen, spoke of that literature with admiration, however politically qualified. He even asserted the *necessity* of Celtic values to English cultural health. Arnold's position then, however contradictory and confusing on race and culture in itself, provided a basis for an argument that the Celts were a separate race, and that their difference was established – despite the devastation of their Celtic world and its languages – by their legends, myths and folklore, in short, by their cultural capital. From the perspective of hindsight, an astonished Arnold might consider himself to have unwittingly been party to the fathering of cultural nationalism – most obviously in Ireland. The striking contrast with Scotland throws light on the Irish development. The Scots had never lost their key national institutions: their Church, their educational system, their own legal system, were all guaranteed under the Treaty of Union. In Ireland no such guarantees existed or applied. In Scotland, therefore, there could exist in the nineteenth century 'unionist nationalism' (Morton 1999; Craig 2005: 58), in which the overt markers of Scottishness – tartans, pipes, clans, regiments – were underpinned by a genuine if limited autonomy. Thus, tartanry and what went with it could indeed function as a proud token of identity, but an identity at ease within the embrace of the Union, which was perceived less as a threat to, more as a confirmation of, Scottish identity (see Devine 1999: 244–5). The Irish, lacking the institutional markers which the Scots had retained, were driven to a more militantly oppositional form of cultural nationalism. The assertion of Irishness, growing in less friendly soil, had to be pushed further to find a definitive demarcation line of difference, separation, even rupture.

Another factor distinguished the different road followed in Ireland. Celticism as depicted by Arnold, as embodied in the old literatures, myths and legends of Ireland, suggested the possibilities of racial unity and a mode of belonging which was profoundly attractive to the Anglo- or Protestant Irish, who played a major role in the construction of a significant Irish literature in the English language. Celticism as presented by Arnold might provide for them a way of resisting exclusivist or essentialist rejection by an increasingly chauvinist Ireland ready to deny to the Anglo- or Protestant Irishman (or woman) Irishness, as tightly defined, on the grounds of blood, or religion, or language. I have written elsewhere (Watson 1994) of the tensions clustering around Irish identity in relation to the opposition between those who were Catholic, of peasant stock and Gaelic-speaking by ancestry, and those who were born or educated in England, or were Protestant minor gentry or professionals, and I will not rehearse the story again here. However, it is remarkable how so many of those who played such a significant role in the Celtic Revival – Sir Samuel Ferguson, Standish O'Grady, Douglas Hyde, George Russell, Lady Gregory, John Synge and Yeats himself – were

Protestants. How gratefully they received Arnold's intimation that in cultural capital could be found the key to what Yeats called Unity of Culture. Standish O'Grady, a Tory landowner and regarded by many of his contemporaries as father of the revival, hits the Arnoldian note perfectly when he writes in his *History of Ireland*:

> a nation's history is made for it by its circumstances, and the irresistible progress of events; but their legends they make for themselves. The legends represent the imagination of the country; they are that kind of history which a nation desires to possess. (O'Grady 1878: 22)

His readership was Anglo-Irish Protestants who like himself had embraced Celticism and converted to its tenets with semi-religious zeal. His treatment of myth grows from a belief in legend as a national collective unconscious which could be tapped at will by the writer of vision to forge a cultural unity which had eluded political solutions. This was of great significance to Yeats, whose first publication, in 1886, was a review of the poetry of Sir Samuel Ferguson, a devout Unionist, who had given much of his long life to rather wooden translations of Irish tales, legends and songs. Yeats enthusiastically hails Ferguson's reworking of his material:

> The author of these poems is the greatest poet Ireland has produced, because the most central and most Celtic . . . Of all the many things the past bequeaths to the future, the greatest are great legends; they are the mothers of nations. I hold it the duty of every Irish reader to study those of his own country till they are familiar as his own hands, for in them is the Celtic heart. (Frayne 1: 104)

The Arnoldian belief in a kind of racial literary essence is clear – the major difference, of course, is that for Yeats Celtic culture is far from entombed, but is big with life. If, as O'Grady had argued, the ancient stories and legends, the best works of the bards, are 'probably hidden in the blood and brain of the race to this day' (O'Grady 1878: 22), then racial unity is not rooted solely or primarily in biological or sociological factors. In a process akin to osmosis, Celtic legend, or the imaginative possession of such legend, works in the blood, transforms the blood and becomes the marker of racial identity. For Yeats especially, this was an important prop to his psychological need for *Gemeinschaft*, a sense of community. It was an added advantage that the key legends were all pagan. Celticist valorising of antiquity was helpful to a poet acutely aware of the confessional or sectarian tensions rife in the Ireland of his time – the Red Branch knights were neither Protestant nor Catholic. (Cuchulain features, somewhat surreally, on contemporary gable ends in both the Shankhill and Falls Roads in Belfast.)

★   ★   ★

Celticism, so prominent in Ireland and to a lesser extent in Scotland in the latter part of the nineteenth century, fades away as a significant cultural movement quite rapidly after the turn of the century, though it had spasmodic life in the pages of journals such as *Celtia* until about the outbreak of the Great War. Yeats, whose early essays and journalism constantly used the word – he even signed some of his early reviews and esays for American journals and papers 'The Celt' or 'The Celt in London', and who was associated in the minds of his contemporaries with the Celtic Twilight – more or less stops using the term 'Celtic' completely. The reasons throw some light on the most contentious area of all in the cultural politics of the time, at least in Ireland, the politics of language (Crowley 2005).

In November 1892, Douglas Hyde delivered his famous lecture 'On the necessity for de-Anglicizing Ireland', which led in turn to the foundation of the Gaelic League in July 1893. The centre-piece of the de-anglicisation process was to be the restoration of the Irish language as the first language of the country. The idea of a language revival was of course intensely and pleasingly idealistic, but it was asking the Irish people to change their language for the second time in a few centuries. This was always going to be difficult; in fact it proved impossible. The result was an increasing desperation in the claims and exhortations of the more extreme language enthusiasts, led by D. P. Moran who, as we have already noted, raged against 'a mongrel thing . . . called Irish literature in the English language'. Pearse also attacked the very notion of a literature that called itself 'Irish' but which used the English tongue. In vain did Yeats cite the examples of Walt Whitman and Hawthorne and Poe as users of the English language who were not thereby constrained to reflect an English cultural experience. In vain did he argue that literature might be Irish for all that it was written in English. Moran – and many who thought like him – would have none of this hybridity, for which he and they saw Celticism as the stalking horse. The very word, therefore, was a red rag to a particularly chauvinist bull; and Yeats, aware of the violent rancorousness of the language dispute, simply decided not to inflame the situation further by using it. The dream that Celticism could somehow produce the much-desiderated unity of culture simply died. By then, however, it was no longer really needed: the work of Yeats and Synge (to name just those famous two from the Irish Revival) provided powerful evidence of the reality of significant cultural achievement.

A few months after Hyde's famous lecture, Stopford Brooke lectured in March 1893 to the Irish Literary Society on 'The need and use of getting Irish literature into the English Tongue'. This was a more modest aim than Hyde's, and the title points towards one positive achievement of Celticism, whether in Scottish or Irish modes: its recovery and dissemination of past worlds and rich cultures which might otherwise, in Wordsworth's haunting phrase (from the Preface to the *Lyrical Ballads*, 1802), have gone 'silently out of mind'. Celticism has its false and weak aspects, and will only ever be a translation of the Gaelic worlds. Not all Celticist writers can give the material, as Yeats can, compelling imaginative life. It could be argued, however, that all written attempts to embody the past, in whatever language, are inevitably 'merely' translations. Certainly, in the case of Celticism, from Macpherson through Arnold to Yeats, Celtic culture asserted itself in a predominantly anglicised environment through 'translation', and proved itself a significant agent in the process of cultural exchange, the 'patterns of interaction' as I have called them, between and among the nations and cultures of these islands.

Notes

1 Macpherson's works were published as follows: (i) *Fragments of ancient poetry, collected in the Highlands of Scotland, and translated from the Gaelic or Erse language.* 1760; (ii) *Fingal. An Ancient Epic Poem, in six books; together with several other Poems, composed by Ossian, the son of Fingal.* 1761/1762; (iii) *Temora, an Ancient Epic Poem, in eight books; together with several other poems, composed by Ossian, the son of Fingal; translated from the Gaelic language by James Macpherson.* 1762. These were then published in a combined edition: *The Works of Ossian, the Son of Fingal.* 1765, and finally, in a revised edition, as *The Poems of Ossian. A new edition, carefully corrected, and greatly improved.* 1773.

The Poems of Ossian and Related Works, ed. Howard Gaskill, with an introduction by Fiona Stafford (Edinburgh: Edinburgh Univ. Press, 1996) is the new standard edition of the poems, with critical notes and a helpful introduction. Also included are Macpherson's dissertations and preface to the 1773 edition of the Works, and Hugh Blair's *A Critical Dissertation on the Poems of Ossian.*

2 The controversy over Ossian/Oisín's origins helped to develop genuine Gaelic scholarship – see Clare O'Halloran, 'Irish re-creations of the Gaelic past: the challenge of Macpherson's Ossian', *Past and Present*, 124 (1989), 69–94.

3 R. H. Super (ed.), *The Complete Prose Works of Matthew Arnold*, 11 vols (Ann Arbor: University of Michigan Press, 1960–77). Vol. 3 (1962) contains *On the Study of Celtic Literature*, 291–395, referred to in my text as Super 3. A ground-breaking essay by J. V. Kelleher was published in 1950: 'Matthew Arnold and the Celtic Revival' in Harry Levin (ed.), *Perspectives in Criticism* (Cambridge, Mass.: Harvard University Press). My emphasis, however, is quite different.

4 See L. P. Curtis Jr, *Anglo-Saxons and Celts: A Study of Anti-Irish Prejudice in Victorian England* (Bridgeport, Conn.: New York University Press, 1968); and also his *Apes and Angels: The Irishman in Victorian Caricature* (Washington: Smithsonian Press, 1971).

5 See Curtis, *Anglo-Saxons and Celts* for a fuller discussion of the wilder shores of racial mensuration.

Bibliography

Alaya, Flavia, 1970. *William Sharp – 'Fiona Macleod', 1855–1905*. Cambridge, Mass.: Harvard University Press.

Beal, Joan C., 2004. *English in Modern Times, 1700–1945*. London: Arnold.

Bolt, Christine, 1971. *Victorian Attitudes to Race*. London: Routledge and Kegan Paul.

Brooke, Stopford, 1893. 'The need and use of getting Irish literature into the English tongue'. London: T. Fisher Unwin.

Brown, Terence (ed.), 1996. *Celticism*. Amsterdam and Atlanta: Rodopi.

Craig, Cairns, 2005. 'National literature and cultural capital in Scotland and Ireland', in McIlvanney and Ryan 2005, 38–64.

Crawford, Robert, 1996. 'Post-Cullodenism', *London Review of Books*, 3 Oct., 18.

Crowley, Tony, 2005. *Wars of Words: the Politics of Language in Ireland 1637–2004*. Oxford: Oxford University Press.

Curtis, L. P. Jr, 1968. *Anglo-Saxons and Celts: A Study of Anti-Irish Prejudice in Victorian England*. Bridgeport, Conn.: New York University Press.

Deane, Seamus, 1985. *Celtic Revivals: Essays in Modern Irish Literature 1880–1980*. London: Faber and Faber.

Devine, T. M., 1999. *The Scottish Nation 1700–2000*. London: Allen Lane.

Edwards, Owen Dudley, 1986. 'Matthew Arnold's fight for Ireland', in Robert Giddings (ed.), *Matthew Arnold: Between Two Worlds*. London: Vision Press, 148–201.

Faverty, Frederic E., 1951. *Matthew Arnold the Ethnologist*. Evanston: Northwestern University Press.

Frayne, John P. (ed.), 1970–5. *Uncollected Prose by W B Yeats*, 2 vols. London: Macmillan.

Gaskill, Howard (ed.), 1996. *The Poems of Ossian and Related Works*. Edinburgh: Edinburgh University Press.

Gibbons, Luke, 1996. 'The sympathetic bond: Ossian, Celticism and colonialism', in Brown 1996, 273–91.

Hazlitt, William, 1818. 'On Poetry in General', in P. P. Howe (ed.), *The Collected Works of William Hazlitt*. 21 vols. London: 1930–4, 5, 15.

Hook, Andrew, 1984. '"Ossian" Macpherson as image maker', *The Scottish Review*, 36, 39–44.

Hyde, Douglas, 1892. 'On the necessity for De-Anglicizing Ireland', in Seamus Deane (ed.), *The Field Day Anthology of Irish Writing*. Derry: Field Day, 1991, vol. 2, 527–33.

Jones, C., 1995. *A Language Suppressed: The Pronunciation of the Scots Language in the 18th Century*. Edinburgh: John Donald.

Joyce, James, 1968. *Dubliners*, ed. R. Scholes. New York: Viking.

Kay, B., 1993. *Scots: The Mither Tongue*. 2nd edn. Darvel, Ayrshire: Alloway.

Kelleher, J. V., 1950. 'Matthew Arnold and the Celtic Revival', in Harry Levin (ed.), *Perspectives in Criticism*. Cambridge, Mass.: Harvard University Press.

Lloyd, David, 1987. *Nationalism and Minor Literature: James Clarence Mangan and the Emergence of Irish Cultural Nationalism*. Berkeley: University of California Press.

Macleod, Fiona, 1910. *The Winged Destiny: Studies in the Spiritual History of the Gael*. London: Heinemann.

McCrum, R., W. Cran and R. MacNeil, 1986. *The Story of English*. Revised edn. London: Faber.

McIlvanney, Liam and Ray Ryan (eds), 2005. *Ireland and Scotland: Culture and Society 1700–2000*. Dublin: Four Courts Press.

Moran, D. P., 1905. *The Philosophy of Irish Ireland*. Dublin: J. Duffy.

Morton, Graeme, 1999. *Unionist Nationalism: Governing Urban Scotland, 1830–1860*. East Linton: Tuckwell Press.

Nairn, Tom, 1977. *The Break-Up of Britain*. London: New Left.

O'Grady, Standish J., 1878. *History of Ireland*, vol. 1, 'The heroic period'. Dublin: E. Ponsonby.

O'Halloran, Clare. 1989. 'Irish re-creations of the Gaelic past: the challenge of Macpherson's Ossian', *Past and Present*, 124, 69–94.

Pocock, J. G. A., 1974. 'British history: a plea for a new subject', *New Zealand Historical Journal*, 8, 3–21.

Stafford, Fiona, 1988. *The Sublime Savage: James Macpherson and the Poems of Ossian*. Edinburgh: Edinburgh University Press.

Stafford, Fiona and Howard Gaskill (eds), 1998. *From Gaelic to Romantic: Ossianic Translations*. Amsterdam and Atlanta: Rodopi.

Super, R. H. (ed.), 1960–77. *The Complete Prose Works of Matthew Arnold*, 11 vols (Ann Arbor: University of Michigan Press.

Trilling, Lionel, 1949. *Matthew Arnold*. London: Allen & Unwin. 1st edn 1939.

Watson, G. J. 1994. *Irish Identity and the Literary Revival: Synge, Yeats, Joyce and O'Casey*. 2nd edn, Washington, DC: Catholic University of America Press.

Watson, G. J., 2005. 'Aspects of Celticism', in McIlvanney and Ryan, 2005, 129–43.

Young, Robert J. C., 1995. *Colonial Desire: Hybridity in Theory, Culture and Race*. London: Routledge.

Afterword

Peter Gray

The nine essays presented here have cast a wide net over the tumultuous seas of debate concerning Ireland and its 'question' in the era of the Anglo-Irish Union. However, a volume of this sort must be, by its very nature, selective – focusing on a small number of the multiplicity of commentators who took it upon themselves to delineate, theorise and prognosticate on the past, present and potential future of Irish society and its problematic relationship with its British neighbour, and concentrating on the decades between the 1830s and 1880s. The selection succeeds, nevertheless, in identifying and illuminating the stances adopted by a number of those who occupied the commanding heights of Victorian social and political commentary, who cast long shadows over the opinions of their contemporaries as well as later generations, and in combining this with overviews of the socio-political contexts of nineteenth-century Ireland and such major themes in the intellectual history of the period as race and Celticism. It is noticeable that virtually all the commentators cited, with the exception of Irish Celticists and a sprinkling of scientific voices, observed the island from without, constructing its social form from recollections and notes taken on visits, or culled from literary and statistical sources perused in their studies or in such repositories of knowledge as the British Museum reading room. The thinkers reviewed include two pairs of Frenchmen and Germans, but it is the voice of the English observer that predominates here. This is to be expected given both the location of political and economic power over the island within Great Britain and the pathologisation of Ireland provoked by the reporting of its social and political upheavals across the Irish Sea and the political preoccupation of Westminster with the 'Irish problem' for much of the century.

Séamas Ó Síocháin is surely right to lament the scholarly neglect of the intellectual history of nineteenth-century Ireland generally, and of social thought in particular, and these essays go some way towards addressing this absence. An agenda for further development of such an intellectual history might seek to move beyond the discussion of individual contributions (essential as these are) to address other issues. Future research that shifted the focus away from the Olympian heights of the canonical thinkers to the range of interactions and practices that informed both the formulation and reception of these 'interventions' would be welcome. A number of the essays here seek to unpick the textured warp and weave of ideas, prejudices and perceptions that informed individuals' writings on Ireland. Further digging into the cultural and political contexts in which these were researched, produced and consumed might throw additional light not only on the meaning of 'Ireland' to the writers in question but on the broader cultural climate(s) of opinion in Britain, Ireland and continental Europe with which they were in dialogue. It might be possible, for example, through locating Beaumont's and Tocqueville's perspectives (see chapter 2) within pre-existing French liberal Catholic constructions of the 'Irish problem' to offer some explanation as to why they came to such very different conclusions about the island and the British relationship to another continental Anglophile liberal, Camillo di Cavour, whose 1845 treatise on the subject was an enthusiastic endorsement of Westminster policy.

The problem of reception and impact is equally important, not least because it is evident that some texts were (and remain) open to a variety of interpretations – some of them decidedly unintended by the authors – and capable of appropriation by those outside the intended 'core' audience. Henry Maine's *Ancient Law*, discussed in chapter 5, is a prime example of this phenomenon. The frenzied (and perhaps misplaced) Irish reactions to Froude's complex interpretation of the Irish past has been carefully analysed in Ciaran Brady's essay in chapter 7; the appropriation of Arnold's constructions of Celticity in Ireland is also thoroughly addressed by George Watson in chapter 9. Yet it would be desirable to know more about the positive, negative or ambivalent reception in Ireland of these and other 'external' voices.

One overarching theme addressed by many of the contributions is that of 'otherness' in the construction of Irish society. What the case studies suggest, in fact, is a range of 'otherings', contingent on what norm Ireland is being contrasted with, on whether its difference is regarded as contingent or essential, and whether this was seen as *sui generis* or in conformity with a pattern of 'otherness' and 'sameness' defined through an exercise of comparison and contrast. 'Otherness' might (and frequently did) imply inferiority, but might also be valorised (by Arnold in chapter 9, for example) as a positive element that might contribute some essential leavening to a diverse United Kingdom and compound British nationality. While this case for interdependent cultural plurality within political unity may have failed to gain sufficient traction to counter growing national antipathies within the islands, it did leave a significant legacy.

One way of approaching the problem of 'otherness' is through the apparent binary of environmentalism and essentialism in writings on Irish society. Posed most simply, the perceived inferiority of Irish society to British or European norms might be attributed primarily to either a set of contingent circumstances relating to Ireland's historical condition that had bequeathed a malign legacy to the nineteenth century but which were fundamentally malleable, or it could be put down to an inherent backwardness that was the outgrowth of the intractable 'facts' of race or topography. Most external observers agreed on Ireland's social backwardness (if perhaps balanced by some compensating cultural characteristics), but the centre of gravity in the environmentalist–essentialist debate shifted over time and according to the wider liberal/conservative and optimistic/pessimistic proclivities of the observer. Broadly speaking, environmentalism appears to have predominated between the 1830s and 1860s in both thought and policy, with a much more polarised division emerging thereafter as Darwinian ideas about Irish racial difference permeated into popular discourse (albeit, as Peter Bowler demonstrates in chapter 8, being largely ignored by practising scientists). One theme emerging from these essays, however, is the extent to which the binary was complicated by writers conflating the environmental and the essential. This may have arisen from the loose and ambiguous application of seemingly incompatible categories of analysis, the result perhaps of the strength of both interpretations of Irish 'backwardness' in British culture. Some commentators may also have been drawn to blend the two in an attempt to explain a perceived 'stickiness' of national character in Irish society's failure to respond as expected to environmental stimuli that should have (in their eyes) produced profound change – such as the removal of Catholic disabilities and the providential intervention of the Great Famine.

Another theme connecting many of these essays is the significance of the 1860s as a decade of change in thought about Irish society, and the application of that thought in Ireland itself. One might have anticipated that the cataclysmic social disaster of the Great Famine in the later 1840s would have triggered such a reassessment of what constituted the 'Irish problem'. Certainly John Stuart Mill and similar heterodox economic thinkers responded to the potato blight by proposing a radical alteration in British policy towards the island, and this is reflected in the *Principles of Political Economy* in 1848. In practice, however, the very scale and massive mortality of the famine tended to drive most British (and some Irish) commentators into rhetorical and ideological rationalisations that stressed the operations of a beneficent providence, the inevitable consequences of slighting the laws of population and rational capitalist development, and the responsibility of 'feudal' landlord mismanagement and legal incumbrances to optimal land use, rather than any governmental failure or economic exploitation, as the causative factors. Many British, and indeed some continental, observers (such as the French agronomist Leonce de Lavergne) drew a remarkably 'optimistic' picture of the outcome of the cataclysm: not only had the excess population been thinned and land consolidated into more 'efficient' holdings, but (it was widely averred), the previous obstacles to English-style rural development had been swept aside through the elimination of potato-subsistence and peasant proletarianisation, the winnowing out of inefficient landowners and middlemen, and the introduction of 'free trade in land'. This optimistic liberal triumphalism is evident in Harriet Martineau's letters of 1852 (see chapter 4), and was shared enthusiastically with the Irish economists of the 'Dublin School', such as William Neilson Hancock, with whom she communicated.

The 1850s saw something of a post-famine agricultural 'boom', marked by recovering land values and higher rents and wages, fuelled by the development of a wholesale livestock export market from Ireland. In this context, the 'optimistic' readings of the famine went largely unchallenged in Britain and amongst Irish elites. As Graham Finlay notes in chapter 3, even J. S. Mill's attention to Ireland, and his support for radical land reform, slipped away in these years. Arguably, it was the first major post-famine agricultural crisis, of 1859–63, that posed more profound challenges to this consensus than the famine itself. Few, if any, died of hunger in these years, but the spectre of famine returned to Irish minds, economists were obliged to revisit and defend their assumptions of sustained development, and agrarian and political unrest received a social boost that had been marginal for a decade. Arguably, the 1859–63 crisis and its consequences both provoked and provided the context for many of the texts discussed in this volume. It may be no accident that De Beaumont's coruscating critique of British famine policy appeared in an 1863 edition of *L'Irlande* rather than earlier. The Irish commentary in the first volume of Marx's *Capital* (see chapter 6 on Marx and Engels) drew heavily on statistical data from the early 1860s; it also seems unlikely that he was unaware of both the preoccupation of contributors to the Dublin Statistical Society's Journal in the 1850s with the necessary and ongoing 'defeudalisation' of Irish landholding, or their descent into a scholarly civil war in the early 1860s over the significance of the downturn and the social costs of depopulation and the 'pastoral revolution' that had ensued. His blistering attack on Malthusianism may also have been provoked by the appearance in 1867 of Lord Dufferin's *Irish Emigration and the Tenure of Land in Ireland* – a pessimistic polemic claiming that the depopulating work of the famine remained unfinished and that no deviation from Smithian orthodoxy was tolerable.

Arnold's lectures of 1865 (ch. 9) and Froude's writings of the late 1860s to early 1870s (ch. 7) may have been less directly composed in response to the social crisis in the countryside, but were nonetheless shaped by what followed: the upsurge of radical nationalism that took its most prominent form in Fenianism, the confident assertiveness of Ultramontane Catholicism that sought to counter both subversive republicanism and the growing Anglicisation (and potentially Protestantisation) of Irish society, and the onus both of these developments placed on British liberalism to respond positively to Irish grievances. Both Fenianism and Cullenism stimulated hostile responses in significant sections of British (and indeed American) popular culture and tended towards a political polarisation on Irish matters that would tend to undermine the initial Gladstonian strategy of reconciliation within the Union and provoke greater support for nationalism within Catholic Ireland. The pattern of much that would follow was thus established in the 1860s.

The decade was, however, also notable for a marked 'turn' in attitudes towards Irish society on the part of many public intellectuals in both countries. Paradoxically, given his later antagonism towards Ireland and pessimism about its prospects for civilised development, the work of Henry Maine contributed significantly towards this shift (see Séamas Ó Síocháin's chapter 5). Maine's *Ancient Law* (1861) was hungrily consumed by others who developed his concept of stadial development in quite different directions. Maine's principal Irish disciple was T. E. Cliffe Leslie; originally taking a conventional Smithian perspective of Irish society in the 1850s, in the following decade Cliffe Leslie embraced a radically historicist and anti-Malthusian position that suggested that Ireland needed to adopt a pathway to development that reflected its specific historical experience and cultural inheritance. This rejection of the universalism of classical economics in favour of a socio-economic theory that recognised Irish difference and recommended policies that valorised rather than sought to eradicate it, encouraged social thinkers such as Cliffe Leslie and the Scotsman George Campbell to draw parallels between Ireland and established 'peasant' societies on the continent and in India. While a number of these ideas had already been pioneered by Mill in the 1840s, it was the rejuvenation of the field by the radical disciples of Maine in the 1860s that appears to have drawn Mill back into the fray and inspired the pyrotechnics of his 1868 manifesto. In this context, 'Celticism' and economic thought might be reconciled, and the previously orthodox Neilson Hancock and A. G. Richey collaborated on editing the first volumes of the *Brehon Laws of Ancient Ireland* before penning historicist defences of Gladstone's land legislation of 1870 and 1881. While this historicism was rejected as obfuscation by Marx and by neo-Malthusians (including of course Maine himself), it offered a new 'optimism' about Irish social development within the British polity in the 1860s that survived the political fall-outs of 1885–6 in the form of 'Constructive Unionism' as well as Gladstonian reformism.

In conclusion, the forms of social thought reviewed here might be dismissed as contributing little to the trajectory of British–Irish relations in the later nineteenth and early twentieth centuries. While Marx's Irish commentaries, although somewhat opaque and incomplete, offered some inspiration to James Connolly, the latter's role in the revolutionary moment of 1916 was limited and the Marxist strand he embodied was marginalised in the struggle that followed. The social thought of Arthur Griffith's Sinn Féin self-consciously rejected the accommodation with liberalism that had marked parliamentary nationalism and sought inspiration from the autarkic and protectionist ideas of social development associated with continental thinkers such as Friedrich List. Catholic corporatism of a description that would have been anathema to nineteenth-century British liberals influenced social thought in the independent Irish Free State. Of the ideas reviewed here, Celticism obviously cast the longest shadow in Ireland, although in forms that were, as George Watson observes, often at odds with each other and incapable of offering much in the way of concrete guidance on building a post-independence society.

Nevertheless, the ideas focused on in this volume, and especially those which were articulated in the 1860s, did pave the way for a major shift in British policy, an experiment in 'governing Ireland by Irish ideas' advocated by Mill and spectacularly initiated by Gladstone's disestablishment and land acts of 1869–70 (the latter much more significant in its symbolic break with Smithian political economy than in its practical consequences). If unsuccessful in re-legitimising the Union, this *demarche* paved the way for the substantial resolution of the 'land question' in Ireland before 1914 and for easing one of the principal British parties towards recognising the principle of Home Rule for Ireland. If this proved a step too far for many liberal intellectuals, especially in the context of the fear of a revivified and apparently reactionary Catholicism, the belief in Irish meliorism at least offered a meaningful alternative to the pessimistic and racially tinged alternative that drew so heavily on the imperialistic social Darwinism of the era.

Bibliography

Black, R. D. Collison, 1960. *Economic Thought and the Irish Question, 1817–1870*. Cambridge: Cambridge University Press.

Boylan, T. A. and T. P. Foley, 1992. *Political Economy and Colonial Ireland: The Propagation and Ideological Function of Economic Discourse in the Nineteenth Century*. London: Routledge.

Dewey, Clive, 1974. 'Celtic agrarian legislation and the Celtic revival: historical implications of Gladstone's Irish and Scottish land acts 1870–86', *Past & Present,* 64, 30–70.

Gray, Peter (ed.), 2004. *Victoria's Ireland? Irishness and Britishness, 1837–1901.* Dublin: Four Courts Press.

McDonough, Terence (ed.), 2005. *Was Ireland a Colony? Economics, Politics and Culture in Nineteenth-Century Ireland.* Dublin: Irish Academic Press.

Winch, Donald and Patrick K. O'Brien (eds), 2002. *The Political Economy of British Historical Experience 1688–1914.* Oxford: Oxford University Press.

Index